A GREATER LOVE

Splendid
BOOKS

Published in 2011 by Splendid Books Limited

Written by Olga Watkins with James Gillespie

Copyright © 2011 Splendid Books Limited

The right of Splendid Books Limited to be identified as the Author of the work has been asserted by them in accordance with the Copyright, Designs and Patents Act 1988.

Splendid Books Limited
The Old Hambledon Racecourse Centre
Sheardley Lane
Droxford
Hampshire
SO32 3QY

www.splendidbooks.co.uk

British Library Cataloguing in Publication Data is available from The British Library

ISBN: 9780955891670

Commissioning Editors: Shoba Vazirani and Steve Clark
Editor: Amber Ross, Coordination: Annabel Silk

Designed by Design Image Ltd.
www.design-image.co.uk

Printed in the UK

Every effort has been made to fulfil requirements with regard to reproducing copyright material. The writers and publisher will be glad to rectify any omissions at the earliest opportunity.

Photo credits: Olga's own collection
Contemporary photographs: James Gillespie
Page 210 picture: Courtesy of The Buchenwald and Mittelbau-Dora Memorials Foundation
Route map: Anthony Graham / www.illustrativemaps.co.uk

A GREATER LOVE

OLGA WATKINS
WITH JAMES GILLESPIE

Splendid
BOOKS

Olga's Journey

1. Zagreb – Osijek (173 miles)
2. Osijek – Budapest (156 miles)
3. Budapest – Osijek (156 miles)
4. Osijek – Zagreb (173 miles)
5. Zagreb – Vienna (224 miles)
6. Vienna – Budapest via Veszprem (196 miles)
7. Budapest – Komarom (60 miles)
8. Komarom – Vienna (104 miles)
9. Vienna – Nuremberg (311 miles)
10. Nuremberg – Munich via Passau (261 miles)
11. Munich – Dachau (10 miles)
12. Dachau to Erfurt (242 miles)
13. Erfurt to Buchenwald (15 miles)

Total: **2,081 miles**

CHAPTER ONE

I looked around, my eyes wide with amazement. There was water everywhere. It covered the entire ground floor of our tiny house and was lapping at the first step of the staircase. I gingerly put one foot down into the water. It was freezing. I hurriedly hopped back onto the stairs.

Thrilled, I screamed: 'There's water in our house!'

My mother replied from upstairs: 'Olga? What are you talking about?'

I heard her footsteps on the landing and then clattering down the stairs behind me, stopping when she saw the water. My mother groaned and looked close to tears.

I still couldn't believe my eyes – where had all this water come from? The answer, of course, was from one of the three rivers – the Sava, the Kupa and the Odra – which converged in my hometown of Sisak in Yugoslavia. My house was just one of hundreds hit by floods that day in 1926.

For the children it was an exciting diversion – the older ones had a day off school and we all had the chance to float along the streets in makeshift canoes, waving to friends. For a three-year-old girl like myself, it was hard to imagine anything more exciting.

For adults it was a burden, but a familiar one. The rivers that meet in Sisak, 35 miles south-east of Zagreb, were good for business in the town but not so great for keeping the place dry. Even today,

Sisak has few buildings of any note, apart from its medieval castle set on higher ground in the old town.

As my parents began clearing up, they could be forgiven for cursing the waters. My father, Josip Czepf, had particular reason to feel aggrieved. He had invested in high-quality timber from the local factory to clad the walls of our dining room and now the bottom of each plank was soaked. The damp was rising swiftly. He resolved to move to a house on higher ground – but only when he found one with a dining room large enough to take his timber cladding.

A fastidious man who worked as an accountant at a local factory, he was determined that such expenditure would not go to waste. My mother, Slava, who worked for the same company in the sales department, would be so disappointed.

They had met eight years earlier when she was a translator at the Shell refinery in Caprag, a suburb of Sisak, where he was employed in the accounts' department. Tall and striking, with piercing green eyes and youthful energy, she had immediately attracted the attention of Josip. He was eight years her senior and a big, powerful man. He was tall with a full head of dark hair, a moustache, piercing brown eyes and a commanding presence. They married when she was just 19 and I was born the following year, on March 20th 1923.

Sisak was a quiet town and we were regular worshippers at the Holy Cross Catholic church, where my mother sang in the choir.

Many of my mother's relatives lived nearby - either in the town itself or on farms in the surrounding countryside. Her mother, Amalia, was a frequent visitor. A tall, elegant woman, she loved seeing me, but didn't feel the same about her son-in-law, Josip, with whom she frequently clashed on matters ranging from the domestic to the financial.

By 1929, I was six years old and our family was comfortably off, with a house close to the town centre - on higher ground this time. I was making friends at the local school and always felt proud when my mother came to collect me. She looked so beautiful and stood out from the other mothers. All eyes were on her and, if anyone asked, I would puff myself up and say: 'That's my mother.'

As time passed, my grandmother grew increasingly infirm. An independent woman, she lived alone, but that year she suffered a stroke, which left her paralysed on the left side of her body. She could no longer look after herself and we made plans for her to move in with us.

My father was far from keen, but there was no alternative, so my grandmother arrived and took up residence in a bedroom at the back of the house. The stroke had not stilled her tongue and the conflict with my father resumed almost immediately and was unrelenting.

I, however, was glad of the company and frequently took refuge in my grandmother's bedroom, reading to her and being taught German in return.

If we felt our bad luck for the year had been used up with my grandmother's stroke we were mistaken. The Wall Street Crash may have happened on the other side of the world, but the shockwaves were felt even in Sisak. My mother's family saw many of its investments wiped out and farm prices collapsed. In common with many others in the inter-war years our comfortable, middle-class family suddenly found itself living in considerably reduced circumstances.

Tensions in our house between my father and my grandmother increased. Something would have to give – and one day it did.

My mother returned from shopping in the local market to find the house quiet. She checked grandmother's bedroom and found her sleeping peacefully. I was out with friends, but where was Josip?

In the kitchen she found a hand-written note from him declaring that he had had enough of caring for her mother, that the constant arguments had become too much to bear and he was leaving. If circumstances were to change, he might return.

Beside herself and still clutching the note, my mother ran out into the street as if expecting to see her husband standing there. She

Aged about two, with my mother.

asked the neighbours, but no one had seen Josip. She tried the factory, but his workmates knew nothing. Forlorn, she returned home to find me at home, chattering to my grandmother. Josip had simply vanished.

This dramatic change in the family left me relatively untroubled. While my mother struggled to see how we would survive, I had always found my father rather distant and forbidding and readily turned to my mother's family for comfort. The German lessons in the upstairs bedroom continued apace and relatives offered financial support, most of which my mother felt too proud to accept. But, in truth, I enjoyed my new life.

My uncle Drago ran a restaurant on the banks of the river Kupa, which frequently played host to some of Sisak's most important citizens. Every day, there was a barbecue and I would run to the restaurant as soon as school had finished to enjoy the lamb's head that Drago had saved for me. Drago looked forward to the moment I appeared: the rest of the family had sons – I was the only girl.

Despite her best efforts, my mother could not find my father. He had left us with no money and it was impossible to claim maintenance without knowing where he was.

She continued with her work at the factory, but the domestic help she employed to look after me and my grandmother never stayed long. Eventually, my mother quit her job and turned to embroidery to make a living. A skilled seamstress, she could work at home and, what's more, I could help her. So at the age of just seven, I was taught the skills and intricacies of embroidery.

By 1930, electricity had yet to reach the homes of Sisak, so we would work late into the night by the light of a petrol lamp placed high on a cupboard, to prevent the flame catching any of the fabric. The lamp cast a yellow glow over the long table at which we worked. I would sit on a saucepan balanced on the seat of a chair to bring me up to the height of the table, stitching one end of the cloth while my mother embroidered the other end. I learnt quickly and we chatted like old friends as we worked, our heads bowed over the material, fingers flicking quickly in the lamplight. We paused in the evening to eat a salami sandwich before picking up our needles again.

Life wasn't just work, though. One of my uncles owned a large farm on the outskirts of the town, and I would often help him to take food out to the workers in the fields in a fiacre. He would whip the horses into a gallop and we would rattle along the country lanes with me hanging on for dear life until he slowed the horses and pulled up at a barn or gate. Then I would jump down clutching a parcel of food, run to the foreman in charge and hand it over. The rich, warm smell of the salami in the packages always left me feeling hungry and I envied the working men their food.

In the winter, when the landscape was covered in a blanket of snow, our faces would be stung by the cold as the horses kicked up their own snowstorm. My uncle would wrap me in a fox fur stole before setting off. 'I feel so special when I'm there in my fur in the fiacre,' I told my mother.

In common with many children of that era, I had to grow up fast. Soon I was doing the family shopping at street markets, haggling over the prices of cheese, eggs, fruit, vegetables and live chickens. I soon learnt to put the live chicken on the ground and press it with my foot to test for the quality of the meat. The stallholders would tease me: 'Oh, Olga, you're too smart. Why don't you buy this

Pictured with my father around 1925.

scraggy old chicken instead?'

On Sundays my mother and I went to church and had Maryland chicken and apple cake afterwards. During the milder weather between April and October, we would head out into the countryside for picnics. Sitting lazily on the grass, she taught me how to make daisy chains and told stories of her youth.

By 1933, life had settled into a routine. There were no luxuries but we survived. The fact that 750 miles away in the German capital of Berlin, Adolf Hitler had just been appointed Chancellor was a matter of the utmost indifference. Yugoslavia's tiny German population may have been excited, but what possible effect could it have on us? No, there was too much in daily life to worry about - the rest of the world would have to look after itself. In fact, that year I had to face a new problem of my own.

I was just ten years old when one night, leaning over my embroidery, I found myself struggling to see clearly. The neat stitches swam before my eyes. The edges blurred; the colours ran together. I blinked and rubbed my eyes. It felt as if I had pieces of grit in them but rubbing only seemed to make it worse.

Over the next few weeks, my eyes became increasingly painful and my sight deteriorated rapidly. Every time I blinked, it hurt. Our local doctor referred me to an eye specialist in Sisak who, also baffled by the condition, referred me to a clinic in Zagreb.

'They have better equipment and medicine there,' he told my mother. 'They'll be able to help you.'

My mother and I caught the train for the 35-mile journey to Zagreb for a series of medical appointments. For me, the train trip was a new world, full of surprises. Peasants would clamber on board with livestock in their hands or tugged behind them on a rope. Everyone seemed to carry vast quantities of food. Wine was transported in huge flagons which were liable to break when the rattling and jolting of the train sent them crashing against the sides of the carriage. Loud wailing and recriminations followed the breakages.

While most of the passengers headed off to the markets of Zagreb, my mother and I would go to the clinic. I was excited by the bustle and crowds of the city, but despite the optimism of the Sisak doctor, the specialists in Zagreb were no closer to finding the cause of my failing eyesight than he had been. Various treatments were tried, but the condition stubbornly refused to clear up. My excitement over the visits to Zagreb was quickly replaced by fear: my world was shrinking all the time.

'Am I going to go blind, Mummy?' I asked.

'No, of course not, the doctors will cure you,' she replied, hiding her concern and wondering where help would come from.

The payments for travelling and treatment were a heavy burden on my mother, who had precious little money to begin with and now had lost her embroidery assistant. She was forced to sell her best furniture and jewellery.

I had to wear dark glasses to protect my weak eyes and could no longer go to school, so I spent my time sitting in a chair outside the house, listening to other children playing. The days of running to Drago's restaurant to eat lamb's head and riding in fiacres with my uncle were long gone. Now, my dark world was one of very limited horizons.

I was very scared. Losing your sight is a terrifying prospect for a child and I cried often, fearful for my future. My mother was in despair. We had tried the best specialists in Zagreb, virtually bankrupting ourselves in the process. If they couldn't cure me, then who could?

Help, when it came, arrived quite by chance.

A woman visiting another family in our street saw me sitting in my chair, my eyes hidden behind dark glasses, and asked me what was wrong.

I explained, and the woman, who gave her name only as Mrs Brun, asked to have a look at my eyes. She studied them carefully and then from a jacket pocket produced a small magnifying glass. She examined them some more.

'I think I know what's wrong,' she said.

'You do?' I asked.

'Oh, yes, I think so. Is your mother or father here?'

'My mother's inside,' I said jumping from my chair and rushing into the house, shouting.

Mrs Brun explained to my mother that she believed the problem was caused by the fact that I had not one, but two rows of eyelashes, a condition known today as distichiasis. In addition, one of the rows was growing inwards, touching the cornea, known in the medical world as trichiasis. Every movement of the lid was injuring the whites of my eyes and causing bleeding. It was – and remains – a rare condition and in those days was virtually unheard of. Diagnosis is made all the more difficult because the secondary row of lashes frequently has no pigmentation and is difficult to see.

Luckily Mrs Brun believed she could treat my eyes. She returned for two visits, in which she used oil and tweezers to remove the lashes. The pain was intense and there were moments when I wept and wondered whether so much pain could really cure me. But, within a week, my eyesight was clearing and I could blink normally without discomfort.

Mrs Brun visited again and seemed pleased with my progress. I thanked her profusely and my mother offered what payment we could muster. It wasn't much. Mrs Brun refused the money and wished us well. We never saw her again.

***

Letters were not frequent in our household and the arrival of one always caused a frisson of excitement. I looked forward to the opening of any letter with eager, childish anticipation, while my mother had an adult's dread of them – fearing demands for payment and bad news.

The letter that arrived one day from Zagreb, written in careful, neat handwriting contained some sensational news – for both of us. It was from a friend of my mother called Helga, who worked at the main post office in Zagreb. Sorting post a few days previously she had come across an envelope addressed to a 'Josip Czepf' and wondered if it was my missing father.

Helga had made a note of the address and my mother instructed a lawyer in Sisak to find out whether it really was Josip – and if so, to begin legal proceedings for the four years of maintenance payments that he owed us.

It didn't take long to uncover the truth. My father was now working as a chief accountant in an asphalt factory, Res, in Zagreb and living with a wealthy Hungarian Jewish woman, Ilona Ungarl.

The legal proceedings were concluded swiftly and the family court in Zagreb ordered Josip to pay four years' maintenance, plus allowances. It amounted to a substantial sum and he never forgave my mother for taking the action.

It did, however, make life easier for us at home in Sisak. With my return to school and the money finally arriving from my father, it seemed as if our fortunes were finally looking up.

Then, as the cold of winter gripped the town in 1934 and stretches of the rivers froze, my grandmother fell ill. I was then 11 years old and could only watch as doctors came and went. I heard their heavy footsteps on the stairs and their muttered conversations outside my grandmother's bedroom door. No one told me what was going on but for some reason I felt sure my grandmother was going to die.

At the beginning of December, the temperature fell well below freezing. The countryside was shrouded in white and icicles hung from the rafters of every house. On December 3rd, in her bedroom at my home, my grandmother slipped into a coma.

I was taken up to see her. The old woman lay still and pale, her eyes closed. Never again would she talk to me in German; ask me about my day at school or curse my father for his fecklessness. I touched her hand, painfully aware of the wafer-thin skin and the fragile bones, before kissing her softly on the forehead.

Three days later, on December 6th 1934, grandmother Amalia died at the age of 72. In keeping with local tradition the funeral was held within 24 hours. The family gathered and as they filled the church pews I looked around and saw Drago and my farmer uncle who had driven the fiacre at a furious pace, and so many cousins.

They all came back to the house after the service and the hubbub of adult voices filled the rooms. I ran between the groups, talking to people, receiving words of sympathy and catching snatches of conversation.

Entering one room, I overheard my mother talking to a friend, Anna. 'You know, Anna, I feel I'll be the next to go,' she said.

'Oh, stop it,' said Anna. 'After all these problems with Josip resolved and your mother's illness, now you can start a new life. Forget this talk about death, you're only 33. You have your daughter to live for.'

Then they noticed that I was there and turned, all smiles, towards me.

Later, when most of the family had gone, Anna stayed on. My mother gave me some playing cards and I sat with the two women and began laying out the cards. The room was warm and after the excitement of the day, I soon began to feel tired and dozed on the floor. Between waking and sleeping, I heard some of the conversation.

At one point my mother confessed to Anna: 'I worry that Olga will never get married. She is so thin and ugly.'

The remark wounded me deeply. Was I really so ugly? For days afterwards I would stare at my reflection in the mirror, examining my lips, eyes and dark hair. If I was really as ugly as my mother said, what could the future possibly hold?

***

In July 1936, Sisak enjoyed a heatwave. All the children played along the riverbanks; the bolder ones swimming in the cool water while others played in the streets or headed into the country for family picnics. The pavement cafes were busy, the men taking the opportunity for lazy days spent drinking.

For women, the weather offered the chance for spring-cleaning and on July 20th, my mother started on the carpets in our house, taking them outside to hang on a fence and beating them until clouds of dust covered her.

'Olga!' she called. When I went to her, she handed me some small change: 'Go and get us some milk.'

I took the money and ran out of the house, glad for an excuse to be outside in such hot weather and to see other people. By then, I was 13 years old and as I walked to the shop I was greeted by market traders and shopkeepers, who knew me from my weekly shopping.

'Ah, Olga, come and spend your money here!' they cried. I smiled and waved, continuing on my way to buy the milk.

Afterwards, I walked slowly around the familiar streets, greeting people, chatting with my friends, stopping to play from time to time.

I certainly didn't hurry home but as I was walking slowly back up our street, a neighbour suddenly appeared looking scared.

'Go quickly, find the doctor!' she shouted. 'Your mother is very sick.'

I put down the milk and ran to the doctor, who came back to the house with me. Neighbours had taken my mother inside and laid her on a bed. The doctor took her temperature and turned to me: 'Fetch your Aunty Tonka – quickly!' Once again, I set off running and once again, just as it had been with my grandmother, I felt the adults weren't telling me everything.

Aunty Tonka – my mother's sister-in-law – came back to the house but closed the door when she went in to talk to the doctor, leaving me outside the room. Through the door, I heard them speaking in hushed tones. Eventually, Tonka emerged and led me into the sitting room.

'Your mother is very ill,' she said. 'She has pneumonia and has to go to hospital in Zagreb; they have better medicines there than in Sisak.'

I remembered how I'd been told that before – and it hadn't been true then.

An ambulance arrived and I watched as my mother was carried out of the house and carefully placed in the back before it moved off slowly down the street. Aunty Tonka stayed with me, but we said little. 'Your mother is very dangerously ill; the doctors don't know yet if she is going to survive,' Tonka explained.

I was devastated. My mother and I shared a bond more like sisters than mother and daughter; a closeness forged during those long nights together working on our embroidery and the summer picnics in the country. My mother cared for me and loved me. Without her, what did I have? Nothing.

That night, I cried and prayed. 'I'm only 13. Please don't take her,' I whispered in the darkness.

The next day came shattering news. Tonka said she could not stay to look after me – she had to work and take care of her own family. Instead, I was to be sent to Zagreb to stay with my father until my mother recovered.

My father? I hadn't seen him since I was six years old when he abandoned us. The prospect filled me with dread.

The train journey to Zagreb this time held no excitement for me; instead I was full of foreboding. Tonka came with me and when we reached the station a couple were waiting for us. I was introduced to my father for the first time in seven years. With typical teenage truculence, I refused to say hello. Beside him was a short, fat and plain-looking woman, not at all like my tall, elegant mother. This was Ilona Ungarl. Josip was then 41-years-old while Ilona was 49; to me they both looked so old compared with my youthful mother.

Outside the station a chauffeur-driven car was waiting. Nobody spoke on the short journey to my father's home, a house standing behind the walls of the factory where he worked.

It seemed as if, in that short journey, my life changed irrevocably. I had no friends in Zagreb, no cousins, no kindly uncles – and factory walls surrounding me.

Life in the Zagreb house was stiff and formal. Furthermore, I was living with strangers. My father was aloof and clearly not thrilled to find himself suddenly caring for a wilful 13-year-old while Ilona seemed to resent everything about me.

I was given a small room at the back of the house with a window that gave a cheerless view of the factory walls.

I couldn't wait for my mother to recover and then we could return to our happy life in Sisak. My father spent all day at work, while Ilona took me to the shops. Our conversation was stilted and I made no secret of my dislike for the new woman in my father's life. I spent the evenings in my room, alone, wondering about my mother. I asked my father for news. 'If I hear something, I will let you know,' he replied brusquely.

On the Saturday of my first week in Zagreb, July 27th 1936, my father suggested we all went to visit some friends for coffee. As we sat in silence behind the chauffeur on the journey to the friends' house, we passed a hospital which I was convinced was the one in which my mother was being treated, although everyone else in the car was looking determinedly in the opposite direction.

'There's the hospital!' I cried. 'Let's stop and go in and ask how mother is.'

'Oh, come on,' my father snapped. 'We'll be late for coffee and they are waiting for us.'

I slumped back in my seat, overwhelmed by sadness. I wanted to see my mother, but no one would let me. Why not? My fears were growing.

On the Monday morning, I was summoned to see my father in the sitting room. The curtains were partly drawn, casting deep shadows.

There was a long silence between us before he broke the news I had been dreading: my mother had died on Saturday morning.

Stunned, I went back over the events of that day in my mind. If only they had stopped the car I could have seen her for the last time; I could have been with her and held her hand. I was too upset and angry to cry – I bunched my fists and stared at my father with a feeling of hatred. How could he have been so cruel?

That wasn't the end of it. The funeral was to be held that very afternoon, but my father was not going; my 'stepmother', as he called Ilona, would take me instead. I could not believe what I was hearing. After all that he had done to my mother, he didn't even have the decency to go to her funeral.

'Why don't you come to the funeral?' I demanded.

'You're too young to understand.'

'Have you told mother's family about the funeral?'

'No.'

Full of bitterness and fury, I ran from the room. For the rest of my life, I have never forgotten my father's coldness that day.

In the afternoon, I dressed carefully and joined my 'stepmother' and two of her friends. They led me to the coffin before the service and opened it for me to see my mother for the last time.

I could not believe it was her. The fine black hair of which she had been so proud had turned white and although she was only 35 years old, her final illness had left her looking drawn and old.

Too quickly, they closed the coffin, but I demanded it be reopened so that I could say farewell. I put my mouth close to my mother's ear and touched her face gently. 'Goodbye, I love you,' I whispered.

I stood back from the coffin and the other three women watched me intently. I was overwhelmed by emotions: grief, anger, despair – but I was too upset to cry. Later Ilona would tell friends: 'Olga has no heart. She never cried for her own mother; how can I expect her to have feelings for me?'

A few days later, my stepmother and I travelled to Sisak to collect my belongings and clear out our house. My mother's family were appalled and angry that they had not been told about the funeral – and had only just heard about her death.

Drago hugged me to his chest: 'My little girl, what is going to happen to you?' he said. 'If the worst comes to the worst, we will all help to keep you until you finish school.'

All our belongings were sold quickly. I was heartbroken to see the beautifully hand-embroidered table clothes and pillowcases, upon which my mother and I had worked so hard, being sold cheaply.

'Can I keep something to take back with me to Zagreb?' I asked my stepmother.

'No,' she replied. 'You don't need anything. When you need something, we will get it for you.'

I said my farewells to the family and places that had shaped my childhood, taking nothing with me but my own clothes.

As I was saying goodbye to Aunty Tonka, she slipped a diamond solitaire ring into my hand. 'It was your mother's,' she whispered to me. 'She would want you to have it. Here, take it.'

I put the diamond in my pocket and then rejoined my stepmother for the journey back to Zagreb. With one final glance, I gazed around me at Sisak and the people I had known and loved all my life. Would I ever see them again?

Not if my father had anything to do with it. When we returned to the house in Zagreb, he took me to one side and said: 'Sisak is your past. Your new life is here in Zagreb. You will have a different life. You will not be poor any longer. You are going to have all you need. From now on, I want you to call your stepmother "mother", as she will be looking after you.'

I did not reply but simply left the room, leaving my father staring after me.

Not once in my life did I ever call Ilona 'mother'.

CHAPTER TWO

The Second World War took a while to reach us in Yugoslavia. We watched anxiously as Hitler's forces conquered much of Europe and we worried for our own future. Stronger nations than ours had succumbed and our Hungarian neighbours had agreed a pact with the Germans. The signs were ominous and I often heard the adults talking in hushed tones about war and what it would mean for us. It was not just the Germans we had to fear. Mussolini, Hitler's ally in Rome, had territorial ambitions too and had long cast covetous glances at our country.

The Yugoslav Prime Minister, Milan Stojadinovic, presided over a corrupt and failing system. Elections were far from secret – each voter had to declare their choice openly and have the vote entered against their name in the electoral register. It was commonplace for government candidates to offer gifts in return for votes. In some areas, officials bribed voters with a pair of opanke (slippers) - one being handed over before the election, the matching one being given after the vote. Civil servants frequently lost their jobs if they voted for the opposition.

The country was showing all the signs of a nation on the point of fracturing. The enmity between Serbs and Croatians had been with us for generations and was growing steadily worse. Belgrade, the capital, was a Serbian stronghold while our city of Zagreb, the capital of Croatia, had become the focus of demands for a separate state*.

In common with the rest of Europe, a homegrown fascist movement, the Ustasha, had sprung up in Croatia during the 1930s, led by one of its founding members, Ante Pavelic. It called for a Croatian state in which only 'true' Croats would be citizens and a society run on totalitarian lines similar to Germany and Italy. But although there were frequent battles with communist supporters, usually around the university in Zagreb, the Ustasha had little effect on us in our day-to-day lives.

By the time war broke out in 1939, Pavelic was living in exile in Italy, on the run from a death penalty handed down by a Belgrade court for anti-Serbian activities.

His chance to return came on April 6th 1941, when Yugoslavia was invaded by Germany, Italy, Hungary and Bulgaria. Ustasha supporters and the ethnic German minority in Yugoslavia helped the invading troops with acts of sabotage and by encouraging Croats to believe the invasion would bring independence for Croatia. It worked. When German and Italian forces entered Zagreb four days later they were greeted by cheering crowds. The 'liberators' had arrived.

In my home in the Res factory, however, there was no such joy. On the day the invading armies entered the city I had just passed my 18th birthday and was out walking our pet dog with Mrs Graf,

* The attempt to unite six Balkan states in the nation of Yugoslavia began in 1918 in the wake of the First World War. The borders of the new country (although it didn't take the name Yugoslavia until 1929) were established on 1 December 1918. It encompassed six states: Bosnia-Herzegovina, Serbia, Croatia, Macedonia, Montenegro and Slovenia. Conflicting nationalist aspirations meant it stumbled from crisis to crisis until 1941 when it was invaded by Germany, Italy, Hungary and Bulgaria. The new rulers divided up the nation again, installing a puppet regime in Zagreb, where Ante Pavelic and his Ustasha party ruled the new Independent State of Croatia while a German Military Administration ruled Serbia from Belgrade. Bosnia was ceded to Croatia; Macedonia was taken over by Bulgaria; Montenegro went to the Italians and Slovenia was divided among Germany, Italy and Hungary.

Resistance to the invaders united around Josip Broz, who took the name Tito. Although a committed Communist, his partisans won the support of the Allies as well as the Soviets and at the end of the war, in 1945, it was Tito who took control of the re-formed nation of Yugoslavia. His brand of independent, liberal communism gave his people a high standard of living and, unlike the rest of the Soviet bloc, citizens were allowed to travel to Western countries and even work abroad.

An alliance with Josef Stalin in Moscow lasted only until 1948 but Tito survived as leader until his death in 1980. Once he went, the end was inevitable. As the whole communist bloc crumbled in 1989, Yugoslavia shattered into warring nations and was finally wiped from the map.

a family friend. While Mrs Graf tried to control her own two large dogs, I ran ahead. Suddenly, the wailing of the city's air raid sirens halted us both. Fearing we were about to be bombed, we ran back home. But there were no bombs, just silence.

All the family was gathered, waiting to hear what would become of our country, when there was a loud banging on the door. 'Open up!' a voice shouted.

Standing on the doorstep were two men smartly dressed in Croatian uniforms. 'We are here to tell you that a new Independent State of Croatia has been declared,' they said before turning and marching away.

Mrs Graf looked pale. 'We are in danger now,' she said to me, while my father simply remarked: 'We have a new country.' Out of nowhere, the streets filled with Italian soldiers. I sat watching these darkly exotic and good-looking men from the window, but was banned by my father from going outside to mingle with the crowds.

The following day the centre of Zagreb was deserted - a city awaiting its fate. My father spent the day creating hiding places in the house for the family's precious hoard of gold.

Five days later Pavelic returned to Zagreb under the cover of darkness with a few hundred supporters, who spread themselves through the city and took control. Styling himself as Poglavnik' – the equivalent of Fuhrer – he began ruling his now Independent State of Croatia with ruthless brutality.

Ustasha gangs roamed the country taking bloody retribution against their enemies in general and Serbs in particular. As a gesture towards Germany, they brought in anti-Semitic legislation, but they were initially more intent on targeting the Serbs in Croatia than persecuting the Jews.

An air of fear pervaded every street in the city. I was in my final year at the St Vincent de Paul private school, run by a French order of nuns, and my route to school took me along familiar roads.

One morning, shortly after the Ustasha had assumed power, I saw what looked like a bundle of old clothes hanging from a tree. As I approached, still wondering why anyone would put clothes in a tree, I realised with sickening horror that it was the body of a hanged man. Further along the street was another, and then another.

I walked faster, my head bent, my eyes fixed on the pavement, the bodies hanging from the branches above me. By the time I reached the gates of the school, I was running.

It was a terrible time, but apart from food shortages we would have been relatively untouched by these events had it not been for one thing: my stepmother was Jewish. Even so, we didn't immediately feel threatened – believing the Serbs had more to fear. At that stage of the war, in 1941, the full horror of the Holocaust had yet to be unleashed.

So, as far as possible, we tried to continue with a normal life. I was doing well at school, particularly in languages, and was helping to teach Serbo–Croat grammar and literature.

And at last I had at least one friend in the family. Aunt Alice, my stepmother's sister, was an elegant woman, fond of fashionable clothes and full of life. She ran a gold and watch dealers in the centre of Zagreb and brought to the family a sense of excitement and glamour.

When she wasn't working, Alice would take me on shopping expeditions to Zagreb's most fashionable stores, and thanks to her, by the time I was 18, I was the proud owner of a pair of crocodile shoes with a handbag to match, a grey Persian lambswool coat and a sable coat. The sable coat had belonged to Ilona but Alice had commandeered it, telling her sister it made her look fat, before presenting it to me as an 18th birthday present.

She was the opposite of Ilona – and I secretly wished she were my stepmother.

My father had anticipated the food shortages and had bought large quantities of salt, sugar, matches and flour, which he traded for meat, cheese and bread with his fellow workers at the asphalt factory, many of whom came from the countryside.

But it couldn't last. An announcement was made that sent the 11,000-strong Jewish community into panic: all Jews had to be registered with the authorities. What should Ilona do? If she turned up for registration would she be arrested? And if she didn't turn up, would she be hunted down? Too many people knew that my stepmother was Jewish for her to just ignore the instruction, and in those desperate days, families could trust no one.

Ilona decided she would attend registration, which was held in one of Zagreb's government buildings, but my father refused to go with her. Despite my feelings, I couldn't let her go alone so I volunteered to accompany her.

There was a short queue when we arrived but soon it was our turn to approach the desk, where a stern Ustasha official demanded my stepmother's name, date of birth, place of birth and home address. She was then handed a black Star of David on a yellow background and told to wear it at all times. The official then turned to me and demanded the same information.

'But I'm not Jewish,' I said.

The official paid no attention. 'Name?' he barked. 'Address?'

I answered the questions and then I too was presented with a yellow star to wear. We both hurried away, Ilona so relieved that she had not been arrested that she smiled and laughed all the way home. When we got back, my father produced his camera to take a picture of the two of us with our new stars – a moment of misplaced humour before the reality of the horror struck home.

Soon Jewish people in the city began disappearing overnight, nobody daring to ask what had happened to them. Homes and businesses belonging to both Serbs and Jews were raided frequently, the owners arrested and their property handed over to 'true' Croats, who, more often than not, were friends of the Ustasha regime.

My father and stepmother noticed that many of their friends

Marta, my best friend, in 1944.

stopped visiting and the frequent dinner invitations they were used to receiving dwindled to next to none. Even their chauffeur, never an admirer of Ilona, became openly hostile, forcing her to travel by taxi. I was often delegated to accompany my stepmother when she went out because my father feared for his position if he was seen too often with his Jewish wife.

The relationship between my stepmother and me underwent a subtle change. Although Ilona was still careful to dress well, with her hair swept back into a bun and always wearing a necklace, she was clearly frightened by her new status as a social pariah and, for the first time, I felt some stirring of sympathy for her.

At 18 years old, I didn't understand the politics of the age, nor the reasons for the war, but for the first time in my life I realised that no one was safe. The laughter of my stepmother after we had registered was tense and brittle, even to my young ears. Our Stars of David marked us out from the crowd and we walked along the streets accompanied by glances of fear and hostility.

Our lives had changed forever. A cloud hung over the family – when would the knock on the door come? My father, although not Jewish himself, was terrified of the future and would do anything to avoid drawing attention to the family. He and Ilona left the house together rarely and shunned public occasions, socialising only with those they could trust who were often in the same situation as themselves.

I couldn't understand why anyone would consider Ilona an enemy. It seemed outlandish and unbelievable but I had seen the bodies hanging from the trees; heard the stories of killings and knew people who had disappeared. These were no longer ordinary times and that cloud of fear would hang over us for four more years, growing worse as the intensity of the persecution of the Jewish people grew and the terrible slaughter swept across Europe.

Our home became a place of refuge and the factory walls that surrounded us now seemed to be a blessing rather than a curse.

It was a lonely time for me, though. Friends from school were banned from visiting because any unexpected callers had to ring a bell at the main gate of the factory to be let in by the porter. My father thought it was too much to expect the porter to be opening the gates for schoolgirls – so I had no visitors.

Virtually all of my stepmother's remaining friends were Hungarian and I understood very little of the language. The only place where I could meet young people of my own age was the Hungarian Social Club, where my father and stepmother were members.

The club was an unprepossessing, single-storey building with a red tiled roof on Duga Ulica, a street which ran up from the city centre into the old town of Zagreb. Behind the grander facades of the buildings fronting onto Duga Ulica was a jumble of small offices, workshops and homes and among them was the Hungarian Club. Despite its rather drab appearance it was a friendly place, full of Hungarian ex-pats and renowned for generous helpings of food and lively music.

It was also the place where I would meet the man who would change my life forever.

I liked the club straight away, and soon made friends, particularly with Marta, a pretty fair-haired girl my own age. Her mother was Hungarian and her father was rumoured to be a relative of partisan leader Josip Tito. No one dared ask if it was true, as the Germans had recently offered a 100,000 Reichsmark reward for his capture, dead or alive.

I began taking Hungarian language classes two evenings a week and soon learnt the csardas, the Hungarian national dance.

If the Hungarian Club became the focus of my social life then my family life revolved mainly around aunt Alice.

Every day after school, I headed to Jelacica Square, the very centre of the city, and past the looming statue of Ban Jelacic astride his horse, sword pointed to the heavens. I would make my way through the flower sellers' stalls and then run up the steps leading to Trznica Dolac. On the left at the very top of the steps, just where the vegetable market spreads onto the square, was Alice's gold shop.

It was as good a place as any in Zagreb to have your business, the spires of the cathedral towering over the buildings on the other side of Trznica and the clock tower above the row of shops ringing out the hours. (The building still stands today, although Alice's shop is now a restaurant.)

Aunt Alice and I would chat happily, surrounded by gold in all shapes and sizes. I would look at the precious items and try to guess how much it was all worth. Every guess would be greeted with laughter from Alice: 'No, no, Olga, it's nowhere near as much as that' or 'Really, Olga, it's worth much more than that'…I was always left guessing but still I could dream of what it would be like to go out dripping in gold jewellery.

I watched fascinated as five elderly watch repairers bent their heads over the bench and carried out their intricate work. Alice had a contract with Helvetia, the Swiss watch company, trusted to do the maintenance and repairs of one of the world's leading brands.

The gold dealership was a family affair. Ilona had a share in the business and my father helped with the accounts. Alice had been widowed twice and had one son, Ferdinand, who was married to a model, Blanka Fredhan.

30

In my naivety it never occurred to me that a Jewish woman with such a lucrative business would be an obvious target for the Ustasha regime. Alice was just my aunt – vivacious, glamorous and fun. Surely there was no one on earth who could hate her?

Every Sunday Alice took me to visit my mother's grave, always buying flowers for me to place on her headstone. Afterwards we would go out to lunch together.

For the first time since my mother had died five years previously, I felt loved.

***

It was past two o'clock one morning in August 1941 when we were woken by a loud hammering on the front door. My father quickly pulled on a dressing gown and went to answer it. On the doorstep were two uniformed members of the Ustasha militia.

'We are here to inform you that Alice Keller has been arrested and is now in the cells at Petrinjska.'

'Why has she been arrested?' my father asked. The two men looked blankly at him as if the question was preposterous. 'Can we visit her?'

'Yes.'

'When?'

'Now.'

My father roused the family and we dressed hurriedly. My mind was whirling. Who were these men who had come to our door at this time? And what did they mean aunt Alice had been arrested?

The news shocked me to the core but then I reasoned with myself: only people who had committed crimes were arrested, Alice had never committed a crime, therefore it was all a terrible mistake and once we got to the police station she would be released amid a flurry of apologies and smiles.

We all dressed hurriedly and took a taxi in the dead of night through the deserted streets of Zagreb. We passed Jelacica Square, shrouded in darkness, and turned sharply into Petrinjska Ulica, which led away from the city centre towards the railway station.

Unlike the other streets there was more life here. Uniformed men were coming in and out of buildings, light spilling onto the pavement when the doors were opened, and in the shadows stood the prostitutes who worked that part of the city.

This was the home of law and order in Zagreb: the grand buildings contained police stations, interrogation centres for the secret police and cells. A forbidding and sombre place, my earlier optimism faded amid the atmosphere of menace. My father and stepmother were quiet but noticeably nervous. The taxi driver was sullen and keen to be rid of us.

No one spoke, but were we heading into a trap? Perhaps we too would be arrested when we walked into the police station.

I thought of aunt Alice, alone in one of the many cells, able to hear the bustle of the street outside but no longer part of it, just taken at random and thrown into prison.

We were led through the entrance of the main police station on Petrinjska and there, in a reception room, we met a tearful and very frightened Alice. She had not been given any reason for her arrest and could tell us nothing about what would happen to her.

As she spoke hurriedly to my parents, I was gripped by fear, not just for Alice, but for all of us. The new regime had reached out and torn us apart with a brutal suddenness that I could barely grasp.

The hostility of the guards and officials was plain – there would be no apologies or smiles.

Unspoken among us was the knowledge that the Ustasha had just built Croatia's first concentration camp at Jasenovac, 60 miles south-east of Zagreb. Jews and Serbs were now regularly being taken from the city prisons and transported to the camp. What became of them, no one knew. We did not know then that Jasenovac had been earmarked as an extermination camp for those deemed enemies of the regime – including a special camp for children. The number of people killed there during the war remains a subject of bitter controversy, estimates range from 50,000 to 600,000.

Standing there in the grim room I was hit by the sudden horrifying thought that I might be seeing my beloved aunt Alice for the last time. I did not cry, but embraced her with a smile and told her we would soon be back in the shop, keeping an eye on the watch repairers. She smiled through her tears and held me close. We both knew it wasn't true.

After just a few minutes and some more hurried embraces the guards ushered us out and we were once more sitting silently in the back of a taxi heading back to the Res factory. The war had hit home.

After a brief discussion when we all tried to raise our spirits by pretending Alice would be freed soon, I was sent to my room but I heard my father and stepmother talking long into the night.

I lay awake in the darkness thinking of Alice and of all the times we had enjoyed together. Now she was in a cell fearing for her life. How could such a thing happen? My feelings were a mixture of terror and anger: who was doing this to us? And why? When the Government, the police, the law courts are all your enemies, who do you turn to for justice?

My father was panic-stricken that his family would lose all its wealth. Two of the partners in the gold dealership – Alice and Ilona – were Jewish and the third, a solicitor, Mr Bratic, was a Serb. Shortly after Alice was seized he, too, was arrested and sent to Jasenovac. The family could find no trace of what had become of him. (In fact, he survived the war and later became president of the High Court in Zagreb.)

All we could be sure of was that we still had the gold that my father had hidden away in the bathroom at the first sign of invasion. We would have to depend upon that.

However, if we thought the worst was over, we were wrong.

***

Since the invasion of Yugoslavia, partisan activity had spread rapidly, particularly in rural areas where people fled to the forests and mountains, launching attacks on the occupying Axis armies and the Ustasha. My hometown of Sisak made its own small mark in history when on June 22nd 1941 the First Sisak Partisan Brigade, formed in the Brezovica forest nearby, became the first armed resistance unit to be created in occupied Europe during the war.

In Zagreb, one girl from Sisak would soon be planning her own act of resistance.

Shortly after Alice's arrest, partisans killed six German soldiers and their furious superiors in Zagreb ordered a dreadful retribution: for every officer, ten Jews were to be executed. Alice Keller's name was put on the death list.

She was still behind bars in the Petrinjska cells, but for how long? The Ustasha ran the cells but the Germans could turn up at any time to take away those on the execution list. Alice could have only hours left to live...

Although, officially, we could still take food to her every day, my father and Ilona feared it would be too dangerous to go, as it would just be inviting arrest.

I was torn. I loved Aunt Alice and could not just sit back as she was murdered, but what could an 18-year-old girl do? Perhaps my parents were right and any attempt to help would only lead to my arrest, and Alice would be executed anyway.

It was an agonising decision; who knew what the risks might be? Disappearances and murders were commonplace, something we dared not reflect on too much, but in the end, my love for Alice overcame my fears and I decided that, if nothing else, I would take her food. If I was risking arrest, so be it.

We packed a basket of ham, cheese and bread and I headed into the city centre. At the top of Petrinjska, I took a deep breath and walked towards the main police station, on the right of the street. The pale, painted walls dotted with tiny windows guarded by steel bars towered above the pedestrians below. When I reached the entrance, however, it looked like an ordinary office building.

Once inside, my papers were checked carefully, I could hear the sound of shouting and orders being barked behind the heavy steel doors leading from the main entrance hall. I felt like turning and running just to get away, to feel fresh air. After checking my papers, a uniformed warden opened a steel door and led me into another cheerless room, divided in two by a line of wooden tables.

He ordered me to place my basket of food on a table and wait. Another guard then appeared from a door on the opposite side of the room and collected the basket. He disappeared with it and reappeared shortly afterwards to return the empty basket to me. I didn't see Alice.

After my initial visit, I went to the prison every day to leave food for her. Never seeing Alice left me wondering if I had become a player in a macabre drama where I delivered food to a woman who was already dead.

The shocking sight of bodies hanging from trees in the streets of Zagreb took on a dreadful new importance: was Alice among them? I couldn't bear to look and would hurry past, my head bent, convincing myself that if I kept taking food and no one told me to stop, then surely Alice must still be alive.

I started asking anyone I could – members of the Hungarian club, friends with relatives in the Ustasha, anyone in fact – whether they would be able to find and help Alice. Some gave vague but empty promises, others just turned away. Who wanted to risk their life to help a Jew?

My father and stepmother wanted Alice freed, but were hampered by their fear of putting themselves at risk. I was young, naïve and didn't really understand the strength and ruthlessness of those ranged against us. Surely we could get Alice out.

Then one of Ilona's friends arranged for me to meet a high-ranking member of the Ustasha. He wouldn't give his real name, saying only that we could call him Ivo, but claimed he could arrange for Alice to be freed. However, there was a price: one kilogramme of gold. I was immediately suspicious. How could I trust him? Wasn't he more likely to simply take the gold and betray me? I asked around, but no one could help, so I was left alone with a terrible decision: trust a member of the brutal Ustasha or walk away and leave Alice to die?

I spent a sleepless night turning all the dreadful possibilities over in my mind. By the time dawn broke I was no less frightened and no more convinced that I could trust this man, but one thing was clear: if Alice were to be saved, this was my only chance.

I met the Ustasha man a second time and decided that if I was going to take a gamble on him, then it was all or nothing. 'I will pay you if you will get Alice out of Petrinjska and then take her to Split,' I said, feeling sure that my shaky voice betrayed how nervous I was.

Ivo smiled. The town of Split, on the Dalmatian coast, had been annexed by the Italians and controls were known to be much laxer there than in other parts of Croatia. It had become a magnet for Jews trying to escape the country. Alice's son Ferdinand – who had deserted from the Croatian army – and his wife Blanka were already there, aiming to make their way to Cuba.

Ivo agreed: 'I'll take her to Split and say that she's my mother.'

I felt relieved, but was still haunted by the thought that I was being lured into a trap. The next words from the Ustasha official hardly instilled confidence. 'I will need the gold first, of course, and if anything goes wrong… I shall say I never met you.'

We made arrangements for me to bring the gold – about the size of a large egg and which my father took from the gold salvaged from Alice's business – and hand it to Ivo. After that there was nothing for me to do except continue with my daily food visits to the cells in Petrinjska and wait.

A week passed and I heard nothing. Approaching the prison once more carrying the basket of food, I was beginning to despair, convinced that I had been betrayed and the Ustasha official had stolen the gold and would not help Alice.

In the main reception area my papers were checked again, even though the guards were beginning to recognise the dark-haired 18-year-old girl who arrived every day. This time the guards seemed nervous and avoided catching my eye. There was none of the usual chatter.

A steel door opened behind me and a gruff voice shouted: 'Hey, you! Come here.'

I felt my legs would give way. The blood rushed to my head and I thought I was going to faint. This was the moment I had been dreading: the Ustasha official had betrayed me and I was about to be arrested.

Slowly I turned and walked towards the guard.

'Olga Czepf?' he asked.

'Yes,' I replied, in a whisper.

'This way,' he said, pushing the steel door open and standing back while I stepped through.

I found myself in the prison office, surrounded by filing cabinets and desks. A low bench ran along the far wall and sitting on it, looking pale, thin and very frightened was Alice. Her face lit up when she saw me and we rushed to embrace. Alice wept with relief: she had had no idea where she was being taken when she was brought from her cell and had feared the worst but instead was in the arms of her niece.

The guard snapped: 'She's free to go. You can take her home, but go now.'

I grabbed Alice's arm and dragged her to the door. Within moments we were in the street hurrying away. I hailed a passing cab and gave the address of the friend of Ilona's who had helped

A picture of me taken at my confirmation at the age of 17.

to arrange the escape. As the car accelerated away along Petrinjska Ulica we sat hugging in the back, weeping and smiling.

***

Once the euphoria of getting Alice out of prison began to dissipate, I felt very frightened. So far, we had succeeded in only half the plan: if Alice were to survive she had to get to Split and then out of the country. But by helping Alice, I was putting myself in terrible danger. Anyone caught helping a Jew escape from the country would at the very least be sent to the concentration camp at Jasenovac – or simply be executed on the spot. The Ustasha contact, Ivo, was supposed to take Alice to Split, but would he turn up?

The woman who had helped us was visibly relieved when she saw Alice and me on her doorstep. 'Come in quickly,' she said, ushering us in before any of her neighbours saw us. She embraced us both and demanded all the details of what had happened.

I told her and asked: 'Have you heard from Ivo? Is he going to come for Alice?'

The woman looked down and shook her head. 'I've heard nothing. We just have to hope.'

We waited anxiously in the flat as the morning dragged on. Looking out from the window, I could see military vehicles passing in the street. Every one, it seemed to my nervous mind, was looking at me. Were they preparing to raid the flat? Were the soldiers I could see standing on the street corner the ones who would come storming in to arrest us all?

There was a sharp knock on the door. Alice and I froze while the other woman went cautiously to the door and listened. There was more knocking – louder, this time – and then a voice, speaking Croatian. The friend flung open the door and Ivo walked in. He greeted all three of us tersely.

'You've got one hour to get ready,' he said. 'We leave this afternoon. We're booked on a plane to Split.'

With that, he left, announcing he would return in exactly one hour to collect Alice. Only she was to go with him, he insisted. We would have to say our goodbyes in the apartment.

I quickly prepared a bag for Alice, including some spare clothes and food. It was very little, but it was the best I could do. We were all terrified something would go wrong, but after an hour, Ivo reappeared.

Alice and I embraced. 'My dear, Olga, thank you so much,' she said. 'You've been so brave and so kind. I will never forget you and will always love you.'

I held her tightly. 'Be careful, Aunt Alice. Be careful. Let us know when you get to Split. Let me know you're safe.'

The Ustasha man was clearly impatient with the tearful farewells and was soon hurrying Alice out of the flat. I ran to the window and looked down into the street in time to see the pair of them getting into a car, which I watched until it turned a corner and was lost to view.

I stayed alone in the flat, keeping an eye on the clock as the minutes ticked past. The flight was due to leave Zagreb later in the afternoon so I ate some lunch and then lay down on the sofa in the sitting room and dozed fitfully.

At four o'clock I was woken suddenly by knocking on the door. I sat up, tense with fear.

'Who's there?' I called out.

'Ustasha!' a voice replied.

I looked around frantically but there was only one way out of the flat and no hiding place. Trembling, I opened the door. The first person I saw was Ivo, and next to him, looking exhausted and tearful, was Alice.

'What…what are you doing here?' I asked, dreading the reply. The Ustasha man pushed past me into the flat, dragging Alice with him.

'There's fog at the airport. All flights have been cancelled. We will have to try again tomorrow morning when the airport reopens. I'll call tomorrow morning.' And with that, he turned and left, his heavy footsteps echoing on the stairs, leaving Alice and me together. Once again we embraced and Alice explained they had got all the way to the airport before being told their flight was cancelled.

The strain was taking its toll. 'I can't stay here,' she said, gripping my arm. 'I just can't. They will know where to find me. I must stay somewhere else tonight and come back in the morning to meet the Ustasha man. Then if they come in the night for me, I won't be here…' She was clearly terrified.

I ran to a friend's house. 'Could you help my aunt, please? Can she stay here tonight?' I asked. The first door was closed in my face. The next family I tried, however, said yes. Quickly, I rushed back to collect Alice and took her to the new flat, which was close to the old town, a few hundred yards from the one we had been in.

There we spent the longest night of our lives in the overheated sitting room of the apartment. To our anxious minds, every sound from the street seemed to herald the arrival of the Ustasha or the Gestapo. A vehicle passing slowly outside, its shrouded headlights illuminating the darkened street was surely the first in a convoy of vehicles arriving to take us away for execution. Sleep was out of the question. The clock on the mantelpiece in the sitting room where we spent the night ticked each second off painfully slowly towards dawn.

It came as a relief to us when the first light of day spread over the city. We walked slowly back to the other flat and, once again, we waited. The Ustasha official was as good as his word, arriving on time and ushering Alice into the car. She turned and waved to me as the vehicle pulled away.

It was the last time I ever saw her.

***

A couple of weeks later a letter arrived at our home. It was postmarked Split and although unsigned told us that Alice had made it there and needed money to escape to Cuba with her son and daughter in law.

If someone could go to the Hotel Esplanade in Zagreb at a certain time they would be met and could hand over the money. My father and stepmother read the letter several times and turned to look at me. No one spoke. I knew they wouldn't do it. Once again it would be down to me. 'It's all right, I'll take the money,' I said.

We didn't have much cash, so we packed a briefcase with jewellery and gold and on the appointed day I headed to the Esplanade, Zagreb's most prestigious hotel. A commanding building near the station, it overlooked carefully manicured lawns and had become a favourite among high-ranking Ustasha officials and German officers.

The front door was held open for me by the liveried doorman and I stepped inside clutching the briefcase. My heart fell as I looked around. I had never seen so many German uniforms before, as all the most senior Nazi and SS officers wandered around or sat laughing and chatting, ordering meals and drinks. Those who weren't German were clearly Ustasha members and the lobby resounded to loud male voices and laughter.

I felt like dropping the briefcase and running. It would take just one person to ask to see what I was carrying and all would be lost.

In fact, no one paid me the slightest attention. A few glances, perhaps, but just what any 18-year-old girl would get in a hotel lobby full of men.

I found a seat on a small sofa away from the main door and placed the briefcase on the floor next to me. My thumping heart was finally beginning to calm down when a tall, elegant Slovenian woman approached. She sat carefully on the chair next to me, the briefcase between us on the floor.

'Hello,' she said, gazing around at all the German officers. 'I'm a friend of Alice.'

I smiled nervously and we made polite conversation for a few minutes, but neither of us wanted to linger. I stood and said my goodbyes. We shook hands and I headed for the exit. When I glanced back the woman had disappeared with the briefcase.

I was glad to escape from the Esplanade and went back home to tell my father about the handover of the jewellery.

For four agonising weeks, we heard nothing. And then a letter arrived. The handwriting was unfamiliar, but the postmark showed again it had been sent from Split. A note inside said that Alice Keller, her son, Ferdinand, and his wife, Blanka, had left on a boat bound for Havana, Cuba.

They were free.

CHAPTER THREE

On August 20th 1942, a fighter plane of the Royal Hungarian Air Force took off from Ilovskoye in the Soviet Union.

No one knows why, but shortly after it left the ground, the pilot lost control and the plane crashed, exploding in a fireball. The pilot died instantly.

It would have been a sad but unremarkable death had it not been for the fact that Flight Lt Istvan Horthy was the 37-year-old son of Admiral Miklos Horthy, the Regent of Hungary and Hitler's ally. The younger Horthy was deputy Regent, a sensitive and hugely popular figure in his home country. In his letters home to his father he expressed deep concerns over the German army's excesses, particularly the SS, as it swept across Russia. Those who had allied themselves with Berlin would one day find themselves held accountable for this brutality, he predicted.

His death stunned Hungary and the country was plunged into mourning. The spirit of national dismay spread quickly to Hungarian communities around the world, and Zagreb was no exception. A memorial service was organised at our Hungarian Club on Duga Ulica, to which all members were invited along with the entire staff of the Hungarian Embassy.

For Marta and me it was an unusual event, bringing important people to our club, including handsome young men. Marta was thrilled and although I was less excited by the prospect, it didn't

My dear friend Marta and I.

stop me going.

The diplomatic corps turned up smartly dressed, some in uniforms, and took their places in the seats reserved for them. We sat three rows behind. Throughout the service one of the diplomats, a fair-haired man with pale blue eyes, kept turning to look at us. As soon as he turned away, we were convulsed with giggles. Hardly acceptable behaviour at a memorial service but when you're young everything in life is funny.

It was a hot summer's day, so food and drink were served in the club's small garden after the service. We were enjoying ourselves and we kept an eye on all around us as we clutched our plates of food and our drinks.

While we were standing chatting, a woman approached and introduced herself as Mrs Tackas. She told us that she ran a restaurant near the Hungarian Embassy and knew most of the diplomatic staff. 'One of the gentlemen would like to be introduced to you,' she said to us.

We assumed he was interested in Marta with her curly blonde hair and ready smile. 'Oh, yes,' said Marta, 'I wouldn't mind being a diplomat's wife.'

Mrs Tackas disappeared into the throng and didn't reappear. Marta soon lost heart. 'He must have changed his mind,' she said.

We were just turning away when Mrs Tackas reappeared accompanied by a pale, slightly-built, blond man who, I thought, was surprisingly short. But I did notice his striking blue eyes and he had an engaging smile.

'Here is the gentleman who wishes to meet you,' she announced, introducing Marta.

'This is Julius Koreny from the Hungarian Embassy,' she said. The diplomat took Marta's hand, kissed it in greeting and said to Mrs Tackas: 'Would you now introduce me to her friend?'

He repeated his hand-kissing ritual with me and smiled warmly. Turning to Mrs Tackas he said: 'This is the girl I wanted to meet.'

We were all surprised by his bluntness; I caught Marta's eye and fought back laughter. Who was this rather unprepossessing man? What he lacked in traditional good looks he more than made up for in self-confidence – but I was unimpressed.

As the day turned to evening, dinner was served in the club. Julius Koreny made sure to sit with me on one side and my stepmother on the other. He quickly charmed Ilona, so much so that Marta whispered to me: 'Look! Your stepmother has stolen your admirer.' We laughed again. I couldn't have cared less. I didn't find Julius handsome and his attempts at charm struck me as false and unconvincing. 'You may like me,' I thought, 'but I don't like you.'

When the party broke up in the early hours Julius came to say farewell and as he bent to kiss my hand, he turned to my stepmother and said: 'Yes, 12.30 will be fine. I'll look forward to it.'

On the way home, Ilona was full of praise for the bright young man and told me that she had invited Julius to join us for Sunday lunch. My heart sank. A family lunch with my difficult father, awkward stepmother and a rather boring admirer? What a dull prospect.

**

At our house behind the walls of the Res factory, the guests began to gather early for lunch that Sunday. Julius Koreny, the diplomat from Budapest, was to be the VIP guest, someone new to add to Ilona's dwindling band of lunch companions. He didn't disappoint, proving good company and a lively conversationalist. He told us he'd been in Zagreb for 18 months and had previously

45

Julius Koreny, pictured in Zagreb in 1943.

served in Romania. He loved the Croatian people, he said, because they were friendly and good fun. But there was a surprise: he was divorced with a one-year-old son, Gabor, who was at home with his ex-wife in Budapest. I noticed that he still wore a wedding ring.

Through further questioning I worked out that he was 29, exactly ten years older than me. Another mark against him in the romance stakes.

'Of course, I visit Budapest regularly so am able to see Gabor often and help look after him,' he told us.

Ilona saw an opportunity. For some time she'd struggled to make contact with her father who lived among Budapest's beleaguered Jewish community. Letters and parcels never seemed to reach him. Could Julius help?

He responded commendably: 'Yes, of course, if you give me his name and address I'll take money to him next time I'm in Budapest.' Ilona was delighted and the other guests were impressed by Julius's cool defiance of Hungary's pro-Nazi Government. He rose in my estimation.

When the meal was over and the guests were preparing to leave, Julius told Ilona he was going to Budapest at the end of the following week. Would she like him to take some money this time? My stepmother rushed to find her handbag and gave money to Julius, squeezing his hand and saying: 'Oh, thank you! It's so difficult at the moment… Well, you know…' Everyone knew what was happening to the Jewish community across Europe. We lived with that same fear every day. They had come for Alice and any day they could come for Ilona.

He was back within a fortnight, having seen Ilona's father and handed over the money. He carried a letter from him, which brought tears to her eyes. Julius became a regular visitor at our home, always welcomed by Ilona and increasingly by me too. 'He's good for company,' I thought, 'but not for romance.'

***

At the time of the invasion of Yugoslavia almost 11,000 Jews lived in Zagreb, a city with a total population of around 250,000. By the end of the war, 8,000 of the Jews had died in the holocaust, others had fled and barely 1,000 were left.

As the purges of Jews intensified, an elderly aunt of Alice's first husband, Mrs Hirsch, was rounded up by the Ustasha and taken to a lunatic asylum at Vrapce, in the western suburbs of Zagreb. Many Jewish people were detained there, often before being sent to the camp at Jasenovac. A proper and very grand lady, who smoked with a diamond-studded cigarette holder, Mrs Hirsch was in her seventies and Ilona wanted to send her food and money. Once again she thought of Julius. The next time he visited the house an opportunity presented itself.

'Look,' he said to us, producing a document bearing his picture, 'this is my diplomatic pass – I can go anywhere with this and it is accepted by everyone.'

'Really?' said Ilona, 'in that case, can I ask another favour of you, after your kindness to my father?'

Julius, no doubt aware that I was watching him keenly, answered promptly: 'Of course, what is it?'

Ilona told him the story of her relative and asked whether he could visit Vrapce. Ilona pleaded with him. 'Just some food and money, that's all you'd have to take. She's an elderly lady, she can't escape and she can't hurt anyone. Please…'

Julius agreed: 'But on one condition.' We looked at him across the dining room table.

'What's that?' my father asked, nervously.

'I would need to take my wife. A diplomat travelling with his wife attracts very little attention: everyone assumes you're just sightseeing. A man on his own attracts much more attention and I don't want to face any awkward questions.'

There was a long silence. His wife? What was he talking about?

'But,' said Ilona, 'you're divorced. Your wife is in Budapest; how can she help?'

'She can't, but I have an idea…' He produced another document from his pocket, bearing the picture of a young woman. 'This is my wife's diplomatic pass. If we take her picture off and substitute one of Olga, she can come with me; that way we can travel safely.'

Everyone turned to look at me. It had been more than a year since I had rescued Aunt Alice and the memories of those terrifying days were beginning to fade. Julius seemed to be offering me an adventure and some excitement. I was only 19. I said yes.

**

It was only as we were approaching Zagreb central station for our first visit to Vrapce that I realised the danger of what we were doing. My initial excitement of embarking on what seemed like a rather inconsequential adventure was overtaken by anxiety: the station was alive with troops, Ustasha officials and Germans.

The feeling of fear took me back to those minutes spent in the Esplanade lobby surrounded by the SS. I felt sure it would take only one inspection of our papers for us to be unmasked. However the first inspection passed without incident. Julius's confidence hid my nerves and everyone saw us exactly as we had intended: a young married couple exploring the city.

Julius smiled and me and squeezed my arm. 'Don't worry,' he whispered as we walked along the platform towards our train.

There seemed to be uniforms wherever I looked: on the platform, at the ticket barriers and even on the trains. Each of those uniforms, whether they were German or Croatian represented danger. Not only was I travelling on a fake diplomatic pass but – far worse – I was using it to visit and help a Jew.

At least this time, unlike when I had helped aunt Alice escape, I was not alone. Julius chatted and did his best to make me laugh – to give the impression of a young couple with nothing to fear.

Fortunately, the train journey was short. Vrapce was nothing more than a suburb of Zagreb and the station was quiet. One cursory examination of our papers and we were out in the street, walking quickly towards the old hospital building. Inside, the grounds were crowded with people who stared at us with suspicion. Some of them were clearly mentally ill, but others were not. Children approached with hands outstretched asking for food, for money, for anything.

I had never seen anything like this before. What was this place? Why were people who were healthy sent here?

We couldn't be seen helping a Jewish resident so we made our way quickly to the grand main building, more reminiscent of a building on the banks of the Seine in Paris, than a hospital in Croatia. Inside, miles of corridors led off in every direction. Julius approached the reception office and rapped on the glass window, to be answered by a surly Croatian woman.

She directed us to the room where Mrs Hirsch lived. There we were greeted by an elegant 75-year-old lady dressed in black whose face creased into a bright smile when we explained who we were and why we had come.

'Come in, come in,' she said, ushering us into the small room.

'You are the first people from outside that I have seen since I came here,' she told us. 'How is Ilona? How is the family?'

I sat with her and told her the family news while Julius stood at the window, wishing to be gone. We couldn't stay long. All three of us were aware of the risk we had taken visiting at all, and when I handed over some money and food, we all felt it would be better for us to go.

Julius and I retraced our steps and both breathed a sigh of relief once we had passed through the main gate of the old hospital and were back in the street.

We had an hour to wait for the train back to Zagreb, so we found a café where we sipped coffee, ate cake and talked. Julius told me about his life in Budapest, the son he'd left behind and his former wife. I told him the story of my early days in Sisak, the death of my mother and aunt Alice's escape from Zagreb. We laughed at the misunderstanding over our first meeting at the Hungarian club.

As we sat at the café table, I finally began to relax. We'd pulled it off. Our papers had been examined, we'd been scrutinised and no one suspected anything. The journey back to Zagreb was straightforward and the fear of arrest receded. Julius and I chattered on, ignoring the uniforms around us.

Back home, Ilona was delighted to hear of the success of the first trip. 'Oh, it sounds easy. You can go again in a few weeks,' she said. I readily agreed.

And so the pattern was set. Every few weeks, I would become Mrs Koreny and travel with Julius on the diplomatic pass. We were stopped countless times, but no one suspected us and we became almost blasé about our deception.

After visiting Ilona's relative, we would sit in the same café, and, like any young couple, would chat and flirt. Our friendship was growing into something more. I found myself looking forward to the trips, no matter how dangerous, while, I suspected, Julius was falling in love with me. The shared sense of danger and excitement forged a bond between us and our easy companionship was something I'd never experienced with a man before. My early unflattering assessment of Julius had long been forgotten.

It was on one of our trips to Vrapce, when we were waiting again in our usual café, that Julius slipped his arm around me, pulled me close and kissed me softly on the lips.

It was the first time I had kissed a man – it felt as if the world had stopped. 'Oh,' I said, as if that was what all girls said when they were kissed. Julius smiled gently at me, his eyes flashed blue and we sat there silently in the small café surrounded by smoke and conversation, in our own little world.

The next invitation from Julius was not to accompany him to Vrapce but to go to the opera. I could barely contain my excitement. My father was unsure whether or not he approved, but he could hardly complain about his daughter going to such a public place. He didn't need to worry about chaperones: there would be hundreds of them.

The Hungarian Embassy kept a box at the opera in Zagreb and I was thrilled as Julius led me to my seat for the opening night of Tosca. Not only did I like this unusual man, but also he was introducing me to a new and glamorous world. As the house lights dimmed we smiled at each other in the darkness before the soaring music swept us away.

Afterwards, Julius saw me home, kissing me tenderly before we reached the factory gate and rang for admittance.

By day we visited Vrapce as Mr and Mrs Koreny; in the evening we went to the opera as Mr Koreny, Hungarian diplomat, and his friend Miss Czepf. Often two women from the embassy joined us in the box. They would talk rapidly to Julius about subjects I didn't even begin to understand. I was always glad when the lights went down and we could sit close together in the dark.

Julius still made his regular visits home to Budapest to see his son and ex-wife. We soon fell into a habit where I would accompany

51

him to the main railway station in Zagreb from where he caught the train to Hungary.

It was never easy to say farewell: I missed Julius when he was away and worried for his safety. We would part with a kiss and I would spend the next days thinking of him and waiting anxiously for his return.

On October 15th 1943, as we set off for the station, I was gripped by an uneasy feeling. Something was going to go wrong, I just knew it. Julius laughed at me. 'This time,' I said, 'you will not return.'

'Of course I will. Don't worry,' he replied. 'Why would I not return? Anyway, I've left my Leica camera, my winter coat and other belongings here. I've got no choice – I have to return. I will see you in a few days.'

We laughed and embraced but still I could not rid myself of the feeling of anxiety.

As the train built up a head of steam and the guards ran along the platform shouting 'All aboard!', I gazed through the compartment window at Julius and wondered when – and if – I would see him again. With a huge blast of steam the engine slowly began to edge out of the gloomy station into the daylight, with its line of carriages clanking along behind.

Julius leant out of a window to wave to me, and I kept my eyes fixed on him until he was hidden in a cloud of steam.

Soon the last carriage had pulled away and the train disappeared eastwards out of the city. As I turned away, I hoped that I was wrong and that everything would be all right and, just as Julius predicted, he would be back in a few days.

In fact, amid the steam and noise of Zagreb central station, everything had changed. My life would never be the same again.

CHAPTER FOUR

For three weeks, there was nothing but silence. I missed Julius. In the past few months he had become the most important person in my life; now he was gone.

Then, after what seemed like a lifetime, the phone rang one day while I was sitting in my bedroom.

My father answered and through the walls I heard a brief conversation, then the receiver was replaced and there was silence. A few moments later I heard Josip's heavy footsteps approaching my bedroom and the door opened.

'That was Julius on the phone,' he said. 'There have been some problems in Budapest but he hopes to be back next week.' There was a pause. 'He wanted you to know.'

My father had made clear his disapproval of the growing friendship between his daughter and the now 30-year-old divorced man with a son.

I was delighted at the news – at least I knew Julius was alive; nothing bad had become of him. Or so I thought.

Then I was beset by doubts. What sort of problems had kept him in Hungary? Surely it couldn't be his former wife, otherwise why would he have called me?

Having been freed from the anxiety about Julius's safety I now wished my father had asked more questions. Perhaps he did, and just wasn't telling me? But if it was bad news for us, my father would have been only too pleased and would have delighted in telling me…

The situation was impossible. I couldn't work out what was going on, so resigned myself to waiting.

The following week, there was another call and once again, my father answered. This time the conversation was longer and as soon as he put down the phone I went through to the sitting room to find out what had been said.

It was bad news. 'Julius is under investigation by the authorities,' my father said. 'He's not able to leave Hungary and has to stay in Budapest…'

His voice trailed off and I realised there was more.

'Yes?' I said.

My father seemed to be struggling to find the words; the expression on his face was dark.

'He asked for my permission to marry you.'

I stood there, speechless. Marriage? I'd never even considered it. 'But I've missed him so much, since he's been away…' I thought.

My father was speaking again: 'He wants you to travel to Budapest and stay with his sister, Shary, until all this is sorted out and he's free.'

Julius had also asked if I could collect his winter coat and Leica camera from the embassy in Zagreb.

My mind was made up straight away. 'Is this what love feels like?' I thought, smiling to myself. 'I'm going to Budapest,' I told my father.

He was furious. 'You're only 20!' he shouted. 'You can't go off chasing after this man. He's too old and he's divorced. Anyway, how would you get there, when we're in the middle of a war?'

I shouted back, saying I'd do what I pleased. My stepmother came running to find out what all the noise was about and, of course, took my father's side.

But I was in love and had only one aim: to rejoin Julius. If I had to go to Budapest to do that, then so be it.

I'd never felt at home with my father and stepmother, so why not go to someone who really cared for me?

Further, I believed that Julius might have been in trouble because he had helped Ilona and her Jewish family, and he had done that to impress me.

Realising he would not dissuade me, my father gave me the address of Ilona's brother in Budapest in case I needed help, and some money.

'But from now on,' he told me, 'you're on your own.'

Later that day, I called Julius's number in Budapest and spoke to him with all the shyness of a girl in love. I said I was preparing to travel to Hungary and he told me not to worry, that everything would be sorted out soon so I wouldn't have to stay in Budapest for long and then we could return to Zagreb. The call was hurried, the line unreliable and so much was left unsaid.

Had we known what was to follow, the conversation would have been very different.

***

The Hungarian Embassy in Zagreb was a large three-storey building next to the Botanical Gardens on Marulicev Trg, close to the Opera House. I wasn't sure what to expect when I went there to collect Julius's belongings, stepping through the imposing entrance and then up some marble steps to the main hall.

On either side were corridors of offices with people bustling in and out. The staff seemed distant and faintly hostile when I told them my reason for being there, but one man, Mr Angel, disappeared down a corridor and reappeared with Julius's coat and camera. He handed them over without a word and joined some embassy staff in one of the offices. They all stood staring at me.

I was glad to leave the oppressive atmosphere but was haunted by the looks and the whispered conversations while I was there. What sort of trouble was Julius in?

I spent my evenings poring over maps and train timetables, calculating a route to Budapest and how long my money would last.

It was less than 200 miles from Zagreb and while travelling was obviously difficult because of the war, it was not impossible. I would have to stop en route and work to raise some money to complete the journey, but, I told myself, it could be done.

When I made closer checks at Zagreb's main railway station, however, I found to my dismay that it was impossible to get on direct trains between the two capitals. They were always full of military, business, government and diplomatic staff and a girl of 20 on her own would need a special permit to travel. I had no chance of getting on board.

There was another way. I could take a train to Osijek, 130 miles east of Zagreb, and close to the border with Hungary. I didn't need a permit to make that journey and there I could work for a short time, raise more money and then find a way across the border and travel north to the Hungarian capital. My decision was made. Now I could take the first steps on my journey.

***

The turn of the year brought dreadful weather to Eastern Europe. In January 1944 temperatures fell to minus 15 degrees in some areas and snow covered most of Croatia.

The war was far from over and in the north-eastern corner of Croatia, the city of Osijek was filling up with German troops as the Axis forces began the long, bloody withdrawal towards Germany and defeat.

Sitting on the River Drava, the town was important for its close proximity to the borders of Serbia and Hungary, and also for its oil refinery. Hitler needed oil and the Allied bombers often targeted the refinery.

Was it any more dangerous than staying in Zagreb?, I wondered, as I boarded the train for the four-hour journey to Osijek. The train pulled out across the flat lands to the east of Zagreb, running parallel to the blue hills in the north, before leaving them behind and speeding through farmland where makeshift homes stood next to the tracks, each piled high with wood for the fire.

From time to time, the train would pull to a stop at a nondescript low platform and passengers would clamber down, clutching their belongings and disappear into the surrounding countryside.

We passed scattered villages, clustered around red-roofed churches, looking picture-postcard pretty in the snow.

Occasionally, I would see a horse and cart, making its way along a straight road next to the railway line. It reminded me of those long-ago days in Sisak when my uncle took me galloping through the snow in his fiacre.

The train's progress was painfully slow but we were lucky. No bombers appeared in the skies above us and as we headed further east trees appeared close to the tracks and a string of low hills shielded us from Allied aircraft.

I ate what little food I had brought and dozed fitfully as the train ploughed on. Eventually, we slowed and drew to a stop alongside a long, low station building bearing the sign 'Osijek'.

Most passengers left the train, walking across the tracks and into the station building before heading out into the town. Long straight roads led north towards the River Drava and, not knowing the town at all, I simply followed the crowd.

The main street was Zupanijska Ulica leading towards the huge red-brick building of St Peter and St Paul's Parish church, which everyone called 'the cathedral'. Another short walk and I was on the banks of the Drava, staring across the wide waterway towards the north. The real border between Croatia and Hungary was about

12 miles away, but the Hungarians had occupied a swathe of land, effectively bringing the border down to the Drava. Cross the river and you were in Hungarian territory.

Nearby, children were breaking ice on the edges of the water, shouting and laughing.

I turned back into the town and asked directions to the labour exchange. I jumped on a tram, which headed into the town centre, and within minutes I was offered a job with a local undertaker back on Zupanijska Ulica. Not a cheery occupation, but given the times a pretty reliable one.

Now, I needed somewhere to stay – and a new heel for my shoe, which I had broken during the journey. I found a cobbler, Mr Bariaktar, a few doors along the street from the undertaker's and handed in my shoe, asking at the same time if he knew anyone who let out rooms. The old man asked me to return in a couple of hours – he might have something for me.

When I went back he said he had spoken with his wife and they could offer me a room. Soon I was installed in a small bedroom at the back of the cobbler's shop.

Mr Bariaktar sang every evening in a choir so Mrs Bariaktar, who was Hungarian, was delighted to have some female company and what's more, one who could speak some of her native language.

We got on famously and I found my new accommodation gave me a valuable insight into the people of Osijek. Everyone needed coupons to buy shoes and Mr Bariaktar knew virtually everyone in the town.

Mrs Bariaktar was also a useful source of information about travelling to Budapest. Her view was simple: don't. People seeking to travel from Osijek across the border had to be resident in the town for at least a year, she told me. What's more, the trains were unreliable and subject to Allied air attack. She hadn't been back to her hometown since war broke out. Why on earth would I risk it?

I kept my counsel and carried on with my dispiriting work at the undertaker's recording the names of the dead, allowing relatives in to view the bodies and helping to organise the funerals.

In the evenings, after Mr Bariaktar had finished singing, the Bariaktars would take me to clubs in the town where Hungarian musicians played. A hotel on Zupanijska Ulica became one of our regular haunts and it was also popular with some less reputable elements in the town including a notorious horse racing gambler, known simply as Giner. He limped on his left leg after what he claimed was a war injury but others guessed came from a beating. He held court at one of the tables there and whenever I appeared with Mr and Mrs Bariaktar he would catch my eye and smile.

Shortly after we had sat down at our table a waiter would appear with a tray of cakes, which he presented to me with a flourish.

'Giner sent these,' he would say and just then Giner would raise his glass to me and smile broadly. I laughed and enjoyed the cakes, but I had no desire to take his obvious approaches any further. I didn't need any more trouble; I had enough of my own.

During the day, I often walked through the city and watched the trains pulling out of the station, heading north. They were always full and at the station everyone's papers were checked before boarding. I saw people turned away if their papers were not in order. Ustasha guards and – increasingly – the Gestapo took a keen interest in anyone trying to travel to Hungary.

Hitler's patience with the Hungarian Regent, Admiral Horthy, was wearing thin. There was even talk of Hungary trying to make a separate peace with England and the US – an intolerable betrayal in the eyes of Berlin. To add to the suspicions of the guards on the cross-border trains, Budapest had become known as a relatively safe city for Jews. Before 1939 the city's Jewish population had numbered 200,000 and although Horthy's Government passed the anti-Semitic laws required by all the German allies, there had been little of the physical brutality seen in other countries. So in the early 1940s Jews from other European countries headed to Budapest as their 'least worst' option and hoped they could sit out the war in relative safety among a large number of fellow Jews and a less virulent government.

They were wrong, of course. The horror reached them just as it did millions of others. As I stood watching the crowds in the low railway station at Osijek I could not have foreseen the terror that was about to engulf them all.

Anyway, the state of relations between Budapest and Berlin didn't matter to me. I was preoccupied only by thoughts of reaching the Hungarian capital, and Julius. Leaving Zagreb had been easy, but that was only an internal journey and in Osijek I understood for the first time just how difficult it was to cross a border in time of war.

Eventually I confided in Mr and Mrs Bariaktar. 'I must get to Budapest – my fiancé is under investigation and I need to help him,' I said, realising with a start that it was the first time I had referred to Julius in this way.

Mrs Bariaktar was not surprised. She had wondered why a young girl from Zagreb – who could speak some Hungarian – would travel to Osijek for no apparent reason. She warned me of the dangers. 'The war will end one day and your fiancé will come back. Wouldn't it be better if you waited for him in Zagreb then he knows where to find you?' she said gently. 'Budapest is a very dangerous place.'

I knew that Mrs Bariaktar was right, but who could really tell how long the war would last? And Julius needed me now.

Quietly, Mr Bariaktar mentioned one of his customers, known in the town as Dr K, who could get anyone across the border. Mr Bariaktar would arrange for me to meet him.

I was delighted, never imagining it would be so easy, and went to sleep that night excited at the thought that my journey was assured and soon I would be with Julius.

The next day, after work, Mr Bariaktar told me that he had been in touch with Dr K. We could meet the following day in a café and he would make arrangements for me to travel to Hungary.

Thrilled at the prospect, I dressed carefully in my best clothes for the meeting: a brown woollen coat with a fur trim, new shoes (courtesy of Mr Bariaktar), matching handbag and brown felt hat with three pheasant feathers.

Looking at myself in the mirror I could hardly fail to be pleased. Staring back was a pretty young woman, with long black hair, dark eyes and a dazzling smile. How far I'd come from my mother's description of me as 'thin and ugly'.

I arrived in plenty of time at the café near the church of St Peter and St Paul and waited. Feeling self-conscious under the gaze of the other customers, I began to fear that Dr K would never appear but a short time later, the door opened and a gust of cold air preceded the arrival of a large man, covered in a heavy dark coat, with a hat and scarf obscuring much of his face.

His attire made no difference; everyone seemed to recognise him and there was a muffled chorus of greetings. I was convinced I heard the name 'Dr K', and sure enough he stood just inside the door, nodded his head in acknowledgement of the other customers and looked around, his eyes coming to rest on me.

'Miss Czepf?' he asked.

'Yes,' I replied, standing awkwardly to shake his hand. He sat opposite and signalled to the waiter to bring him a coffee.

'I know that you want to cross the border,' he said, studying me closely, 'and I can help you, but it is absolutely essential that you keep this secret. You mustn't mention it to anyone. Do you understand?'

I nodded vigorously. 'I understand, of course. I will tell no one.'

Dr K studied me some more and sipped his coffee. 'Why do you want to go to Hungary?'

I told my story once again and he seemed satisfied. He gave me the address of a place to meet the following day and, with that, he shook hands and left.

I rushed home, full of excitement, and told the Bariaktars that it was all arranged. 'Tomorrow, I'll be in Budapest,' I said.

After a sleepless night, I dressed again in my smartest clothes and packed a bag. This was the day. By the time night fell, I would be with Julius.

Dr K was at the meeting place and greeted me with a handshake and a slight smile before leading me towards the bridge across the river.

As we walked, I could feel my fears rising, wondering what would become of me. Within minutes we were close to the bridge and Dr K strode confidently towards a wooden hut full of Croatian border guards. His heavy coat billowed like a cape as I trailed along in his wake.

Once inside, Dr K did all the talking. I stood mute behind him while the guards listened and scrutinised me. After a rapid exchange, two guards stood and led me out of the hut. I looked back, expecting to see Dr K coming with us, but instead the door closed quickly and I was alone with the guards.

'Come,' one of them said, and we set off towards another cluster of huts on the other side of the bridge. We passed some coils of barbed wire and I realised as we walked that I was in no man's land, just a few steps from Hungary.

The guards greeted me warmly and with great courtesy – my spirits rose. While the Croatian guards waited a few yards away, I told the Hungarians my story and reason for wanting to visit Budapest. One of them watched me closely and then turned and disappeared into the hut.

'He is asking our commanding officer,' one of them told me. There was nothing to do but wait. Behind me was Croatia; in front, Hungary, Budapest and Julius. There was only one direction I wanted to go and I was growing more and more sure that I would be allowed across. The guards had been so friendly. Finally, the one who had gone to seek permission emerged, his face set and determined.

He looked at the other men and then shook his head once and uttered the word: 'Nem.'

With that he turned his back and left us. The Hungarian guards shook their heads in sadness and held out their arms to signal that I should turn back.

Stunned and close to tears, I picked up my bag and began walking slowly back across the bridge.

I paused and looked over the parapet at the dark waters of the River Drava. Just then, a strong gust of wind whipped the hat off my head, sending it spinning into the water below. I gazed down and saw the three pheasant feathers bobbing on the water before sinking out of sight.

My hopes went with them.

Once back in Osijek I told Dr K I was determined to cross the border. 'I doubt you will,' he said. 'If I can't get you across, no one can.'

I felt tears sting my eyes. I had to find a way to Budapest, otherwise my journey would be over before it had even begun. But who could I turn to now?

Help came from an unlikely source. My father had family near Osijek and when I visited them, one mentioned a Hungarian border guard whose work involved examining the papers of passengers who went for day trips to Hungary.

I arranged to meet the guard the following Wednesday, when he was on duty. He seemed unconcerned about any risk in taking me across the border, but insisted on payment. He named his price – an outrageous sum of money.

'I'm sorry,' I said, 'I can't afford it.'

The earnings from the undertaker were enough for me to live on, but little was left over. The money my father had given me was rapidly disappearing and the only item of any value that I owned was the solitaire ring that had belonged to my mother.

The guard had already noticed it. 'If you can't afford to pay me in cash, then the ring on your finger will do very well,' he said.

I asked for time to think about it. The thought of using my mother's ring as payment was deeply upsetting. It was my last link to her and even though she'd died eight years previously, those days with her in Sisak were times when I had felt safe and loved.

Just as when I had met the Ustasha officer who had helped my aunt Alice escape, I had no idea whether I could trust the guard. I was told he had helped others and no one suggested he betrayed them.

A few days later, I returned to the guard's office. I told him my decision: he would get the ring on condition that he took me all the way to Budapest. He promptly agreed and told me to meet him at Osijek railway station the following Thursday.

The die was cast.

***

On the appointed day, I packed two suitcases and again said goodbye to Mrs Bariaktar, who embraced me and whispered: 'Good luck! Let me know you're safe.'

At the station, I met the border guard, who took my arm and led me past the officers checking papers and into a carriage with six seats. We took places by the window, facing each other, and after what seemed an interminable delay, the engine expelled a cloud of steam and slowly the train pulled out.

It crossed the bridge over the River Drava, where my hat had been lost, and then ground to a halt. Armed guards appeared alongside the tracks and began climbing aboard the train, shouting for papers. They were approaching along the corridor, each carriage door thrown open followed by a demand for passports and identity cards.

Eventually the door in our carriage crashed open and two guards appeared. They looked at my companion and me and stopped dead. Slowly, their faces broke into smiles and they began chatting to the guard from Osijek. They shook hands warmly and both the border guards cast a few interested looks at the young girl travelling with their colleague. They didn't ask to see any papers.

Soon the doors were slammed shut as the guards jumped down from the train and the engine once again built up a head of steam and began the slow journey north.

I watched with relief as we moved past the border posts and huts to which the armed guards were returning. My companion smiled at me. 'There. I told you everything would be all right,' he said.

I smiled weakly back. 'We're not there yet,' I thought, but allowed myself some elation that finally I had achieved my first objective: I was in Hungary.

Our next stop was at the town that I had always called Pechuh but today is more often known as Pecs.

It was only about 35 miles from Osijek and soon the train was rattling through the outskirts of the town. The guard stood up. 'I told you I was your friend. You're safely across the border and I must leave you now,' he told me, holding out his hand for payment.

I was shocked; I hadn't expected to be left alone so soon and I had no papers.

'What about me?' I said.

'From here, you're on your own,' he replied, coldly, hand still outstretched.

I pulled the ring from my finger and passed it over. The guard pocketed it, gave me a quick kiss on the cheek and was gone.

A lot of passengers got off the train and more joined. My carriage soon filled up. The seat opposite was taken by a ginger-haired man in a suit who looked keenly at me before turning his attention to a newspaper.

The train began moving and I looked around the carriage. No

one met my gaze. Everyone was quiet. I had expected the guard to stay with me to Budapest and now here I was, once again alone.

This wasn't what I had planned at all.

***

When I arrived in Budapest, stepping down from the Pecs train into a maelstrom of noise and rushing people, I was stunned by the sheer size of the place. Not just the station, which was huge, but also the city itself. Sisak and Osijek were tiny in comparison and even Zagreb had not prepared me for the scale of Budapest.

I was overwhelmed by the noise and atmosphere. The trams ran rapidly through the streets; everyone seemed to be in a hurry; each face bore signs of strain and anxiety. Smiles were in short supply. None of this was surprising given that Hitler, fed up with the Hungarian leader Admiral Horthy, had finally seized control of the country. What would become of Budapest now?

Whatever the future held for the city, the day I arrived it was freezing, seeming to me to be even colder than Osijek. I needed to find some warmth and shelter.

I picked up the two suitcases I had brought and headed for a telephone booth. Scrabbling for change I found enough money and dialed Julius's number, expecting to hear his voice. Instead, I heard only the dull tone of a disconnected line. Suddenly, I was frightened. Now that I was here in Budapest I had expected everything to be easy but Julius had disappeared. What had become of Julius?

I was looking in my bag for my stepmother's brother's address that my father had written down before I left Zagreb, when a man's voice interrupted: 'Can I help you? You look lost. Is anything worrying you?'

With a start, I realised it was the ginger-haired man from the railway carriage. Had he been following me? Why would anyone be interested in me? I dismissed the idea and told myself not to be foolish.

I answered the man in all innocence: 'My fiancé's phone has been cut off and my uncle's number is not in the phone book…'

The ginger-haired man seemed genuinely concerned. 'Oh, dear. Do you know your way around? Have you been here before?'

'No, this is my first time here. I don't know Budapest at all,' I replied, showing the stranger my uncle's address. He looked at it and smiled.

'What a stroke of luck! I'm going in the same direction. I'll take you to the tram stop. I'm going two stops further on, so we can travel together.'

He picked up my suitcases, glancing at the coat I was carrying on my arm and the Leica camera in a shoulder bag. 'Where are you taking those?'

'To my fiancé who lives in Halmi Utca. I am going to leave my suitcases with my uncle then I'll take these to him.'

The ginger-haired man gave me a thin smile and led me out of the station onto the crowded pavement. We joined a group of people waiting for a tram, standing in silence until it arrived. He politely helped me aboard and sat next to me. The tram set off and it wasn't long before it juddered to a halt at a stop not far from the station. Helping me down with my suitcases, the ginger-haired man pointed to a corner and told me that was the street I needed. With that, he stepped back onto the tram, gave a small wave and settled back into his seat.

***

My uncle was delighted to see me. 'We get so few visitors,' he said, ushering me into the front room of their large house where his wife was sitting by the fire.

'It is very difficult for us all at the moment… But we are the lucky

67

Myself, pictured in 1942.

ones, you know. So many others have suffered so much more.'

His wife fussed around, preparing food while I retold the story of my journey to Budapest – and why I was there.

The couple looked at each other, anxiety written on their faces. 'It's dangerous here,' my uncle said. 'No one knows what is going to happen. You should go back to Zagreb, go home. Ilona will look after you.'

I wasn't impressed by that suggestion but, not wishing to offend my hosts, said nothing.

'I really must get to Julius now,' I said, standing. 'Before it gets dark.' The couple looked at each other. 'But you're staying here tonight?' my uncle asked.

'Oh, yes, please, if I could.'

'Well you must have lunch before you go. You don't need to rush. He will still be waiting for you.'

'Shouldn't I go now?'

'No, no. You must have lunch…'

So I stayed, chafing at the slow progress of the meal, the endless courses and the glasses of wine that left my head spinning.

Finally it was over. I hugged them both and with messages of good luck ringing in my ears headed back into the street to find the bus stop to take me to Halmi Utca – and to Julius.

I approached the bus stop and joined the waiting group, huddled together against the cold. I looked again at a small map my uncle had drawn, showing the route.

As I waited, a man approached and smiled: 'How remarkable – we meet again!'

He doffed his hat and revealed the ginger hair of the man who had boarded the train at Pecs. I froze; who was this man? I took a step back, trying to lose myself in the crowd, but there was nowhere to go.

The man smiled. 'Don't be frightened. I want to help you.'

Just then the bus pulled up and the crowd surged forward. I pushed my way to the front and scrambled on board, desperate to get away. It seemed as if the bus would never move as more and more people got on, but there was no sign of the strange man. As the driver finally engaged gear and the ancient vehicle jerked forward, I relaxed and turned my gaze to the back of the bus. There, sitting comfortably in one of the few available seats, was the ginger-haired man. He met my gaze with a slight nod of the head and a faint smile.

It wasn't far to Halmi Utca and soon I was stepping down from the bus on a tree-lined road of large villas. I stood on the pavement watching the other passengers disembark, but there was no sign of my constant companion. As the bus pulled away I caught sight of him in his seat, still staring at me.

I watched until the bus was out of sight before setting off slowly along the street, clutching the hand-drawn map and the coat I had brought for Julius. The street was on the Buda side of the Danube, in a quiet residential area not far from the river. It had wide pavements shrouded by overhanging branches and houses set back from the road.

Many of the homes had entrance gates and the door numbers were difficult to see. I concentrated on each of the houses in turn. Perhaps that's why I didn't hear the sound of a vehicle approaching.

It wasn't until the large, black car pulled up at the kerb and a man in a dark suit got out that I realised what was happening. The man stepped in front of me, his jacket falling open to reveal a gun as he snapped: 'Papers!'

For a split-second I thought of running; would he really shoot a woman in cold blood in the street? But the moment passed. He would chase me down and then my punishment would be even greater.

'I…I don't have any,' I said quietly.

'Why are you here?'

'I'm visiting a friend…'

The man grabbed Julius's coat and pulled it. 'Whose coat is this? Give me the coat!'

'No!' I cried, pulling it back towards me.

'You're under arrest,' he shouted, and dragged me by the coat towards the car.

He pushed me into the back, climbed in beside me and slammed the door. He gave a terse command to the driver and the car swung around on the wide street and headed fast towards the Danube.

My mind was racing: the border guard in Osijek and the ginger-haired man on the train must have been working together. But was there someone else involved in the plot against me? I must have been watched every step of the way.

As the car sped on, I was left with a bitter sense of betrayal and, looking at the cruel-faced men who'd arrested me, a feeling of terrible fear.

CHAPTER FIVE

Today, Andrassy Utca in Budapest is one of Europe's most attractive boulevards. The travel guides describe it as 'the Champs Elysees of Budapest' and for once, they're not wrong. It's a tree-lined avenue with international designer names occupying the boutiques on the ground floor of the elegant buildings, and some of Budapest's most expensive apartments and offices above. It all has a feeling of grandeur and class.

There is only one building that intrudes, striking a discordant note: number 60. The imposing four-storey structure built in traditional stone with large windows would not seem out of place but for a rather odd stencil-like awning that extends from the roof high above the street below. The letters in the awning are designed so that the sun shining through them will spell out a word on the exterior of the building, appearing in different places on the fascia at different times of the day. The word says simply: 'Terror'.

This is the House of Terror, the place where first Hungary's own Nazi Party, the Arrow Cross, had its headquarters from 1937 to 1944, and then where the Nazis themselves set up an interrogation centre after they arrived in Budapest. Later, it would become home to the Communist Party's secret police when it was their turn to be in charge.

The basement, carefully hidden from the street outside, is a labyrinth of corridors and cells – Budapest's very own Lubyanka.

(top) One of the cells in the House of Terror today, similar to the one in which I was kept for two weeks in 1944. (bottom) 60 Andrassy Utca, Budapest – the House of Terror as it looks today. It was here that I was taken for interrogation after being arrested in the city.

It was here, in March 1944, that I was taken.

As the black limousine that had picked me up in Halmi Utca crossed the river, I dared to turn and take a last look out of the back window of the car. The Buda hills rose high above us, with the city's castle perched on top.

Soon we were onto the broad sweep of Andrassy Utca; the car accelerated past the grand buildings until it reached the forbidding entrance at number 60.

The two men got out and marched me to a steel door, which was opened by more guards. Inside, everything was a brilliant white; the walls, the floors and the ceiling. Music was playing from speakers fixed high on the walls. I was led to a side room and locked in. The guards disappeared and I was left completely alone except for the music, which sounded louder now.

When the door opened again, a female guard in full uniform strode in and ordered me to take off all my clothes.

Petrified, I did as I was told. The guard searched me intimately before allowing me to get dressed. With that, she disappeared and I was once more alone.

What was to become of me now? I was angry with myself for being so easily caught and frightened of what would happen. I didn't know, at that stage, what a terrifying reputation 60 Andrassy

Utca had and how much worse that reputation would become in the next few years.

After what seemed like hours, two male guards appeared and told me to follow them. I was marched to a flight of steps and taken down into the basement.

Still accompanied by the incessant music, I was marched along a corridor lined with steel doors until one opened and I was pushed inside.

The cell had a barred window with opaque glass, high in the wall. A single bed draped with a Hungarian flag sloped up towards it and when I lay down, I was surprised by how comfortable the bed was. Through the window I could hear traffic and the footsteps of passersby on Andrassy Utca.

The cell door had a small flap attached to the outside, and from time to time it would be opened and a guard would look in to check on me. Apart from that there was nothing – except the sound of music.

I paced the cell wondering what would happen next. I was a 20-year-old woman, entirely at the mercy of guards who were used to doing whatever they wanted to the prisoners.

The first time the door opened it was for a soldier to deliver a surprisingly good dinner and when he returned to collect the tray, he left writing paper and a pen, saying I could write to whomever I chose and the guards would post it.

'What do you want with me? When will I get out of here?' I asked, but got no reply.

As dusk fell, the lights still burned in the cell and the corridor. The only way I could tell that day was turning into night was the fading of the light from the window. When I asked to visit the lavatory, the guard accompanied me along the corridor and waited outside.

I found it hard to believe what had happened. Why on earth would they arrest me? I had done nothing. I didn't even know why I had been arrested. I was scared and tired, but convinced that it was all a terrible mistake. Soon I would be freed.

I lay down on my prison bed, going over all the day's events in my mind. I cursed myself for not realising sooner that I had walked into a trap. Finally, I fell into a troubled sleep, not knowing where I was or how long I would be there.

It was three o'clock in the morning when the cell door was flung open.

'Come!' a guard shouted. Stunned and drowsy, I got up quickly and followed him along the corridor to a lift. We went up four floors and I was led to an interview room and ordered to sit opposite two men who were waiting there.

I looked from one man to the other. Both were smartly dressed with carefully cut hair; one dark, the other, fair. The fair one, younger and almost effeminate, had the shadow of a moustache on his upper lip, as if to emphasise his masculinity. Of course, it had the opposite effect.

They began to ask questions: 'Who are you?'

'Why are you here?'

'Who sent you?'

'Where are your papers?'

'Are you a spy?'

'Why did you have a camera?'

'You know what happens to spies?'

'Who is Koreny working for?'

'Who else was there when you met him?'

'What do you know about his activities?'

'How did you meet him?'

'Have you come to Budapest before?'

'What were you going to do when you met Koreny?'

The questions just went on and on, delivered so rapidly I could barely understand them – never mind give a coherent reply.

Sometimes one of the men would stand and walk round behind me, firing questions all the time while the other sat watching closely. At other times they would both sit, or stand. They smoked incessantly and the atmosphere in the room was heavy with their threats and my fear.

I did what any innocent person does in such circumstances: told the truth.

'I've come to see my fiancé, nothing else,' I told them. 'You have to believe me. He wants to marry me and I brought his coat and camera from the embassy in Zagreb. I'm going to stay with his sister until this is all cleared up and then we will get married.'

My voice was desperate but I was determined not to cry. I would not give them that satisfaction.

'What is cleared up? Do you know what has happened?'

'No, no. I only know that he is under some sort of investigation. I don't know any more than that.'

'When did you last speak to him?'

'Weeks ago.'

'So you don't know what's happened to him?'

'Oh, no!' I cried in despair. 'What has happened?'

Neither man answered. Moments later, I was escorted back to my cell.

The pattern had been set. Every night between three and four o'clock, the cell door opened and I was taken to the top floor for questioning.

Sometimes the interrogators were the same men; other times, different faces appeared. The questions, however, never changed. They were all about Julius and his 'activities'. My head would spin with all the questions but I knew nothing. Surely they couldn't be talking about our visits to Ilona's Jewish relative in Vrapce? Why would they care about something that took place in Zagreb? Maybe Julius was helping the Jews here in Budapest, I thought.

'What did Julius tell you?' they asked, time and time again.

'I don't know. He never told me anything,' I replied. It was nothing but the truth.

Then, suddenly, after 14 nights, it stopped. I was told that the following morning I would be sent back to Croatia. I felt overwhelming relief at the prospect of being free again, but dismayed that I did not know what had become of Julius. My first thought was of how I could return to Budapest.

The following morning two officers from the secret police led me to a waiting car. It was a short journey to my uncle's house, where one of the officers collected my two suitcases while I sat in the car. I was not allowed to see my aunt or uncle and was puzzled by the courtesy which the secret police showed towards the occupants of the house, who were Jewish, after all. As the car pulled away and I looked back at the imposing home, a terrible thought began nagging at the back of my mind...

Soon we were at the station and settled in a train carriage for the journey to Pecs. The guards were obviously enjoying their trip out with a young woman and as my fears for my own safety began to disappear we chatted, sharing ham rolls and drinks. We reached Pecs at lunchtime and the guards treated me to a meal of szekely gylyas, a local dish of sour cabbage and pork. I said how good a glass of wine would taste with the meal.

'If you have any Hungarian money left, I'll buy some,' one of the guards offered. I found some change and he bought a bottle of white wine for us to share.

It was a bizarre moment. I was sitting enjoying a pleasant meal, yet I was still a prisoner and only a few hours previously I'd been in a cell in Budapest's most notorious interrogation centre.

After we had eaten I was taken to Pecs prison to spend the night before completing the journey the next day. The two guards from Budapest wished me good luck.

'Well, hopefully, I'll have better luck next time,' I replied. They laughed and left me.

I didn't sleep that night. The dark stone walls in the prison seemed even more forbidding than my familiar cell at 60 Andrassy

Utca and I was troubled by fears for Julius. The moment I felt myself slipping into sleep, I would see his face and suddenly I was wide awake again.

The next day, I was on the train to Osijek with two different guards, who asked how I was. I replied: 'In need of a good long sleep.'

The train rumbled to a halt at midnight, a few miles short of the border. I could see pinpricks of light in the surrounding countryside but apart from that, only darkness. The guards got up. 'This is where we leave you; we're getting off here.'

'What?' I said, beginning to panic. 'How do I get to Osijek with no papers and what will I tell the Croatian police about where I've been and what I was doing here?'

One of the guards turned and said coldly: 'You should have thought of that before you decided to cross into Hungary. You didn't ask our advice then. Don't ask for it now.'

With that, the two of them clambered down from the train, walked along the low platform and disappeared into the darkness.

I was left alone in the carriage with two suitcases, no papers and no reason for being there. Just then the train gave a jerk and began moving slowly forward. The next stop would be the border.

As the train approached the barbed wire lines and the security huts, I made my decision. Grabbing my suitcases, I waited until the train had slowed to walking pace and jumped, landing on the dusty ground a few hundred yards short of the border crossing.

I approached the nearest hut of the border patrol and knocked on the lit window. The door was opened quickly, casting light out onto the dark railway tracks and standing there was the guard who had first taken me across the border. Recognising me, he laughed and invited me in. 'You met your fiancé, everything's fine and you've decided to come back?'

I was furious. 'You betrayed me! I know you kissed me when you left me on that train so that other man would know who to follow… Judas!' I hissed at him. The guard laughed again. 'Some coffee? You're really most ungrateful. I jeopardised my position to help you and this is all the thanks I get?'

Still angry, I sipped the hot coffee and added: 'Well, don't worry I'm sure your name will be on the next list of honours.'

'You made your own choice; you have to live with it.' But he was beginning to soften and suggested I wait in the hut overnight until a direct train to Zagreb arrived at nine o'clock.

'If you try to lose yourself in the crowds, it will be easier,' he added.

But my luck had definitely run out. Standing the next morning among the small crowd waiting for the Zagreb train, which was more than half an hour late, I was the only passenger with a sizeable amount of luggage. Two suitcases was an unusual load to be carrying and a couple of Croatian guards approached and demanded that I open them.

Inside they found a carefully crafted Hungarian doll in national dress and some powdered red paprika – both gifts from my uncle that I didn't know he'd packed in the suitcase.

Two more guards arrived and began questioning me as the others went through my belongings under the inquisitive gaze of the waiting passengers.

'Where did you buy these items?'

'I didn't – they were a gift from my uncle.'

The guards were sceptical and one suggested I was a black marketeer. 'No, no,' I said, and told them the truth about my journey.

'For crossing the border illegally you will spend two weeks in prison,' the senior guard announced. With that, all of my belongings were gathered up and roughly stuffed back into the suitcases and shortly afterwards two guards and I boarded the Osijek train.

Once more I crossed the River Drava back into Osijek. I was taken to the jail in the old town and put in a basement cell. Freezing cold, I sat huddled in a corner, trying to keep warm. My journey had become nothing more than a procession of prison cells. Suddenly, I felt a light touch on my leg and screamed. Rats. I looked around: the floor appeared to be alive, constantly moving; it was infested. I was terrified and longed for my cell at 60 Andrassy Utca.

During my two weeks in the Osijek jail, a fellow prisoner told me why there had been constant music playing in the Budapest cells: 'It's so that you can't hear the beatings and the screams.'

The guards in Osijek were certainly less threatening – almost bored, in fact. From time to time, I was taken for some desultory questioning about my illegal journey, but the interrogators' hearts weren't in it. They knew they were dealing with a foolish young girl – not a spy.

Sitting shivering in my cell, warding off the rats and trying desperately to keep warm, I had time to reflect. I was convinced the betrayal had begun the moment I made contact with the border guard. The authorities watched me all the way to Budapest to see who I would contact and arrested me. Why had they not arrested my uncle as well? After all, he was Jewish. Could he have been part of the plot? I couldn't believe it. I dismissed the idea.

All this plotting to arrest me and find out more about Julius. But why? What had he done?

My cell door opened for the final time and I collected the two suitcases. As I began walking slowly back towards Mrs Bariaktar's home, I was struck by the recollection of one thing the interrogator in Budapest had said: 'So you don't know what's happened to him?'

What had he meant by that? Standing alone in the street, there was one question that now haunted me: was Julius already dead?

CHAPTER SIX

News was hard to come by during the war. In places such as Osijek it was often difficult to distinguish between fact and rumour. All the news on radio and newspapers was controlled by the Germans and the Ustasha – it was illegal to listen to foreign broadcasts, the BBC in particular.

But by June 13th 1944 we had all heard: the Allies had invaded Normandy the previous week. The Germans claimed they were turning the Allies back and driving them into the sea. Some believed them, some didn't and predicted that it marked the end of the war.

I wasn't sure. How could I tell? For me, and millions of others, it seemed to change nothing. It was just another battle and we'd heard about so many; it seemed unlikely this one would be any different.

It was hardly surprising, though, while all eyes were on northern France, that few observers either knew or cared what was happening in the small Croatian town of Osijek.

We'd suffered before at the hands of the US bombers as the town's oil refinery made it a target – but not a tremendously important one. The damage often came as planes were turned back by the guns at Ploesti in Romania, Hitler's key oil refinery. Osijek was a good location en route home to offload unused bombs.

We hoped that apart from the occasional raid on the refinery, we'd largely be left alone.

It was not to be. By June 1944 a growing number of German

soldiers were moving into barracks in the Tvrdja area of the town. Around them were factories, a sugar plant and an oil refinery. For the bombers, it was an obvious target.

It was not an area of the town I visited regularly. The combination of warm weather and the river was irresistible to the mosquitoes and walking there was like trying to force your way through a moving green curtain of insects.

June 13th was St Anthony's Day and celebrated widely among the Catholic population. It was also the name day of the Ustasha leader, Ante Pavelic. So the bombers had a target and a perfect time to attack.

After my return from Budapest I had nowhere else to go but back to the Bariaktars, where they had kept my room clean and tidy and all my belongings neatly stored away.

When I knocked on the door the day I was released from prison, I resolved not to tell them of my spell in the town jail. Budapest they could know about, but not my shame in Osijek.

'Olga!' cried Mrs Bariaktar, when she opened the door and saw me standing there, bedraggled and forlorn, with my two suitcases.

'Come in, come in,' she said, giving me a big hug. I held her close. It felt good to experience some kindness after all the hostility in Hungary.

She fussed around, making tea and finding food, demanding to know all about my adventure. She was dismayed at my betrayal and imprisonment but glad that I was safe and back in Osijek.

I felt relieved but also a failure. What had I achieved? Nothing. If anything, I might have made matters worse for Julius. As Mrs Bariaktar helped me unpack my suitcases and chattered about how we could again go to the music clubs we used to visit, I had already made up my mind to return to Budapest and find Julius.

I wouldn't tell Mrs Bariaktar straight away. First, I had to make plans.

I went back to my old job at the funeral parlour. If I thought it had been grim work before, I had no idea how depressing it would become. The bombing raid on June 13th changed everything.

The first I knew of the raid was the thud of explosions and the tremors from the blasts. The streets emptied as everyone rushed to find shelter and soon a pall of black smoke hung over us. Wave after wave of bombers swept over and the town's anti-aircraft guns sent up a stream of bullets.

When the last of the bombers turned and headed back to the west, I looked out and saw the fires burning and the clouds of dust from collapsing buildings rising high in the sky.

I could hear the screams of terrified survivors and the distant wailing of sirens. I got ready quickly and ran the short distance along Zupanjiska Ulica to the funeral parlour. It was the worst raid the town had suffered. I dreaded to think how many people had been killed.

When I got there everything was in chaos. Already bodies were being brought in and stories were circulating that several hundred people had died. 'It can't be that many,' I thought. 'It just can't be.'

In fact, it was worse. In all 1,300 people had been killed in the raid and because of the stifling summer heat, families wanted their loved ones buried within 24 hours.

It was heartbreaking to see the bodies of entire families being brought in, the young children often looking completely unharmed, as if sleeping.

The bombs had missed much of the industrial area, landing instead in the densely populated streets of the old town. Very little was left standing; more bodies were being found all the time.

We were too busy for emotions. The funeral parlour soon ran out of coffins, as did all the others in the town. Makeshift ones were hammered together by carpenters and tradesmen while funerals were being conducted around the clock. I worked through the day and night, dealing with grieving families, writing names on makeshift crosses to mark graves, allocating bodies to particular graveyards. There was no time for the proper paperwork to be done and, inevitably, mistakes were made.

Families found their loved ones buried in cemeteries of a different religious faith and insisted they be reburied. They were not slow to complain to me about the error and a Catholic priest turned up to accuse me of neglect. I'd worked solidly for more than 24 hours helping the grieving families and wanted to snap back: 'Where were you when we needed you?' But I stayed silent, too tired and sad to bother arguing.

For me the bombing was the final straw. What was I doing in Osijek when my original plan had failed so badly? I'd only moved there to cross the border – and I couldn't risk that route again.

There had to be another way, but it meant going back to Zagreb and by June 1944 you needed papers and official permission even for that domestic journey. I applied and by July, my papers were ready.

With a heavy heart I said goodbye to the Bariaktars again and all my friends in Osijek before boarding the train for what should have been a straightforward four-hour journey home.

It took two days.

Not long after leaving Osijek the anti-aircraft guns carried on flat wagons at the front and back of the train exploded into life, spitting fire at the Allied aircraft lining up to attack.

'Quick! Get out!' the guards shouted. We threw open the doors and jumped down onto the track.

I helped another woman down from the train and we fled across the railway into the undergrowth and flung ourselves into a ditch. Soon the planes were directly above us, the sound of their machine guns raking the carriages.

I pressed myself into the ground and covered my head, deafened by the sound of gunfire and bombs exploding. All around me I could hear people muttering prayers or sobbing quietly. Some of the bombs landed so close that great showers of mud rained down on

Julius in Zagreb before his arrest.

us where we lay hidden. When the aircraft finally turned away, everything was deathly quiet until a guard came along giving the all clear. We scrambled to our feet and headed back to the train, which had escaped serious damage, but many of the windows had been shattered by gunfire and, worse, the track ahead had been hit by bombs and was now impassable.

There was nothing to do except sit in the train until the track was repaired. We chatted and dozed for hours, and, eventually, the train jerked forward. We were on our way again – but not for long. Soon we reached another part of bombed track and the whole ponderous process of repairing it began again.

Next, there was a rumour of partisans ahead, planning an ambush. Again, we were ordered off the train and we all lay in the fields and bushes, waiting for hours before finally being told the way was clear.

Fortunately, I had brought food but others on board had nothing. I shared my rations – salami, bread and cheese – among them. Finally, after spending a night on board the train, it dragged into the central station in Zagreb.

Exhausted, hungry and dirty, I looked around the familiar station, made my way to a phone box and dialled my father's number. His voice was cold and unwelcoming.

He had heard from my uncle in Budapest about my arrest. 'I can't have you coming here,' he told me. 'The risk to Ilona would be too great.'

I was hurt and shocked. Even after all the arguments we had had, I never imagined he would turn his back on me in this way.

Zagreb was my home city, but I didn't have a home there any more.

I looked around the station at all the people hurrying to their homes and felt terribly lost and alone.

I picked up the phone again and called my friend Marta, from the Hungarian club, who'd been with me that day when I first met Julius. Unlike my father, she was delighted to hear that I was back and invited me round.

Her mother was appalled at my father's behaviour and I winced when she called him to tell him that he was not behaving as a father should and she would help me instead. After that, they were always the fiercest of enemies.

I was given a small room next to the kitchen, which had been used in the past for a maid.

As I settled in that first night back in Zagreb I realised that to many people it would appear that I had lost everything: work, family and home. What's more, I hadn't found Julius – and didn't even know what had become of him.

I saw it in a different way. I was more determined than ever to be reunited with Julius, the man I loved. After all I had been through I had everything to gain – and nothing left to lose.

CHAPTER SEVEN

The trains waited in the sidings at Radnicka Cesta in Zagreb for days at a time while they slowly filled with people. The long rows of cattle trucks were destined for the Reich and the passengers were travelling north for work.

By July 1944, Germany was desperate for labour to keep the war going. Apart from the prisoners of war and the concentration camp inmates, they also demanded 'volunteers' from their allies.

Zagreb was one of the places expected to come up with its share of volunteers for the greater good of Germany. Those who went did so for a host of reasons: money, escape, regular work, a belief it would benefit them if Germany won the war. I doubt that anyone else made that journey for the same reason as I did: love.

Watching another of those trains waiting in the sidings at Radnicka Cesta early in July, I asked one girl who was clambering on board with a suitcase where it was headed.

'Vienna,' she replied.

'What do you need to volunteer?'

'You have to have identity papers, of course, and be over 21. If you're not old enough, you just need your parents' permission,' she said, smiling briefly before heading into the darkness of the railway truck to find a place to sit.

'When do you leave?' I called after her.

'Tomorrow,' came the voice from the shadows.

Vienna was perfect. The train could carry me across the borders into the Reich without fear of arrest and once in Vienna it was a relatively easy 150-mile journey to Budapest.

Life, however, is not that simple. I had no identity papers and the idea of asking my father for his approval was out of the question – he would not help me in any way. But how closely would the Germans running the train look at ID papers? All they were worried about was returning to Germany with the requisite number of volunteers. I had no desire to help the German war effort, but every desire to find Julius.

I packed a suitcase at Marta's home that night and left the remainder of my belongings there. Early the next morning I was at Radnicka Cesta, picking my way across the railway tracks and looking along the long line of cattle trucks to choose one to board. I ruled out the first and last carriages – too obvious – and opted for one somewhere in the middle, guessing that if they were checking papers they'd be bored and rushed by the time they reached my carriage.

I threw my suitcase in and climbed up behind it. Someone offered me a hand and soon I was standing in the truck and as my eyes adjusted to the darkness I realised it was already almost full.

After a few muttered apologies and smiles, I found a place to sit, next to a dark girl with gentle brown eyes, wearing a turban. She avoided my gaze and I got the feeling that she too had no papers – there was certainly something strange about her. It was a hot summer's day and the heat in the carriage was stifling, so why was she wearing a turban?

We studied each other surreptitiously and sat in silence.

The more I examined her the more I became convinced that she was Jewish. I dismissed the thought just as quickly – she was dark and looked Jewish, but in that case why on earth would she be volunteering to work in the Third Reich?

No one else in the carriage was paying us any attention. I

caught her eye and spoke very softly: 'I know you are Jewish; my stepmother is Jewish as well and I know many Jewish people.'

She froze, her whole body stiffened, but she still didn't look at me.

'If you are, don't worry,' I continued. 'I shall never betray you.'

With those words, she relaxed and finally looked at me.

'Promise?' she said.

'I promise.'

Her name was Hermina but all her documents gave it as Herta, so from then on that was how I addressed her. Quietly, so that no one else in the carriage could hear, she told me her story.

Herta was only 22 years old, barely older than me, but she had spent time with Tito's partisans, launching attacks on German troops and the Croatian army. In one encounter an SS doctor had been badly injured and was left behind by his fleeing comrades.

As the partisans withdrew, Herta stayed with the doctor, who gave his name as Karl, and nursed him back to health. He was an Austrian from Vienna who had been injured on the Russian front and was partially blind. Not knowing that she was Jewish, he promised that in return for saving his life if she ever wanted help, she need only ask.

Now, he was due to meet her at the station in Vienna and take her to the Croatian Embassy. His influence would secure her a better job.

'Isn't it very dangerous?' I asked, shocked that a Jewish girl would choose to take such a risk.

'What isn't dangerous these days?' she replied, with a thin smile.

'Look at me,' she said, pointing at her turban, 'I've had typhoid and lost all my hair, that's why I have to wear this thing.' She lifted the edge of it and I could see that her hair was growing back, but to remove the headgear would have brought too much unwelcome attention.

When the train finally began to inch forward out of Radnicka Cesta towards the north and Austria, we settled back, chatting, both relieved to have found a companion for the journey.

It's only about 230 miles from Zagreb to Vienna but it was as tortuous a journey as the one I had made from Osijek. The train frequently slowed to a halt as guards ran alongside, banging on the sides of the wagons shouting: 'Air raid! Everyone out!' and we would jump down and run for shelter beside the track until the bombers had passed over.

Sidings and railway stations were always targets for the bombers, and a train moving across countryside heading into the Third Reich was too tempting a target for the Allied air crew. If no bombs were dropped, then some of the accompanying fighters swooped down and strafed the train with their machine guns. Our train had anti-aircraft guns, but what effect they ever had, I don't know. Herta and I would lie together in the fields listening to the gunfire and the explosions, wondering how we had got there, and what we were doing making such a dangerous journey.

Occasionally, I looked up and watched the bombers high above us, moving slowly through the gentle cotton-wool clouds while the fighter planes darted around them and took it in turns to come screaming down towards us, firing all the time.

Damage to the tracks ahead delayed us the most, and we had all become so exhausted from running for shelter that on some occasions at night we would just lie on the floors of the wagons and pray the aircraft would pass overhead without seeing us.

After a full day and night, we halted at the Austrian border, still 35 miles short of our first intended stop of Graz. I peered through the wooden slats of the wagon and saw a line of soldiers beside the track, standing there in the light of dawn.

I shivered, not just from the cold air but from fear. This was when I would be discovered. I was certain. I had no papers and no permission to be there. But what could I do?

I sat back down and Herta squeezed my hand and smiled. Neither of us should have been there, but her risk was far greater than mine.

We sat at the border and listened to the shouting of the guards. There were footsteps outside and then the door of our wagon was thrown open. A tall German officer stood there, accompanied by two other soldiers, all of them carrying guns.

The officer shouted some words at us in German. We all looked blank – although I spoke some German I certainly wasn't going to draw attention to myself by speaking to him.

He repeated what he'd said, but more quietly this time. Still no answer. He turned to the other soldiers, spoke sharply to them, and I overheard the word 'Schnell'. One of them clambered up into the wagon.

'Here it comes,' I thought. 'He's going to ask for papers.' But the soldier said nothing. Instead, he studiously counted us and wrote the tally on a piece of paper, which he handed to the officer. Then he jumped back down and the other soldier grabbed the sliding door of the wagon and heaved it shut.

Everyone in the carriage let out a sigh of relief, none more so than Herta and me. We couldn't believe that it had been so easy but the Germans were so desperate for workers I suspect they didn't care too much who they were. There were no prizes for the soldiers in preventing workers getting to the Fatherland.

Amid much shouting, the wagons on the train clanked together and we were once more on the move. Now we were in Austria, officially part of Nazi Germany. Welcome to the Third Reich, I thought.

Austria was a dangerous place. In March 1938 the people had welcomed the annexation of the country by Hitler with unbridled enthusiasm. Anti-semitism was rife and attacks on Jews had begun even before the Nazis arrived. Photographs of Austrian Jews on their knees being forced to scrub the pavement were seen around the world and almost 500 Jews killed themselves in Vienna alone.

It was all a long way from the Vienna I had been brought up to admire. I had dreamed of visiting the city, listening to a Johan Strauss concert in the Stadtpark in the summer or wandering the corridors of the beautiful Schonbrunn Palace, once home to the Habsburg ruling family.

When I finally made it to the city, it was in very different circumstances. I'd used some of my precious money to buy smoked fish when we stopped at Graz, but it had only made me ill, so by the time we crawled into North Bahnhoff terminal I was sick, hungry and exhausted. It was not at all what I'd hoped for.

We climbed down from the wagon with our modest possessions and made our way to the platforms and there, waiting for Herta, was the SS doctor whose life she had saved. How odd it seemed to see such a man embrace a Jewish woman and be so glad to see her.

Herta introduced me and the doctor quickly ushered us to his car and drove us to the Croatian Embassy in Annagasse.

The others who had travelled with us on the train had joined long lines of people, waiting for transport to their places of work.

At the embassy, a Croatian priest told us he had work for both of us at a radio factory, Horniphon, in a town just outside Vienna called Modling. Saying our goodbyes to the doctor and promising to visit him, we joined the priest in his car and he set off to the south-west, in the direction of Baden.

It was only when we had cleared the city centre and were on a longer, straighter road that I glanced behind us – and froze with fear. The police were following us.

I turned to the front; memories of what had happened to me in Budapest came flooding back. Surely I hadn't been betrayed again?

Herta was smiling and talking to the priest. She hadn't noticed the following car and we had picked up speed.

I risked another glance behind, hoping the police car had gone.

But it was still there, closer than ever and as I watched, it pulled out to overtake us.

When it passed the police driver gestured to the priest to pull in at the side of the road. All the chatter in the car ceased; a heavy atmosphere of fear silenced us.

The priest gripped the wheel tightly as the policeman got out of the car and walked towards us.

'Where are you going?' snapped the officer.

'I'm taking these two girls to the Horniphon factory in Modling, where they are going to work,' the priest replied nervously.

'Do you know why I've stopped you?'

'No, no, I don't.'

'You were going too fast,' the officer said. His face creased into a smile as he looked at Herta and me. 'We have speed limits you know, try to keep to them.'

All three of us in the car smiled broadly and nodded vigorously. 'Of course, officer, of course. Sorry,' said the priest.

The officer looked at each of us and then waved the car on.

'Heil Hitler,' he said.

CHAPTER EIGHT

I hadn't given much thought to where I would end up when I jumped on the train in Zagreb; all I knew was that we were heading for Vienna, an elegant, beautiful city of parks, music and Wiener schnitzel.

My dreams were shattered the moment we pulled up outside the camp for volunteer workers at Neue Erlaa near Baden. It was a huge complex, parts of it surrounded by barbed wire with barrack huts stretching away into the distance.

'This can't be where we will live,' I thought. 'No, we must be waiting here until we go on to a better place.'

As if reading my thoughts, the priest turned off the engine and climbed out. He opened the boot to get our suitcases and dumped them on the ground.

'This is where I leave you,' he said. 'If you report to the office they will show you where you are staying. Good luck.' He shook hands with each of us, climbed back into the car, revved the engine and was gone.

We picked up our suitcases and headed with heavy hearts into the camp. It was run by Germans from the Reich labour corps and their quarters were at the entrance to the camp, next to a small medical centre.

Further along were the kitchens, which produced food so bad I can still remember the taste of it today. Herta and I were sent to a hut divided into rooms, each of which contained four bunk beds with three tiers, so there were 12 girls crammed into a tiny space.

As we'd arrived late in the afternoon we were given bread, margarine and some jam – rations that were handed out to all the workers on Saturday lunchtime. It was just as well that we ate them, because the dinner, served in a large dining hall, was inedible. We knew how bad the food must be when we joined the long queue and saw all around us, on untidy tables, plates still full of food, abandoned by the previous sitting.

This was wartime: everything was rationed, no one left food uneaten. Except at Neue Erlaa – and I soon saw why. When I reached the head of the queue, the sight alone of the baked potatoes covered in thin gravy was enough to turn my stomach.

Herta and I took our plates and sat at one of the cluttered tables. We didn't know whether to laugh or cry.

'This wasn't what I was expecting for my first meal in Vienna,' I said. Neither of us ate anything – we would have to look elsewhere for a decent hot meal in Austria.

As newcomers, we were soon approached by the camp's numerous black marketeers. We bought some high-priced coupons for meat, bread and butter but there were no restaurants or cafés nearby so we would have to wait until we could reach Vienna.

The chance came on the Monday when two Yugoslav girls offered to show us the sights of the Austrian capital. We dressed carefully in our best clothes – after all, it was Vienna – and I still had my crocodile shoes and matching handbag. We looked too smart for the camp but we were ready to see the city and, with a little bit of money and our newly-bought food coupons, we were determined to enjoy ourselves.

Prater, the girls told us, was the place to go with its large ferris wheel, clubs and even a Croatian restaurant. There was a small train that ran between our local station and the centre of Vienna and we waited on the platform, full of excitement. We would begin work at the factory the following morning, but this day was ours. Eventually the small electric train appeared, painted in a metallic blue except for one carriage which was a lighter colour and bore a large sign: 'Ausslanders' (foreigners). There were no seats in the carriage; we had to stand for 25 minutes as we passed through Siebenhirten and other stops before reaching the city centre.

Herta and I decided in future we would use the other carriages – after all, we could speak some German and we looked the part.

'Why should we be treated as second class citizens?' I said, forgetting for a moment that Herta was Jewish and the minor inconvenience of being made to stand on a train was utterly irrelevant when set against the suffering of her people.

The two girls took us to a good restaurant near the Opera House, where Herta and I had our first edible hot meal since arriving in Austria. Afterwards we strolled around the streets and stopped for coffee and cakes. It was a rare treat and at last – if I ignored the bomb damage – I saw the Vienna of my dreams: chic and elegant, with the magisterial buildings of the Habsburg Empire still dominating the wide streets.

We strolled in Stadtpark and gazed in awe at the enormous Schonbrunn Palace, mercifully untouched by the bombs.

For a moment I could forget the war – and why I was there.

Not for long though. The next day brought a rude awakening. The camp guards roused us early for our first working day and there was a stampede of young women to the few cold water taps that were supposed to serve us all.

Herta and I couldn't get anywhere near them – we would have to be quicker off the mark if we wanted a morning wash and resolved that the following day we would be at the front of the charge.

After a quick breakfast, we ran to the station and caught the train to Modling, on the edge of the Vienna woods. The Horniphon factory was a two-storey yellow building, with offices on the ground floor and the production line on the upper floor, where about 40 of us (all women) coiled different coloured wires onto circuit boards. These were eventually used in the manufacture of torpedoes.

On the first day, Herta and I reported to the main office and when they discovered we could both speak some German we were given some translating tasks in addition to the regular work. Not that much translation was required; it was just a matter of passing on instructions about the work to the other girls and occasionally stepping in as a peacemaker when the factory's two female cooks – one Croatian and one Serbian – began their own small war.

The outbreaks were signalled first by the sound of raised voices, followed by screaming and a great crashing of pans. I would race to the canteen, urged on by the other girls, to find the red-faced cooks standing facing each other and clutching a tureen of boiling soup apiece, ready to dump it over the head of the other. I talked to them both and calmed them down enough so they could return to work. It was vital, not just because I didn't want to see either of them burnt by boiling soup, but also because if they were unable to work, the rest of us wouldn't eat.

Despite the tension in the kitchen, the two women produced surprisingly good food – there was always plenty of meat in the stews – and they kept their working area spotlessly clean.

As time passed, my peacemaking skills were called upon less frequently as they seemed to realise they could get along, and both retained a fondness for me, their kitchen diplomat.

But these little domestic dramas were nothing compared with the far greater drama in which we were all trapped – the war.

While the factory was comfortable and pleasant it was also on the direct approach to Vienna for the Allied bombers. As soon as the aircraft appeared over the border area of Karnten in the west, heading towards Steiermark, the sirens began wailing in Baden, then Modling and eventually all the way across Vienna.

If the weather was good, we fled the factory and ran across the road into the Vienna woods, where we sat listening and watching for the planes coming from the west. As soon as they were spotted, the boom of the anti-aircraft guns began and we saw their shells exploding high in the sky. I was amazed by how many planes just flew on, apparently indifferent to the explosions around them. They looked so fragile to me; I couldn't understand how they could remain in the air. But remain there they did.

Although the Allied losses were heavy, enough bombers always got through to cause major damage and great tragedies, which affected us all.

Sometimes we had enough time to reach Baden, where the best air raid shelter in the area had been built into the side of a hill. Hundreds of people streamed in when the sirens sounded and sat listening to patriotic German songs on loudspeakers to drown out the sound of gunfire and explosions.

Our area was rarely targeted – the Horniphon factory was small and didn't seem to attract attention. Most of the bombs fell in a low-lying district where there was an oil refinery, but a factory near the camp was also a regular target, although it was never hit. The surrounding houses, however, were flattened so we never met any of the locals – they had all moved elsewhere.

When the sirens sounded we made our way from the camp to the shelters in the nearby town, but the alarms were coming so regularly by then that Herta and I were often slow in getting there. 'Your laziness will get you killed if you're not careful,' the shelter warden told us sternly.

It seemed as if his words were about to come true one day, when, slow as ever to leave the camp as the sirens sounded, we made our way to the best shelter in the town just as they were closing the door.

'Sorry, girls, we're full, there's no more room,' the warden told us.

We could hear the bombers approaching. We'd left it too late.

'Please!' I begged. 'They're coming. Please let us in!'

Me, wearing a hat made by my stepmother Ilona.

The door slammed shut in our faces. Herta and I turned to each other just as the first bombers appeared and the anti-aircraft guns opened up.

The noise of plane after plane thundering overhead was deafening as we ran along the street towards the only other shelter. Just as the first bombs began to fall, we flung ourselves through the entrance to safety while a series of huge explosions made the ground shudder.

It was a particularly heavy raid and it was many hours before we heard the welcome sound of the all-clear. Emerging from our shelter, we found the streets of the town alive with weeping people. I could hear the screams of women coming from further along the street and Herta and I made our way towards a crowd that had gathered near the shelter where the door had been slammed on us.

There was nothing there, just a huge bomb crater filled with rubble – the shelter had suffered a direct hit and everyone inside killed. A man nearby told me 200 people had been inside when the bomb exploded.

Herta and I were shaken: we could so easily have been among them, but our laziness, far from costing our lives, had saved us. Would we be so lucky again?

A trip to Prater became our regular weekend treat, our

opportunity to forget the hardships of the camp and our work. The Viennese equivalent to the Bois de Boulogne in Paris, it was a large public park in the Leopoldstadt district of the city. The roads in the area were full of bars, shops and cafés and we would often stroll along the Hauptallee (main avenue) between the lines of towering horse chestnut trees. After the war, the area – and its ferris wheel – became famous when the Graham Greene film The Third Man was shot there.

Despite our weekend escapes, the hardship of the camp was beginning to take its toll on both Herta and me. I suffered frequent stomach upsets and the local doctor gave me additional coupons so I could get better food. Of course, I shared these with Herta and they were the basis for our excursions to Prater, but my health continued to deteriorate. I was diagnosed with anaemia and sent to hospital.

It was wonderful, as if I'd been given a room in a hotel. I even had a hot bath – a luxury unheard of in the camp – but I was not kept there for long and had to return to the depressing daily routine of work.

I was getting restless; after all, I had no reason to be there other than to get to Budapest and Julius. I began to make careful inquiries about trains from Vienna to Budapest, but without papers travelling would not be easy. I thought back to my first experience in the Hungarian capital and had no wish to repeat it.

I wrote to my father and Marta in Zagreb, but got no answer from them. A letter to Julius's sister Shary in Budapest produced no response either.

I was beginning to feel lonely and abandoned; apart from Herta the rest of the world seemed to have forgotten I even existed. But Julius – if he was still alive – would be desperate to know what had become of me.

I had to get out.

Then, to add to my gloom, I returned from work one day to find that my suitcase, which had been stored under our bunk bed, had vanished. I reported it to the local police but they could find no trace of it. Presumably the contents had disappeared swiftly into the camp's highly-organised black market. On the day of the theft it was so cold I had been wearing a Coypu fur coat, otherwise I would have lost that as well. My other coat was gone and all my shoes, except the pair I was wearing, had disappeared.

It was impossible to get coupons to buy new shoes (all leather went on army boots), and those available on the black market were horribly expensive and often in the wrong size. Before long my shoes were wearing out and I was reduced to wearing rags on my feet, in common with many of the girls in the camp. It seemed to be the final humiliation, a public sign of how desperate we had all become.

There was something to lighten our dreary days, however: a camp romance. Another girl from Yugoslavia, Maria, had been prevented from marrying the man she loved by her parents who didn't consider him good enough. So she had come to Vienna to escape her family – hoping that her boyfriend would follow. All of us were thrilled when he turned up at the camp to claim his bride. It was a bitter-sweet moment for me: it saddened me to think of my similar mission to find Julius, but also gave me heart to see the young couple so happy. Maybe that would be Julius and me soon…

The pair set the date to wed on a Sunday and chose a hotel near Prater for their honeymoon.

Everyone was excited and a collection was organised for a wedding present. Without family or close friends, Maria invited some of us from the camp to join them for the ceremony. We were delighted and began trying to find enough decent clothes to pass muster at a wedding.

It was when I was looking through my few remaining items of clothing that a letter arrived from the police. It instructed me to attend the police station at 11 o'clock on the Sunday of the wedding to make a statement about the theft of my suitcase. I had no choice.

Sadly, I told Maria I couldn't make the wedding and neither could Herta who had promised to come to the police station with me.

On that Sunday morning, we boarded a train but no sooner had we arrived at the police station then the air raid siren sounded.

'Not again,' said the policeman, who clearly just wanted to take a quick statement from me and then get rid of us.

'Please, let us stay here during the raid,' I begged. 'We don't know where the shelter is.'

He seemed reluctant to help, but an older officer appeared and took us all down to a bunker beneath the cells. Even down there we could feel the earth trembling as the bombs fell around us.

It was unusual for the Allies to raid on a Sunday; if they continued to do so it would put an end to our weekend trips to Prater and the only day of the week when we felt safe.

The all-clear did not sound until two o'clock. The policemen produced a cup of ersatz coffee – it was made from roasted wheat – took my statement about the theft, and then sent us on our way.

At the station a hastily-written sign told us that no trains were running in the direction of our camp as the tracks had been damaged in the bombing.

Taxis and private cars were now a rarity for civilians because of the fuel shortages, so we had no alternative but to start walking. We weren't sure how many miles it was to the camp, but in order to preserve my last pair of shoes for as long as possible, I slipped them off and walked barefoot.

By the time dusk fell, we were still nowhere near the camp – but had no choice other than to keep going. Soon, darkness fell and we could see the stars in the cloudless sky above us. We met not another living soul as we walked on in the eerie quiet of the night.

There was a haunting beauty in the darkness, with only the moon and stars giving us light and the profound peace that came from the utter stillness around us.

It was all in such startling contrast to the maelstrom of the bombing raid and the terrible death toll; as if the night arrived to cleanse us of all that the day had done.

At four o'clock in the morning we saw the outline of our camp in the blackness, and were greeted with a stern reprimand by the camp guards: 'Where have you been until this time?'

We explained that we had had to walk because of the bombing and, to prove it, I pointed to my feet, all blistered and covered in blood. One guard prepared a footbath of water and disinfectant for me but my injuries were still enough to guarantee me the next two days off work.

By the time I'd recovered we were all eagerly awaiting the return of our newlyweds who had been granted a couple of days leave to spend in the honeymoon hotel. When they didn't turn up we assumed, amid much giggling, that they had enjoyed themselves so much they were breaking the rules and spending a few more days together.

Three days later I was called to the office for translation work. It was the worst possible news and I had to tell the other girls. Our newly-weds had been in their hotel when the Allied bombers arrived over Vienna on the day of their wedding and had gone with the rest of the staff and guests to the basement, hoping the bombers would pass over them.

But that day, Prater itself had been a target and one of the bombs landed directly on their hotel, burying them in the rubble.

They had been married for less than an hour.

CHAPTER NINE

My luck finally ran out. The moment the guard started pulling names out of a box and reading them aloud, I knew mine would be one of them. Sure enough, in the very first group of names he shouted: 'Olga Czepf!'

I stepped forward and walked to the other side of the hut. One of the chosen.

The Germans were demanding 'volunteers' to join work parties digging anti-tank trenches on the Austria–Hungary border, near the Austrian town of Gols and the larger Hungarian one of Sopron. By late 1944 the war had turned against Germany. We all knew how it would end – we just didn't know when.

The Russian Red Army – of which we were all terrified because we had heard such dreadful stories about its brutality – was advancing rapidly towards Budapest and the Germans obviously feared that once that city fell, the way would be open for the Red Army to push west into Austria.

They wanted to bolster the border defences and they needed 'volunteers' to help them. I had just been volunteered.

Those of us chosen packed what belongings we had and said our tearful farewells to those staying behind. Most difficult for me was saying goodbye to Herta, who had been such a good friend.

We embraced amid words of whispered encouragement before stepping apart and looking at each other one last time.

Those being sent to the border generally felt pretty despondent, and so did I. However, a look at the map changed all that. Gols was on the main route from Vienna to Budapest, only a handful of miles from the border. Just as I had come to Vienna courtesy of the Germans, I could make it to the Hungarian border the same way. Once I was there, the rest was up to me.

It was madness, of course. Not only were all the borders closely guarded, but to go south towards Budapest was to head straight into the path of the Red Army – the eye of the storm.

What else could I do? Julius was in Budapest and I couldn't abandon him. I had come this far. Almost 12 months had passed since he had proposed marriage and in that time my love had only grown. I would not find peace until I knew whether he was dead or alive – and, if he was alive, whether his feelings were still the same for me.

Once more, we were loaded into cattle trucks at the local railway station and again the train sat there for hours before moving forward at an agonisingly slow pace. Then it stopped. We waited and it started again.

So we proceeded at snail's pace towards Vienna and then turned south on the line towards Gols. It was not long before we shuddered to a halt again and heard the sound of guards running along the train shouting 'Air raid! Everyone out!'

We fled into the fields as the anti-aircraft guns began their staccato firing and watched the explosions high above us.

This time the aircraft ignored us, heading straight towards Vienna and dropping their bombs on the beautiful city.

'How much they must be suffering,' I thought, not knowing that the city to which I was heading, Budapest, would suffer far, far more.

***

After a night on the train, we crawled to a halt near some abandoned farm buildings and were ordered to get down. There were no people and no houses in sight, just rolling countryside. I had hoped for a town that would provide chances to travel across the border. Looking around I could see no such opportunities existed there. My spirits fell.

A group of about 50 of us were told to go to the top floor of one of the buildings, where straw lay scattered around. There were no beds or blankets and the cold, damp November weather seeped through the wooden walls. As the one who could speak German, I was urged by the group to ask for blankets.

'No blankets. Cover yourselves with your coats,' was the curt reply.

On the ground floor, there was one toilet and three taps for all of us. Armed guards stood watch outside – we were more prisoners than 'volunteers' now, and the tension among the soldiers watching us was palpable. This was not the front line, but one day not far in the future, it would be and they knew it.

We settled as best we could, trying to keep warm with a combination of coats, straw and body heat. The women slept on one side, the men on the other. During the night the temperatures fell and the biting wind cut through the wooden walls. I shivered uncontrollably.

I woke to the sound of guards shouting and orders being bellowed. We stumbled around, feeling as if we hadn't slept at all and made what attempts we could to wash.

Hard, dark bread with a little margarine was handed out for breakfast – which we were required to sign for – and we were promised that coffee would be provided on the way to the trenches. By the time it came, it was stone cold and bitter.

We climbed into lorries and were driven part of the way towards the border. After that, we had to march another three miles. When we finally arrived we were each issued with shovels, directed towards a trench that was half dug and set to work.

It was gruelling, desperate labour: the trenches had to be deep and wide to have any chance of stopping tanks. When we had finished the German army engineers would move in and build concrete and iron anti-tank traps. We were just the labourers.

After our first day we returned to the farm building, tired and sore. I lay down on the straw, utterly exhausted, but I couldn't rest; instead, I was scratching. The skin on my head felt as if it were crawling across my skull.

One of the girls sleeping close to me was a tall, slim blonde who spoke hardly a word of German. She had not said anything since we'd arrived at the trenches but she looked lonely and despondent.

Now, she watched me scratch. I smiled at her and told her my head was itching. She smiled back and said in faltering German: 'It's lice. They have laid their eggs in your hair.'

I was horrified, but there were no mirrors; I couldn't look to see if she was telling the truth.

'Where do you come from?' I asked.

'A few miles from here. I am Hungarian.'

'So let us speak Hungarian,' I said, and her face lit up at the prospect of being able to talk to someone in her native language. She introduced herself as Lenke and although tidy, her clothes were threadbare and poor. She seemed nervous and restless, as if something was constantly worrying her.

Lenke helped me wash my hair, scrubbing hard to drive out the lice and, as she did so, she confided in me that she had volunteered to come and dig trenches in the hope of escaping across the border back to her home country.

'My father is an officer in the Hungarian army and I came to Germany with my mother and sister to work because we were frightened of the Russians,' she said. 'We were separated on the journey and I haven't seen them since. I've been looking for them for two months but I don't know what's happened to them. I might as well go home.'

'But how, Lenke? How will you get home?'

'Oh, I have an aunt in Gyor, which is not far across the border from here. If I can cross the border illegally I can get to her and then I'll be safe.'

I turned to her and looked into her pale blue eyes. Could I trust her? It seemed too remarkable that both of us had come here with the same intention of escaping across the border but it was possible.

'What?' she said. 'Why are you staring at me like that?'

Suddenly, she seemed nervous again, possibly afraid that I would betray her. Instead I sat her down, my hair still wet, and told her my own story.

After she had listened to me, I felt an overwhelming sense of relief that I had found someone in whom I could confide and someone who also wanted to cross the border.

I wasn't alone any more.

I told her all about Julius and my search for him, switching between elation at the thought of being reunited with him and despair at the thought he might already be dead.

Lenke smiled and held my hand. 'You'll find him again. I know you will.'

***

A grey Monday morning and the guards roused us at dawn to begin the march to the trenches. A group of about 50 of us formed outside the sheds after a hurried wash. We wore as many clothes as possible to ward off the cold.

After a shouted command, the straggly line of workers began following the two German soldiers who took us to work. They walked in front, their guns slung casually across their backs.

Slowly, as we walked, the singing began:

Vor der Kaserne
Vor dem großen Tor
Stand eine Laterne*

The haunting opening lines to Lili Marlene had become our constant companion when marching and working. Soon all the voices of the group were joining in and the sound swelled as we trudged on through the quiet countryside.

The guards hardly ever looked round. We were 'volunteers', not prisoners; why would any of us try to escape? In any case, we were heading towards the Red Army – no one would flee into the arms of the Russians.

As the walk progressed, Lenke and I slipped towards the back of the line. Around us were green fields and hedges; occasionally we would pass a small clump of trees or a group of bushes. A pale sun had climbed above the horizon and with it our excitement grew. Surely this was the time.

We reached a point where the road ahead curved slightly taking the front of the column and – more importantly – the guards out of our sight. Lenke and I dropped even further back until there was a gap between the others and us. Then, with a quick glance between us and the briefest of nods, we jumped down from the road into a clump of bushes and buried ourselves deep in the undergrowth.

We held our breath, expecting to hear the shouts of our fellow workers and the sight of angry guards. Nothing happened. The sound of marching footsteps on the dusty road gradually faded and we were left entirely alone.

When we finally emerged from our hiding place we were greeted with the sight of an empty road stretching across rolling countryside. There was not a soul in sight and birdsong the only sound to be heard.

*At the barracks
before the big gate
stands a lantern

I glanced at Lenke, realising that I had no idea how to find the border. Were those fields that I could see in the distance Hungary or just another part of Austria? Lenke smiled. 'Don't worry. I know the way.'

We set off across fields until we joined another road and then we walked slowly south, through gentle countryside peppered with vineyards. Any grapes still on the vine we plucked and ate. We saw no one. It reminded me of my nocturnal walk back to the work camp with Herta after the terrible bombing of Vienna, but now the sun was shining brightly and this tiny corner of the world seemed to be at peace.

My thoughts turned to Julius, each step I took brought me closer to him, but what awaited me if I found him? Only time would tell.

Suddenly, Lenke cried out and pointed to some large white houses in the distance.

'Where are we?' I asked.

'Those buildings are near the border, I'm sure. The town over there must be Sopron,' she said, not looking entirely convinced. Still there was no turning back, so we walked towards them. Suddenly Lenke grabbed my arm.

'Look!' she said, pointing to a large rock, painted white, beside the road. Lenke jumped in the air.

'We're here! This is the border sign.' Sure enough one side of the rock bore the large painted letter D for Deutschland, and the other marked the Hungarian side.

'When we pass this rock we are in no man's land. That hut over there marks the start of Hungary,' Lenke said, pointing to a wooden building, about one 100 yards away. It seemed an awfully wide no man's land to me, but we walked past the stone and headed along the road, which led us past barbed wire fences and defensive trenches.

Suddenly, we heard a shout behind us: 'Halte!'

We both spun round and there, some way, were two German soldiers with their guns at the ready. 'Where are you going? Come back here.'

We froze. They wouldn't shoot two young women, surely? Lenke made the sign of the cross and we put our hands in the air as if to surrender, muttering 'God help us'. Then, just as the German soldiers slowed their run to a walk, we turned and sprinted for the hut in the distance.

'Halte! Halte!'

I waited for the sharp crack of a rifle shot, terrified that I was taking my last steps on this earth. I could hear Lenke's breath coming in short gasps as we kept running. 'Keep going, keep going,' she cried.

I forced myself to run faster; now I could hear my own breathing and the pounding of blood in my ears.

Still no shots.

We were getting close to the Hungarian border hut, but it seemed as if we would never get there. Every time I thought we were almost there it seemed as if the hut had moved further away. I couldn't hear the soldiers shouting any more, but was that the sound of their boots pounding along the road behind us? I didn't dare look...

As we approached the hut, gasping for air, we expected to see Hungarian soldiers but there was no one in sight. Instead, coming from inside the hut, we heard the sound of singing. I couldn't believe it, thinking: 'Here we are, running for our lives and you lot are singing.'

We hammered on the door, but the deep, booming voices of the singers just carried on, and then, beside me, in a sweet, clear voice, Lenke began singing as well, joining in with the Hungarian song coming from inside the hut.

I dared to turn round. The two German soldiers had come to a halt a short distance away and were staring at this extraordinary spectacle.

Inside, the sound of singing slowly died out until Lenke was left singing alone. Two faces appeared at the windows of the hut and there was a rattling at the door as a guard unlocked it and stepped outside. He looked down at us in amazement as Lenke's singing faltered and stopped. A broad smile spread across his face.

'Miss Lenke! What are you doing in this part of the world?'

'Andras,' she replied, looking amazed and then smiling happily. 'Please help us; the Germans are chasing us…'

Andras looked across at the two Germans and then opened the door to the hut.

'Come in,' he said and we scrambled gratefully into the warmth inside as the German soldiers approached.

We watched through the window as Andras spoke to them.

When he returned, he told us: 'I said you were our sisters and they said you could stay in Hungary.'

Lenke introduced me and explained that Andras had served with her father in the Hungarian army and they knew each other well. We looked out of the window and saw the two German soldiers walking slowly back across the border.

We'd made it.

CHAPTER TEN

Crossing the border was one thing; what awaited us on the other side was quite another.

Lenke and I were two young women with little knowledge of how the war was going. All we'd heard were reports of great victories and courageous resistance. Since we'd left Vienna we'd seen little of the Allied bombers and the war seemed further away than ever.

In fact, it was getting closer all the time. The Red Army had already swept through the south-east of the country and Russian soldiers were on the southern outskirts of Budapest itself.

The Germans were sending reinforcements and what was left of the Hungarian army was being directed to the capital in a desperate last-ditch defence.

Budapest was about to become a front-line city, the scene of some of the worst street fighting in the Second World War. Yet what was I doing? Heading straight towards it.

The civilian population of Budapest was never evacuated and more than 38,000 people would die there, but how was I to know?

All I knew was that Julius was in Budapest and I had to reach him. Somehow – the madness of love perhaps – I believed that if we were together then everything would be all right.

Sitting in the hut on the Hungarian side of the border on that day early in December 1944 I was just overjoyed to be in the country again.

The soldiers gave us some food and wine but urged us to move on quickly as the area was alive with German soldiers who were checking papers and were nervous about the forthcoming battle.

They loaded us onto a lorry carrying supplies and told the driver to take us as far as possible towards Gyor, where Lenke's aunt lived and which was only 70 miles from Budapest.

Our journey was painfully slow, even by the standards of wartime. The traffic was heavy with refugees fleeing west from Budapest and columns of soldiers and artillery moving towards the capital and the Red Army.

Time after time, our lorry was halted to allow military vehicles to go forward. Lenke and I sat gazing at the silent, heavily-laden refugees heading west and the nervous faces of the young soldiers heading east.

'How many of them will die?' I asked Lenke.

'Too many…'

Then the engine of our lorry would roar and we would move slowly forward until, inevitably, we were stopped again. There was nothing we could do. To walk was to risk being questioned by the Germans as were all civilians heading west. No one but soldiers was heading in the same direction as us.

Eventually, the concentration of troops began to ease and we could drive more freely, but soon our driver stopped and told us he was going no further. We jumped down and began walking.

Whenever we saw civilian or Hungarian army lorries we waved them down and begged for a lift. At dusk, we knocked on the door of any house by the road and asked for a room for the night.

It's a tribute to the hospitality of the Hungarian people that we were never turned away. On the contrary, we not only got accommodation but a free dinner as well.

Help often appeared when we least expected it. Everyone was anxious and questioned us for news: 'Is the Red Army coming?'

'Will they kill us all?'

'Do the Germans think they can still win?'

We had no answers to their questions but as we travelled further east the people we met were more fearful and despairing; some seemed to have lost all hope.

To add to the gloom and feeling of defeat, the weather was closing in. Each day brought grey clouds, freezing temperatures and rain with flurries of snow. It was not a good time to be travelling.

After four days we had covered less than 50 miles, but had at last reached Gyor. However, disappointment awaited us. We went to the address of Lenke's aunt, only to find the house deserted. The neighbours had disappeared as well; presumably somewhere along the packed roads to Austria we had passed Lenke's aunt amid the thousands of refugees flowing west.

Lenke was bitterly upset. She didn't know what had become of her mother and sister, and now she'd lost her aunt as well.

'Where's your father based?' I asked her.

'He's in Veszprem with the army,' she said, naming a town about 45 miles south of Gyor. It was hardly a direct route to Budapest, but I didn't feel I could abandon her.

We resumed our daily routine of walking and hitching lifts, but as we travelled further south, more and more people warned us to turn back.

'The Russians are coming, they are trying to surround Budapest,' they told us.

It gave a new urgency to our travels: Lenke wanted to reach her father before he was caught in a battle with the Russians and I wanted to get to Budapest before the city was besieged.

We knew the Red Army was south and east of Budapest, but no one seemed to know exactly where. Rumours were rife, most suggesting that we might be walking straight into the arms of the Russians.

'Turn back, girls. Don't go that way,' one woman said, offering explicit descriptions of what would happen to us if we fell into the hands of the Red Army.

The rumours and warnings took their toll. Every time a military vehicle appeared heading towards us we had a moment of intense fear: was it the Russians?

In fact, we reached Veszprem without incident and although the town was tense and full of the military, it was quiet, an air of dreadful expectancy hanging over it.

We had passed many of the residents on the roads heading north – they were running while they still could.

Lenke and I said our farewells and she went to find her father, whose unit was stationed on the outskirts of the town. I walked through the town centre until I was on the main road to Budapest.

For once, I was lucky and a lorry stopped. I climbed onto the back and squeezed myself in among the goods piled high on the lorry.

The journey was surprisingly quick and before long we came over a small hill, and there in front of us, were the waters of the Danube and the beautiful city of Budapest.

CHAPTER ELEVEN

It had taken me two weeks after crossing the border to reach Budapest. I was tired, cold and wet. I hadn't slept in a proper bed since leaving the camp near Vienna and I was stiff and sore from sitting in different lorries travelling over potholed roads.

Once I had been dropped in the city centre, I wanted to get to Julius's sister, Shary, as quickly as possible. Julius had given me her address near Vaci Utca in the city centre and, when I found it, my search would be over. Surely Shary would know where he was?

I exchanged some of the Reichsmarks that I had earned in the work camp for Hungarian currency and went in search of Shary's home, which turned out to be a private hostel for young professional women. The porter said Shary would be home after five o'clock, leaving me hours to fill.

Budapest was a revelation. The city was on the eve of its destruction, but you would never have known. Walking along one street I was halted by the mouth-watering scent of newly-baked bread. There was a small queue at the baker's door and I had no idea whether ration coupons were needed but I joined the line anyway. A few minutes later, I left the shop with four warm rolls – such luxury! I hadn't seen anything like this in Vienna and here I was, a few miles from the front line, happily devouring my fresh Hungarian bread.

Along the streets men shouted out the prices of roasted

chestnuts and the corn on the cob they were cooking on open fires. It was livelier than Vienna and seemed strangely untroubled by the advancing Russians who, in three short weeks, would surround the entire city, causing food shortages that would make the days of bread rolls, chestnuts and corn on the cob seem like a distant dream.

Of course, people were frightened by the stories of the Red Army, and there was much talk about how everyone would fight for Budapest, but it was hard to believe it would actually come to that.

Demands from Hungary's own Nazi party, the Arrow Cross, for civilians to present themselves for work building the city's defences were greeted with almost universal indifference. Barely anyone turned up.

For most of the people of Budapest, life went on. Relatively few even bothered to flee.

It was a dangerously deceptive lifestyle. Like so many of the residents, I soon found myself succumbing to the belief that the war wasn't that close; that it would pass the city by.

It was an illusion and when it was shattered, tens of thousands of people would die.

The Jewish population were under no such illusions. As the Red Army approached, the intensity of the German and Arrow Cross attacks on them increased. Thousands were forced to march to the concentration camps of Germany, beaten and harried every step of the way. Meanwhile, the banks of the Danube became a regular slaughter ground for the Arrow Cross militia, particularly at night.

Early in December 1944, however, much of Budapest was enjoying its last few days of freedom, largely unaware of the full extent of what was going on in the surrounding countryside and cruelly exposed to the terrible fate awaiting it.

After my breakfast of bread rolls, I walked the streets and found a sauna where I had my hair done, a hot bath and a massage. When I emerged back into the wintery sunshine, I felt a different person.

The aches and pains of my journey had faded and I was

filled with a sense of optimism. When I passed a shoe shop, a pair of boots caught my eye. They were made of grey and black felt, with wooden soles, identical to a pair that Julius had bought me in Zagreb. How long ago that seemed.

I entered the shop, expecting to be told they didn't have my size or quoting a price that I couldn't afford. But a few minutes later I was back in the street, the proud owner of a wonderfully comfortable pair of new boots. My transformation was complete: bathed, hair done and now with new shoes.

I found a café playing Hungarian music on a gramophone and drank a surprisingly good cup of coffee. The music took me back to the carefree days in the Hungarian Club in Zagreb, where Marta and I would dance the csardas and where I first met Julius.

It was 16 months since that fateful meeting. Who would have believed then what would become of us?

Sipping my coffee, I reflected on all that had happened. Again my spirits rose at the thought that it would not be long now before I was reunited with Julius. Once we were together, then we could let the war roll by and get on with our new life.

First, though, I had to see Shary. Leaving the café, I walked along Vaci Utca, its Gothic architecture towering over the pavements below, giving the street a gloomy feel even when the sun was high.

I turned into Shary's street and presented myself once more at the hostel. The porter recognised me and directed me to the first floor where, after ringing a doorbell, I was greeted by an elderly lady who led me to a cheerless waiting room. A few chairs were placed around the walls and in the centre some magazines had been scattered on a low table.

It was deserted but as I sat down I heard the bell ring again and the elderly lady appeared with another woman. In a low voice, the older woman said: 'There is somebody else waiting to see Miss Shary…'

The newcomer gave me a cold look as she came into the room

and sat opposite me. She was well dressed, neatly groomed and wearing a green turban – the latest fashion at the time.

We did not speak and she picked up a magazine to avoid my gaze. She did not know who I was, but I recognised her straight away.

Her features were immediately familiar from a photograph I had seen on a diplomatic pass back in Zagreb… a photograph that had been replaced with my own when Julius and I had travelled to Vrapce.

The woman sitting opposite me was Giska, Julius's ex-wife.

Seeing her brought all the memories of him flooding back: the risks we had taken together; the happy time spent waiting in the café for the train back to Zagreb; the nights at the opera; our farewells when Julius left for Budapest; our talk, our laughter.

The waiting room was deathly quiet. On the wall the clock ticked, the hands showing twenty past five. Giska studied her magazine, seemingly determined not to meet my gaze, when the door opened suddenly and a beautiful blonde woman with Julius's blue eyes appeared. She was dressed in a black coat with a silver fox collar. Giska rose quickly and kissed her on the cheek.

'Shary,' she said.

'Come in, Giska,' Shary replied coldly.

They disappeared and for half an hour I was left alone with only the ticking clock for company.

When they reappeared their parting was formal, lacking in warmth. They weren't, I guessed, the best of friends. Once Giska had left Shary turned to look at me. The silence stretched until finally she said: 'Come.'

I followed her to a small single room in which there was only room for a day couch and a camp bed for the night. She sat on the couch but left me standing.

'You must be Olgi from Yugoslavia,' she said. Julius liked the Hungarian form of my name and must have used it when telling his family about me.

'I am,' I replied.

'Well, it must be my lucky day,' she said, her voice heavy with sarcasm. 'First, Giska comes demanding money for Julius's son and now you. What are you doing here? What do you want? I didn't expect you.'

With the harshness of her words and the chill in the room, I began to shiver. Suddenly, the long months of being on my own, of hiding the truth from so many and the constant fear of exposure and arrest overcame me. I started to cry.

Sobbing, I turned to leave but Shary called me back.

'Wait, let's talk,' she said. 'I'm sorry, but you must understand we are all very unhappy about Julius being in prison. We are a very respectable family, our mother is heartbroken and she thinks that if he hadn't gone to Zagreb and hadn't met you none of this would have happened.'

In prison? This was the first I had heard that Julius was in jail. What on earth had happened?

'Giska keeps asking for money for Gabor and my parents have had to sell part of their land to raise cash,' Shary said, hurrying on and apparently unaware of my shock. 'Inflation here is terrible: prices are rising astronomically from minute to minute.

'I'm sorry I was so rude, but I've had a terribly difficult day at the bank where I work and now this. I know you came to find Julius – I got your letter from Vienna but I was frightened to answer and give details. I never expected you to get to Budapest. How did you do it?'

For the first time, she gestured for me to sit down while I told her my story. I left nothing out and then said: 'Where is Julius?'

'He's in Komarom prison,' she replied. My heart sank. Komarom was almost 60 miles from Budapest, close to the Czech border. I had expected to find Julius in Budapest and now it turned out he wasn't even there any more.

'Our lawyer says there is no case against him but still they keep him,' Shary continued.

'Why was he arrested?'

She looked at me in surprise. 'We were hoping you'd know that. No one will tell us. It's the war, I suppose.'

'I have no idea,' I said, truthfully. 'Has anyone seen Julius?'

'I've tried to get permission to visit him in jail but they won't let me. You've got to get a permit from one particular minister apparently, and it's virtually impossible. After all, the Russians are almost here and people have other things to worry about.'

She looked at me hard. 'You're strong, would you try to see Julius?' she asked.

Of course I would, why else had I come to Budapest? Shary hurried on: 'If you try I can give you some money to help you and him. The family would be very grateful.'

She seemed to have warmed to me. 'I have great faith in you,' she added.

I left shortly after, with an envelope of money (not knowing how much it would be worth in the morning), the name of the minister and the address of his ministry.

Shary had failed to get permission to visit Julius and she had a lawyer on her side. What chance did I have?

***

By December 1944 the Arrow Cross – or Nyilas party – was tightening its grip on Hungary. Installed in power by Hitler, its members would strut around the streets of Budapest wearing uniforms almost identical to those worn by the Nazis in Germany, except that their armbands bore the motif of four arrows formed into a cross.

They brought a terror to the city that it hadn't experienced before under Admiral Horthy. The sound of gunfire from the banks of the Danube became a regular nocturnal ritual, signifying yet more merciless executions.

Jews were being rounded up, crammed into cattle trucks and sent to the camps in Poland. We didn't know then what happened to them but the city was full of terrible rumours about their fate.

Now, in this city being run by barbarians, I had to do a deal with them. Shary had told me that the minister I needed to see had many friends in Osijek, some of whom were members of the Nyilas party. 'Make sure you tell him about Osijek,' she said to me.

I found a tiny room in a cheap hotel not far from Vaci Utca and after a troubled night, disturbed by the sound of gunfire, I woke to a freezing day and no heating in my room.

In the cold light of morning, the impossibility of my task overwhelmed me. The bare walls of my room seemed to reflect my despair. So this was how my journey was to end: in a cold, depressing hotel room in a beautiful city that had been taken over by the ugliest of people.

What possible chance did a young woman from Zagreb have of seeing a Government minister while all around Jews were being slaughtered and just outside the city the Red Army gathered for its final assault?

A formal approach had no chance of success; after all, Julius's family had tried with a lawyer and got nowhere. I could hardly tell the truth – that would only get me arrested.

I needed some way to make the minister sit up and take notice. Our shared connection with Osijek, tenuous though it was, might well be the only way.

I thought back to my days there and could remember being given some political leaflets about the situation in Hungary but had paid no attention. I cared nothing for politics.

A member of the Nyilas party had introduced himself to me once, but that was in the tragic aftermath of the bombing. He had stood in the undertaker's office, weeping over his two dead children.

'My children,' he'd wailed. 'My son was my future – now he has gone.'

I could say nothing to console him then and had long since forgotten his name.

Now, of course, I wished I had taken note of names and those political leaflets. At the back of my mind, I was sure I had heard much talk in the town of the leader of the Nyilas party there. I had heard Mr Bariaktar, my landlord, talking about him.

If only I could remember his name. As for names, I thought it would help if mine sounded more Hungarian so I became Olga Kovach. It sounded suitably Hungarian but also reassuringly common, unlikely to attract much attention or be remembered.

I dressed carefully, pleased that I had had my hair done the previous day and bought new shoes. I looked less like a refugee and more like a young Budapest woman.

I studied my reflection in the scratched mirror hanging on the wall of the bathroom at the end of the hotel corridor.

'This is it,' I said to myself.

***

At the imposing front door of the ministry building, a uniformed porter stopped me. 'Your papers, please?' he asked.

Of course, I had none. Suddenly I was nervous, aware of the risk I was taking. 'Please tell the minister I am a friend of the President of the Nyilas party in Osijek and bring him greetings from his friends there, and would like to talk to him, if I may…'

My voice trailed off rather unconvincingly but to my surprise the doorman picked up the phone on a nearby desk and spoke to someone. After a few moments and some more conversation he replaced the receiver and smiled: 'The minister will see you now,' he said.

Another porter appeared and greeted me deferentially: 'If you would come this way, madam,' directing me towards a wide, richly carpeted staircase, leading up to the first floor.

I was ushered into the minister's office, where a tall, blond thin-faced man was waiting for me. He smiled broadly and welcomed me warmly.

'You have come from Osijek – how wonderful. Please sit down, I want to hear all the news about my old friends there.'

He poured us each a small glass of barack, a Hungarian apricot brandy, and then we sat in armchairs facing each other. He looked at me expectantly.

'How did you enjoy your time in Osijek?' I asked him, hoping to steer him away from specific people whom I did not know.

We chatted about the town, the restaurants and the clubs and whenever possible I would drop the name of one of the town's well-known citizens into the conversation to give the impression I was well connected.

I mentioned Giner, my admirer from the nightclub, and the minister laughed. 'A rogue,' he said.

Then, from nowhere, I remembered the name of the Nyilas party leader so blurted it out in the middle of my inane chatter.

He smiled broadly, 'Ah, yes,' he said. 'He's my great friend; how good to hear that he's well.'

I had no idea if he was well or not, just that he had been alive when I left Osijek. The conversation was going better than I had hoped and despite his senior position with the Hungarian Government, this middle-aged man seemed to be enjoying talking about a small town in Croatia. Perhaps it was less painful than reflecting on what the rest of the day would hold for him.

I didn't want to push my luck, so when there was a pause I took my chance. 'I'm only staying in Budapest for a short time and I wonder if I could ask a small favour?'

'Of course, my dear, what is it?'

'A friend of mine has a relative who has been imprisoned in

Komarom and she's asked me to visit him, but I haven't got a pass and was wondering if you could help?'

'Of course, I will. Tell me his name,' he said reaching into a desk drawer and pulling out a printed form. He wrote Julius's name carefully on it, then mine, 'Olga Kovach' and, with a theatrical flourish, stamped it.

He handed it to me. 'A pleasure to help you, Miss Kovach,' he said.

I smiled and thanked him as he showed me to the door, where a guard waited to escort me to the street. Once there, I felt irrationally proud of myself, elated that my subterfuge had worked and thrilled that I had succeeded on my own where Julius's family and their lawyers had failed.

At the back of my mind, however, was the nagging anxiety that the minister would now pick up the phone to his friends in Osijek to tell them what a great favour he had just done them and I would be discovered, but it was a slender risk. In times of war, and particularly in Budapest late in 1944, phone calls were anything but easy.

As I walked down the street back towards the city centre, I felt confident that my duplicity would not be discovered. I looked again at the green card the minister had given me, now safely stowed in my handbag. Just one word was visible: 'Julius'.

***

Komarom, on the banks of the Danube, lies north-west of Budapest, on the border with Czechoslovakia. By the time I got there it was a key target for both sides. The Germans and Hungarians were building up supplies and men there; the Russians, in a huge sweeping move around Budapest, were approaching from the south, hoping to link up with their eastern flank, north of the capital.

It was also where Hungarian political prisoners, Jews and 'enemies of the Reich' were sent, en route to Germany and whatever fate awaited them there.

Refugees were drawn to it as a staging post on their flight from the beleaguered capital.

At the central station in Budapest all the trains heading north out of the city were packed, their destinations either vague or not announced at all. The passengers just wanted to get out of the city any way they could and as far from the Russians as possible. The gap through the Red Army around the city was getting smaller and smaller; the chances for escape fewer and fewer.

I climbed aboard a train and squeezed into an already overflowing carriage. I was the only passenger without luggage – everyone else seemed to be carrying all their worldly possessions.

Our progress, when we finally pulled out of Budapest, was painfully slow and by the time we reached Bicske, about 25 miles north, the stifling conditions on board and our snail's pace became too much for me.

I jumped down and walked to the front of the station, where I begged a lift from a lorry driver heading in the same direction. It was uncomfortable but progress was steadier, except when we had to wait for military traffic to pass.

The roads were packed with troops and armour on the move. We were in an area that was part of a corridor from the capital to the German and Hungarian troops in the north. The Russians were on either side of us and we could hear the rumble of their guns.

Before long, the Red Army would slam the door shut and the terrible siege of Budapest would begin.

The driver of the lorry warned me that Komarom was a dangerous town.

'There are many unexploded bombs, you must be careful,' he said. 'Why do you want to go there?'

'Oh, the Russians,' I said. 'I must escape the Russians.'

That satisfied him, as it did everyone. The Red Army's reputation for brutality and rape meant that young women seeking to escape were nothing unusual.

We arrived in Komarom at dawn and after thanking the driver for his help, I asked a passerby for directions to the prison.

'Watch out for bombs,' he said, as he sent me on my way.

It was a long walk through a sombre and ghostly town. Many streets were nothing more than ruins, with rubble piled where houses had once been and the occasional chimney left standing, reaching to the sky. Where were the people? Dead or on the roads to Austria, I guessed; their homes, their belongings, all gone now, buried in the rubble of Komarom. Occasionally, the road ahead was blocked altogether and a large warning sign was posted: 'Danger. Keep away'. I would skirt round the area until I was back on the road to the prison.

I found a bakery, nowhere near as good as the one I had discovered in Budapest, but I bought some rolls, sat on a pile of rubble and ate the hard bread. Those people I did see seemed subdued and beaten down, flitting between the homes and buildings still standing and disappearing down alleyways until hidden from my view.

Finally, I stood before a huge building with national flags flying high on its walls. The Hungarian flag was there, and of course so was the Swastika.

'They've put the flags out for me,' I thought, but then I saw an armed guard patrolling on the flat roof and looking down, straight at me. Suddenly it wasn't funny any more.

I headed towards the main entrance, checking that my pass was still in my handbag. I was a bundle of nerves and could feel my blood pounding from fear of being discovered. Had the minister phoned the prison to warn them I was an imposter? There was also the strange nervous excitement at the prospect of seeing Julius again for the first time in 14 months. How had he been treated? Was he ill? Had he been tortured? And what would he feel about me now?

There was another problem. He would be told that a visitor called 'Kovach' wanted to see him. He might say straightaway that he knew no one of that name and the visit would be cancelled.

Just then a voice shouted: 'Halt!' I hadn't even reached the main entrance when an armed guard approached.

'What are you doing here?'

'I have permission to visit a prisoner,' I replied, to this tall, thin man.

'Your pass?'

His expression changed when he saw who had signed my pass and he saluted sharply. 'Follow me, please.'

As we approached the huge entrance door the soldier gave an order and it was pushed slowly open.

Inside, another soldier appeared. There was a rapid conversation between the guards and then one led me along a corridor to a room at the far end. Inside, there was a table and two chairs and some shelves with books. What daylight there was came from a small, barred window.

The guard said nothing, just stood next to me staring at a door in the opposite wall. The minutes stretched, the silence growing more and more oppressive.

Inch by inch, the door in front of us opened and a tall, broad guard stepped through, a gun strapped to his belt. He paused for a moment, nodded to the guard next to me and then moved to one side.

From the darkness behind him a much smaller man, also in uniform, stepped into the room. Thin and pale with sandy hair and those unforgettable blue eyes, he looked at me with astonishment.

It was Julius.

CHAPTER TWELVE

Everyone stood absolutely still. No one spoke.

I stared at Julius thinking, willing him: 'Don't give us away, please.' I stepped forward, held out my hand and said: 'Mr Koreny, pleased to meet you.'

He took my hand and for a moment I thought he wasn't able to speak: his eyes were wide open, his face a picture of surprise.

'Miss Kovach,' he said finally. 'How kind of you to come to visit me.'

The spell was broken, the two guards withdrew through their separate doors, but left them open so they could see and hear what was going on. We were told we had half an hour.

Now it was my turn to be silent. I stared at Julius – wondering if there would ever be another day like this in my life? After 14 months of constant travel, fear and danger, I wanted to step forward and hold him, feel his arms around me, for him to tell me my journey was over, everything was going to be all right.

It was all I could do to stop myself taking that step into his arms, but I couldn't; the guards were watching. I was supposed to be a friend of a friend, nothing more. It was exquisite agony.

We sat in the chairs on opposite sides of the table and began to chat. He was wearing a Hungarian army officer's uniform with the insignia of rank removed. I had never seen him in uniform before; in Zagreb he had always worn a suit.

He lit a cigarette and the smoke drifted lazily up into the light coming through the window.

'I've seen Shary in Budapest, and I've been to Osijek and Vienna,' I said, sounding to my own ears utterly ridiculous. Was that really all I had to say? Of course not. There was so much I wanted to tell Julius: how I had missed him; how worried I'd been; to share with him the risks of my journey; to laugh together at the scrapes I'd got into and what a consummate liar I had become. But none of that was possible. Just outside the doors we could hear the guards shuffling or talking to colleagues.

Physically, Julius looked well and he seemed cheerful, and, once the shock of seeing me had faded, delighted that I was there.

'What about you?' I asked.

'Don't worry about me,' he said. 'I'm being well looked after and I am working in a prison office…'

He seemed to want to say so much more, but couldn't because of the guards.

'Did you get your winter coat and your Leica camera?' I asked.

'Oh, yes, they finally arrived,' he said, smiling.

I longed to ask him why he had been arrested but questions like that were forbidden. Instead we had to carry on with this false conversation. Julius had been the one man in the world to whom I could confess my true feelings and here I was, unable to utter a word other than a string of meaningless platitudes disguising how I really felt.

Half an hour seemed like nothing at all. I was desperate to know whether Julius would be released soon, but, again, I couldn't ask and it was unlikely that he would know.

Fortunately, he was thinking the same thing.

'Are you staying in Komarom long? I think we are soon going to Germany to work and – ' he spoke loudly for the benefit of the guards ' – I'm looking forward to it.'

My heart sank. Germany. Some prisoners were being forced to

march all the way from Hungary, and many didn't make it. Julius wasn't physically strong; how could he possibly survive?

I could see neither guard at the doors, so pulled a piece of paper from my handbag and scrawled Herta's address at the work camp in Vienna, before folding the paper and slipping it across the table to Julius. For a second our hands touched, then he took the paper and put it carefully in his pocket.

'Write to me, I'll come and find you,' I whispered.

All too soon, our time was up. The guards reappeared and as I was led out of the door, I turned and gave Julius a small wave. He smiled at me before the door swung shut behind him.

On my way out I checked at the prison office whether my pass was valid for any more visits. The guard studied it closely, noticed again the signature of the minister and said: 'It is valid for one visit a week for three weeks; you have two visits left.'

I thanked him and was soon back out in the street, making my way to the centre of town. On the one hand I was elated – I had found Julius; on the other, I was more anxious than ever. What did he mean when he said that he was being sent to Germany? Why would they do that?

Among the ruins of Komarom I found a cheap boarding house and rented a small room with the money that Shary had given me. There was nothing to do except wait for my next visit to the grim fortress prison.

The town was becoming more like a military garrison. Every day brought the roar of more tanks and armour moving through, heading south towards Budapest to join yet another offensive against the Red Army.

When I went out, just to walk and get some fresh air, the soldiers would stare at me with hollow, exhausted eyes. Many of them looked too tired to be frightened any more, almost as if they would welcome the end for the rest it brought.

The week dragged by and once again I found myself at the

entrance to the jail. This time it was a bustle of activity: the doors were opening and closing all the time, soldiers were running around and there were even more guards on the roof.

I showed my pass to the guard at the entrance and he sent me on to the prison office. There I was told that all visits had been cancelled – the prisoners were being prepared for their journey to Germany; a long line of cattle trucks was even now waiting in the nearby railway siding.

The news hit me like a blow. Although Julius had said he expected to be sent to Germany, I never thought it would be this soon. I had seen him only once.

I tried not to let my disappointment show but to have come this far and taken such risks, only for Julius to be snatched away from me again, was too much to bear.

As I walked back through the prison gates my eyes misted with tears and by the time I reached the street I was weeping openly. I try never to feel sorry for myself – I believe in fate: what will be, will be. But the combination of war, loneliness and now this latest setback was more than I could stand.

I made my way slowly back to the small rented room, in abject misery. Perhaps it was time to give up? Maybe I should do what everyone kept telling me to do: go home to Zagreb and wait for the end of the war, when Julius would come to find me.

The winter weather was getting colder by the day; the temperature was dropping to -5C and the first snow was covering the surrounding countryside. The streets were a swamp of mud and everyone trudging wearily along wore looks of desperation.

So why did I find it so hard to leave? I could go back to Vienna and return to work at the Horniphon factory. I had carefully kept my employment card for just such an occasion and there I could sit out the war – assuming I survived the bombs – and resume my search for Julius when the world was once more at peace.

It would be the sensible thing to do. The streets of Komarom were packed with refugees. All the boarding houses and rented rooms were overcrowded and once I moved on, I would never get another room. What happened if the Germans cancelled the plan to move Julius to Germany? What if he stayed here, waiting for my next visit and I never came?

I slept badly that night; the noise from the streets never ceased. But mostly I couldn't sleep for thinking about Julius – his delight at seeing me, our love.

The next day dawned bright but very cold. Wrapping myself in as many clothes as I could muster, including my increasingly threadbare fur coat, I headed to the railway marshalling yard near the prison. The long line of cattle trucks was still there and provisions for the guards were being loaded. A kitchen wagon to make food for the prisoners was in the middle of the train.

I stayed for most of the day watching, waiting and chilled to the bone. By the time dusk fell the train was still standing there and my eyes strained to see as it was slowly engulfed by the darkness.

The next day was much the same and I began to think my hunch had been correct: the plan to send the prisoners to Germany had been cancelled.

On the third morning of my vigil, however, there was an atmosphere of tension around the yard. A group of heavily-armed soldiers appeared and formed up along one side of the trucks, then, faintly in the morning air, there was the sound of an approaching train. Looking up, I could see a trail of steam rising high into the sky.

The engine clattered over the points and with a great squeal of brakes came to a halt in the marshalling yard, the line of trucks behind it bumping to a standstill. As soon as it stopped, the guards ran along the trucks throwing open the doors and shouting: 'Schnell! Schnell!'

Prisoners came tumbling out – I couldn't believe how many were crammed into each truck – and were marched straight to the waiting train. They went where they were told, glancing neither to the right nor the left and putting up no protest. The guards harried them along, showing no sympathy to the prisoners in bad physical shape who had to be helped by the others.

After they had all been pushed into the trucks, the doors were slammed shut and the soldiers relaxed. I didn't know where the prisoners had come from – they weren't from Komarom jail; they must have come from further away.

The soldiers didn't leave the yards but remained talking in groups. The smoke from their cigarettes formed small clouds in the cold air while the men stamped their feet to keep warm. At a shouted command from their officers, they threw away their cigarettes, picked up their rifles and formed another line. More prisoners appeared, this time on foot, and the guards began shepherding them towards the cattle trucks.

Some prisoners were sent to collect food from the kitchen wagon, while others were allowed to fill containers with water from a standpipe near the yard fence. It was this group that caught my eye, because among them was a slight, fair figure who I recognised immediately. My heart leapt at the sight of him and I quickly began making my way along the fence towards the water tap.

'Julius,' I hissed, as soon as I was close enough. He turned with surprise at the sound of my voice, and then his face lit up with a broad smile.

'Olgi!' he said, looking quickly back towards the guards. 'We are leaving this afternoon.'

'Where are they taking you?'

'Germany – but we don't know where yet.'

'You must write to me at the Vienna address I gave you. Send a letter there and I will get it.'

'I will, I promise,' he said as I put my fingers on the chain link fence and reached out to him, in the hope he would touch my hand. Just then one of the guards shouted: 'Back to the train – all of you!'

and began walking towards Julius's group with his rifle at the ready.

They all turned and hurried away, Julius pausing to look back as I waved to him.

The prisoners climbed into the cattle trucks and I saw Julius being pulled inside by his fellow prisoners. Moments later, the door was slammed shut and everything was quiet again.

I waited until dusk, but the train didn't move so I returned to my lonely room for another night of fitful sleep.

When I reached the yard in the morning the train had vanished, and with it, Julius.

Staring through the fence at the empty yard, I shed bitter tears. After a year of searching and all the danger I had been through, I had finally found the man I loved – and then lost him again.

CHAPTER THIRTEEN

Christmas was approaching and the stream of people fleeing Budapest and the Red Army had become a flood. A human tide choked the roads. Everyone was there, the young and the old, the sick and the strong – and me, of course.

Those walking carried, wheeled and pushed as many possessions as they could. Every lorry that inched past was groaning under the weight of refugees.

There was no point in staying in Komarom now that Julius had gone. I decided to return to Vienna, contact Herta and resume work at the Horniphon factory. As I travelled I could think of a story to explain my absence.

So I joined the mass exodus from Hungary, hitching lifts in lorries and walking along among the long lines of refugees. We slept in barns and hay lofts, wrapping ourselves in anything we could find to ward off the terrible cold.

By Christmas Eve, I was near Sopron on the border with Austria and had spent the night in a house in a nearby village. It was sunny and dry but very cold. I wanted to cross the border by myself, convinced that a single girl would attract less attention.

Larger groups were often sent on to camps, whereas I had to get back to Vienna. The only address Julius had was Herta's back at the Neue Erlaa camp – there was nowhere else for me to go.

I watched the border crossing from a distance as lorries and pedestrians waited patiently for their papers to be checked before being allowed through to safety.

Their progress seemed relatively swift and the crowds of refugees stretched along the road on the Austrian side of the border, all the way to the horizon.

I felt confident and joined the crush at the border post, walking smartly along behind one of the rare cars in the convoy. The guards gave the driver and passengers a cursory glance, looked briefly at their papers and then waved them on.

I approached the first guard, who looked tired and bored.

'Where are you going?' he asked.

'I am terrified of the Russian army,' I said, 'so I want to go to work in Germany and spend Christmas there.'

'Do you have a passport?'

'No, I have lost mine.'

'Can I look through your bag?'

I handed him the small bag I was carrying which had hardly anything in it, just the last of my money and a few items of clothing.

As he began searching, I remembered too late that it also contained my Horniphon employment card and, sure enough, he found it.

'You were working in the Horniphon factory in Vienna and now you're here, trying to get back?' he asked, his voice suddenly alert. His tiredness and boredom had vanished.

Another guard heard his question and came across to examine the card. I said nothing.

'You deserted from the factory and now find that Hungary is not so good as the Russians are near, so you want to come back to Germany?'

I stood mute. Would they turn me back? I didn't know but I could think of nothing to say that would convince them not to.

'We know that everyone wants to enter the Reich, but we must

137

first find out why you left Vienna,' he said, summoning another soldier who marched across and stood next to me. He dismissed us with a flick of his hand and turned to the refugees behind me, who had been watching my discomfort closely, presumably hoping that my difficulties would make their passage easier. I couldn't blame them; I would have felt the same.

The soldier led me towards a low, white building next to the border post.

'What will happen to me?' I asked him.

'We'll take you to Wiener-Neustadt Prison while we make more inquiries.'

With that, he led me through the front door of the building and into a room where other people were sitting waiting. They looked up anxiously when the door opened and they saw the guard.

My heart sank at the thought of prison again, but at least it was an Austrian jail and less than 30 miles from Vienna – I wasn't being sent back to Komarom.

After a few minutes sitting in silence the door opened and a voice shouted: 'Kovach!' For a moment, I expected one of the others to respond, and then realised it was me he was calling.

I went out and across the hall. An older, fatter soldier was sitting eating smoked ribs with not much meat on them. Watching him chewing on the bones, leaving traces of grease and sauce on his chin, made me realise I hadn't eaten all day. Suddenly, my hunger pangs were intense.

'Can I have something to eat, please?' I asked.

He stopped chewing and slowly looked up at me.

'Those who don't work don't deserve to eat.' He picked up another rib and made a great play of chewing the tiny sliver of meat on the bone.

'I've been put in charge of you,' he said through a mouthful of food. 'We are waiting for the train to come any minute now to take you to Wiener Neustadt.'

With that he carried on eating, leaving me standing there, watching until he had finished. Wiping his hands and chin, he stood and took me outside to a bench by the railway track, where we sat in the freezing cold as the sky darkened, although it was only three o'clock.

The other passengers kept their distance from us, occasionally looking at me and wondering what I had done that required an armed guard. They were all taking food from their bags and still I hadn't eaten.

'Please,' I said to my guard, 'I really need something to eat. I'm starving.'

This time he was more sympathetic and from his own bag he gave me lump of dry bread and a cube of pressed jam. Without a knife to spread the jam, I ate it as best I could, savouring every mouthful.

When I had finished I asked to visit the lavatory. The soldier, grumbling all the way, walked with me to the ladies' and stood guard outside.

Inside, I saw an Austrian woman disappearing into one of the cubicles. She had a kind look to her and I went into the adjacent cubicle and whispered: 'Can you help me, please?'

There was a long, ominous silence from the other side of the cubicle partition before I got an answer: 'What do you want?'

It was not said in an aggressive way, just cautiously.

'Have you got a pen and paper?' I replied. 'I need to send a message to a friend in Vienna.'

Another long silence, then a hand appeared below the partition holding a scrap of paper and a pen. I grabbed them and scribbled a quick note to Herta telling her what had happened and that I was being taken to Wiener-Neustadt Prison. I wrote her camp address at the top and then passed the paper and pen back to the woman.

'Thank you. Thank you very much,' I whispered, before hurrying out to rejoin my guard who led me back to the bench.

I had no way of knowing whether the Austrian woman would betray me. She could just walk along the platform and hand the note to my guard but I had a feeling that she wouldn't. She emerged from the lavatories and, to my relief, went to rejoin her group without even glancing in my direction.

A guard now approached us with a large dog on a lead. There was a brief exchange between the two soldiers and then the original guard left and the new one took his place.

It was going to be a long wait but the consolation was that the presence of an armed soldier meant we had the bench to ourselves so I was able to stretch out, wrap myself in my fur coat and try to sleep. Sadly, the dog wouldn't let me and with its constant snuffling and yapping, I got no rest.

By nine o'clock we had been sitting on the platform for six hours and there was still no sign of the train but at least the guard with the dog was replaced by another soldier; this one without any animals in tow.

More and more people began to appear on the platform and soon everyone was saying the train would arrive within a few minutes. In fact, it was another three freezing hours before we heard the sound of the steam engine and the train inched into the station.

A mad stampede of passengers began before it had even come to a halt, and as soon as my guard and I stood up from our bench we were swept along in the crowd. I was pushed forward until I felt myself being shoved up into a compartment which was so packed I was left standing on one leg. I couldn't even turn round but from what I could see of my travelling companions, there was no sign of my guard. I assumed he was in the next compartment or the corridor but there was not much he could do – there were far too many people on board for anyone to move.

The train set off, first slowly then gathering pace. At least travelling at night we would be spared the constant air raid alarms and the journey would be faster.

People did what they could to make themselves comfortable and I dozed standing up, lulled by the repetitive sound of the wheels rattling over the tracks.

A scream of brakes and the movement of people in the compartment brought me fully awake and I looked into the darkness outside to see signs announcing Wiener Neustadt. Some passengers got out amid shouting and pushing while I waited for my guard to appear. The next sound I heard was the slamming of doors as station staff prepared to wave the train off. It was only when we pulled out of the station that I dared to believe that I had really lost my guard – but I would have to wait until we reached Vienna to be sure.

Soon enough we were crawling through the dark outskirts of the city before the train halted a few hundred yards from the station. This was common practice as railway stations were frequent targets of the bombers, so we all disembarked and walked along the tracks to the platforms. As we approached, I looked around for my guard but there was still no sign of him.

The first time I'd crossed the Austrian border, I'd run from a guard; this time it seemed he'd run away from me. It was a strange Christmas present, but perhaps my gift this year was to be my freedom.

Once again I joined a line of people waiting for my non-existent papers to be checked, this time at the end of the platform. Never mind papers, I had no ticket or money either as the guard had taken my bag at the Austrian border.

All around me, people were smiling and wishing each other Merry Christmas, just happy to be back in Vienna and away from the Russians.

I wished I could share their happiness but instead I felt only fear that, having lost the border guard, I would now be arrested again. I looked around desperately but could see no escape. Guards surrounded the platforms. I began scanning the faces of my fellow passengers; did any of them look kind enough to help?

I didn't get the chance to find out because with a gentle shove from the gentleman behind me, I was suddenly standing in front of the ticket inspector.

'Ticket please,' he said, with a smile.

'I… I don't have one,' I stammered. 'I've come from Hungary and lost all my money.'

'Where are you going?'

'I'm going to Neue Erlaa but I don't know how to get there…'

To my surprise, the inspector smiled more broadly, reached into his pocket and gave me some money.

'Here, that will get you a ticket. Merry Christmas,' he said, and then gave me directions to a nearby station from where I could get the train to Neue Erlaa.

I thanked him profusely and with just one more backward glance to see if my guard had reappeared, I ran from the station as quickly as possible.

That same day, the Russians completed their encirclement of Budapest and the siege of the city began. It would last 100 days, cost 38,000 civilian lives and at the end the Germans would destroy every bridge across the Danube connecting Pest and Buda. More than 80 per cent of the buildings in the city would be reduced to ruins or be seriously damaged by the fighting.

The Budapest of plenty that I had enjoyed a few weeks previously was gone forever.

CHAPTER FOURTEEN

'Olga!' Herta's face was a picture of amazement. 'What are you doing here? How did you get back?'

The questions came in a rush as she ushered me into the dormitory we'd shared at the camp. We sat side by side on a bed while I told Herta everything that had happened since I had been taken to dig the anti-tank trenches.

'We thought you'd gone forever,' she said, smiling with relief. 'I thought I would never see you again.'

When Herta had first answered the door I'd noticed how elegant she looked, wearing a smart black dress, new shoes and even some jewellery – she was going to her SS doctor's house for Christmas lunch.

'Why don't you come as well? I'm sure they won't mind.'

I wasn't so sure, looking at my threadbare clothes, but the thought of a good meal at Christmas, even in the company of the SS, was too tempting. I agreed and Herta began looking for clothes while I washed. With all our activity and chatter we didn't hear the approaching footsteps outside until there was a loud knocking on the door: 'Guards, open up!'

We froze. They must be searching for me, I thought. It wouldn't have taken the border guards long to discover that most of the girls working at Horniphon were living at the camp.

Herta looked at me in panic and then said through the door:

'One minute, please, I'm just dressing.'

'Hurry up,' came the reply, but the door stayed closed.

Herta pointed to a high, wide shelf along one side of the dormitory where the girls put their suitcases. She began pulling some of them down. I scrambled up onto the shelf and lay as close to the wall as possible. Herta pushed the bags and cases back up onto the shelf, hiding me from view.

I heard the door open and the guard came in. 'Are you alone?' he asked Herta.

'Yes, I'm getting ready to go out for Christmas lunch.'

'We're looking for Olga Czepf, do you know her?'

In my hiding place behind the suitcases, I froze when I heard my name mentioned. The border guards had reported me missing and had begun the search. They had kept my work card – so now they knew I'd been travelling under a false name.

I couldn't move or make a sound – to do either would mean a trip to prison. But when you cannot move, absolutely must not move, those are the times when you most want to. You itch all over, you need to sneeze, your muscles seize up and you would give anything to move your limbs. But you have to remain still.

For a moment, it reminded me of hiding from my mother in Sisak when we were playing, but this time it was not a game.

My mind was racing. 'Please, Herta,' I thought, 'don't give me away…'

Then I heard her speaking to the guard: 'Yes, I know Olga, but she left here in November when she was sent to dig anti-tank ditches with the others.'

'You haven't seen her since?'

'No.'

There was silence. What were they doing? Had he seen my hiding place?

Then I heard footsteps and Herta saying 'Heil Hitler' followed by the slamming of the door.

I breathed out heavily and moved the suitcases in front of me. 'Ssssh,' whispered Herta, 'he may still be outside.'

I lay still again until we felt it was safe for me to come down from the shelf but as soon as I got down, we were both seized by a fit of giggles, like a couple of children who think they've outsmarted the grown-ups.

When we had calmed down we spoke in whispers. 'Karl is coming soon to collect me. We'll have to be careful and avoid the guards,' Herta said.

'What if they won't let him in?'

'He's with the SS. They wouldn't dare stop him.'

She was right. As soon as Karl's sleek black car arrived at the camp gates he was waved straight through and we climbed into the back seat well out of sight of the guards.

On the way into Vienna, Herta told Karl that I had been in Hungary but fled from the Red Army's advance and had lost all my papers. It was true – but it wasn't the whole truth. However, he seemed satisfied and when we reached his apartment in the outskirts of the city, he went to explain to his wife why there was an extra guest for lunch, while Herta ushered me into a bathroom to wash.

We were introduced to Karl's blonde wife, who was kind and welcoming, before sitting down at the polished dining room table, where an extra place had been quickly laid with silver cutlery and delicate crockery. It seemed like a lifetime ago that I had last sat down at such an elegant dinner table. Suddenly I felt shy.

Through the windows I could see a small garden at the back of the apartment block, peaceful and undamaged by bombs. It was all a long way from Wiener-Neustadt Prison where I should have been spending Christmas.

Karl came round pouring champagne for each of us, and then he raised his glass.

'Merry Christmas,' he said. Everyone clinked glasses and I looked around the table: the SS officer, his Aryan wife, the Jewess and me, the fugitive. What a strange group to sit down to a meal together in the Third Reich in 1944.

I raised my glass: 'Merry Christmas.'

***

I remained at the house for three days. Herta told my hosts that there was no room at the camp – all the bunks were full – and Karl's wife was quick to offer me the chance to stay. I could hardly refuse; I had nowhere else to go, but there was a limit to how much time I wanted to spend in the home of an SS officer.

Herta came back to tell me that the police had been round to the camp looking for me and she had been questioned again.

We were sitting in the spare bedroom in the house. 'What can I do?' I asked Herta. 'I can't stay here for long.'

'I know a place near the camp which sells milk. I have friends there and I'm sure I could get you a job, but – '

'What? Is there a problem?'

'Well, a lot of the guards from the camp go there to get milk, and so do the girls. Someone might recognise you…'

'Oh, no. I can't risk it,' I said, my hopes of work dashed.

Herta began rummaging around in her bag and then produced a bottle, which she waved in the air, smiling at me. 'Have you ever been blonde?' she said, laughing.

I looked at the bottle – it was bleach. I groaned. I wasn't keen on the idea: my head was still sore from the lice and I was worried the bleach would make it worse. But what option did I have?

Herta told Karl's wife that I'd decided I wanted to be a blonde and she, naturally, thought it was a good idea.

'Olga you'll look lovely,' she assured me. I didn't feel so confident and anyway, I had dark hair: it was part of me. But my feelings made no difference. The next day the operation began and the others took turns in rinsing my hair in bleach and massaging my burning scalp. It was torture; the colour was anything but perfect and yet I became a blonde, for the only time in my life.

Looking in the mirror wasn't quite as big a shock as I'd feared and, with time, I thought I would get used to my new look. What would my mother have made of me now? Still too ugly to find a man?

More importantly, when I put on a pair of dark glasses I looked like a different person. As disguises go, it wasn't sophisticated, but it was certainly very effective.

I was ready to face the world again.

***

My first day at the dairy selling milk and I thought I had found the easiest job in the world. People came in, they paid for milk, I gave it to them and off they went. Even some Serbian prisoners of war came in and I served them as well.

I'd forgotten one thing: ration coupons. I hadn't asked to see any coupons, which wouldn't have mattered that much for the locals and the guards from the camp, but the prisoners of war?

'You stupid Hungarian!' the manager shouted, moments before he fired me.

The only consolation was that he had believed I was Hungarian. Perhaps the disguise was working after all.

However, I was once again without work, had nowhere to live and, above all, there was still no news from Julius. He had promised to write and he had Herta's address… but what had become of him since I saw him in the marshalling yards at Komarom?

We were now into the first days of 1945. Budapest was under siege; Vienna was suffering under more and more bombing raids; the alarms were unrelenting and the casualties shocking.

Herta took me to the employment exchange. 'You have to work, Olga; you need somewhere to live.'

They found me a job at a workers' café in Neue Erlaa, where staff from the nearby factories would come to eat lunch. I was the cook, making the daily stew. The menu never changed. Rations were so scarce that I would put the wrapping paper from the blocks of margarine into the stew, only taking them out when the hot liquid had stripped every scrap of margarine from the paper.

The café owner was a former soldier who limped badly from the injuries he had suffered on the eastern front. He was tall, rake-thin and blond. His wife was a complete contrast: she was short, plump and dark. She looked Slovenian, which was perfectly possible as they came from Villach, close to the border with Yugoslavia.

They were a pleasant couple, who gave me a good room opposite their bedroom. As they believed me to be Hungarian, and Budapest was still holding out against the Russians, they treated me as a friend – an ally of the Reich. I was honest and told them I wasn't interested in politics and although they seemed reluctant to admit it, they didn't seem to be either. He was just an ordinary man who had done his duty and suffered terribly as a result – like millions of others on both sides. He was well known to our regular customers in the café and, as a former soldier, particularly enjoyed talking to the soldiers and camp guards who came in for a plateful of my stew.

It was a comfortable place to be while I waited for Julius to write to Herta telling me where he was. Herta had now found a room in a house in the town, no longer wanting to share a dormitory with other girls at the camp, but she still went there regularly to collect her post.

It seemed that I was coming to the end of my journey; the war was reaching its climax and although we heard the wild rumours about how Vienna would be the next to fall to the Red Army after Budapest, it didn't seem real. The bombers still came to Vienna and people still died, but somehow I never thought I'd be one of them.

Serving in the café gave me a comforting routine for the first time in months. I was up early to prepare the ingredients, then I set the large pot of stew heating on the cooker before the first customers – workers on their way to factories, guards on their way home from night shifts – began arriving for their breakfast. Soon the place was alive with talk and clouded with cigarette smoke. The conversation would fly back and forth, some of the regulars flirting with the blonde Hungarian in the kitchen while the owner would gently admonish them with a fatherly concern.

A soldier came in one morning and chatted easily to the owner but his gaze kept lingering on me. I turned away but when I next looked in his direction his eyes were still staring steadily towards me. As he left, he cast one last glance at me before stepping out into the street and closing the door behind him.

I was 21 years old and newly blonde – perhaps I had an admirer? For some reason, his attention didn't feel like that. I felt uneasy.

The next day, just as the morning rush was at its height, the same soldier appeared, this time in a uniform that reminded me of the guards who had watched over Lenke and me when were sent to dig the anti-tank ditches by the border. My feeling of unease grew.

I avoided his gaze and busied myself with work, but he came up to the counter and again began chatting to the owner. Then he turned to me and asked: 'Where do you come from?'

'Oh,' I said, aware suddenly how hot and smoky the café was. I felt blood rush to my cheeks. 'I'm from Hungary.'

He looked at me coldly. 'Really? You know, I'm not sure where you come from but a few months ago I was on duty near the border, looking after people digging trenches. I started the day with 50 people but by evening two were missing. We never found them.'

The noise and hubbub from the café seemed to fade to a background blur as I stood there, the guard staring at me and the café owner standing between us looking bemused.

'I've come from Budapest to get away from the Red Army, but do tell me more about my double,' I said, smiling at him.

'Oh, I know very little, but you do remind me of her.'

Silence fell between us and then, faintly from the street outside but growing louder all the time, came the one sound that we all hated: the air raid siren. This time it saved me. I grabbed my coat and with the rest of the staff and customers fled from the café. While the others rushed to the shelters or into the relative safety of the Vienna woods, I went in the opposite direction, towards Herta's house. The last thing I wanted was to find myself sheltering alongside the soldier who had recognised me and who would then have hours to question me in detail. No, I would rather take the risk and not go to the shelter.

Within minutes I was regretting that decision. The bombers were not heading for Vienna but for the factories and industrial sites in the Modling area. This time, we were the targets.

After the first wave of bombers passed overhead, I could hear the shrill whistle of the bombs falling and then the whole world around me seemed to lurch upwards in a blaze of flame and explosion. The noise of the blasts was deafening and a hurricane of hot air picked me up and hurled me across the street, where I slammed into a wall and fell to the pavement. Buildings crashed down, and for a terrifying moment I thought I was about to be buried alive. The sky was raining sand, stones and debris while the air was choked with dust.

I'd been in quite a few air raids before, but nothing as intense as this. There were so many bombs landing in such a tiny area that I didn't believe any of us could survive.

As the dust cleared, I heared bombs exploding further away and hoped desperately that they were finished. I strained to hear any more aircraft but the sound and concussion of the explosions had left me temporarily deaf. I struggled to my feet and saw a railway bridge at the far end of the street. I ran to it and found three men already taking refuge there. They sat with their backs pressed up against the brick wall of the bridge, their faces white with fear. One of them clutched a book in his hands. I sat down but none of us said a word. We waited, struck dumb with terror. From all around we could hear further explosions, but our small area stayed relatively quiet. As I looked down the street towards Herta's house, I could see nothing but rubble.

Herta never went to the woods or the shelters now that she had left the camp. She believed in fate.

'Olga, if my number is up, then so be it,' she had said to me on countless occasions. 'I'd rather be at home when the time comes. I don't want to be lying in the snow in the woods.'

Looking through the smoke and dust towards her house from the shelter of the railway bridge I hoped desperately that she was not at home, that for once she had sheltered somewhere else.

After half an hour, the four of us under the bridge were beginning to breathe more easily; there had been no bombs since the first ones. Perhaps, after all, they had passed on to other targets.

But just as we dared to hope, we heard the deep rumble of more bombers, accompanied by the buzzing of their fighter escorts. 'Please, not us,' I thought, pulling my knees up and resting my forehead on them. I could feel the man next to me trembling and as the bombers came closer I closed my eyes and began to pray.

The first explosion brought a building at the far end of the street crashing down in a hailstorm of rubble and flame. From somewhere, I heard a terrible scream. The explosions advanced along the street, ripping vast craters in the earth, hurling everything into the sky. Clouds of smoke billowed under the railway bridge, choking and blinding us as the brickwork shuddered under the blasts.

The air pressure from the pounding bombs swept under the bridge and buffeted us. I glanced at the man with the book and saw that it had shrunk, reduced by pressure and the man's terrified grasp into a tiny ball.

One bomb on the bridge would be all it would take for it to collapse on top of us. Suddenly I felt so desperately claustrophobic, so convinced that I was going to die, that I felt like getting to my feet, ready to run and take my chances in the maelstrom of the streets.

Then, as suddenly as it had begun, it was over. The bombs stopped falling and the sound of the aircraft faded in the sky. Still, none of us moved, none of us spoke.

We were still under the bridge when dusk fell and it was pitch black by the time the all-clear sounded and the four of us emerged, heading off into a world of dust and destruction without a word to each other.

I picked my way past the craters, debris and – worst of all – the unexploded bombs, towards Herta's house.

I got there to find only rubble illuminated by the fires that had sprung up all along the street. Where once had stood a neat, small house, there was nothing. I remembered that terrible scream I had heard when the bombers came in for the second attack.

'Herta! Herta!' I called out, still hoping but deep down feeling only a dreadful despair. There was no answer to my cries. I could see no one. Standing there, I realised I had lost my best friend.

When some people emerged from the woods, I ran to ask them if anyone had seen Herta. 'You know Herta doesn't come to the woods or the shelters,' one told me.

It had grown cold but I sat down on the ground next to Herta's house and wept. Who would help me now?

Some kind people tried to console me, offering me a meal. Those who supposed the destroyed house was mine even offered me a room with them, but it was to no avail.

Before long, the street was deserted once again. What belongings could be salvaged had been and the residents had moved off to find somewhere to stay for the night.

The temperature had fallen below freezing and as I stood I pulled my old fur coat around me as tightly as possible. This, I reflected, is what defeat feels like. All my hopes, all my expectations dashed.

I had nothing: no job, nowhere to live, no fiancé and now, no best friend. I was alone in a hostile world. I couldn't go back to the café - the soldier had seen to that. I would never find out now where Julius was because he would write to Herta and she was dead. His words would go unread, his hopes too would be shattered, and he would assume I had abandoned him.

I was sobbing quietly when another figure approached from the woods. My eyes were blurred with tears and night had fallen, so I could only make out the vague shape of a woman. As she approached, she said: 'Olga?'

I wiped my eyes and looked at her more closely. She looked dishevelled, dirty and shaken, but to my sheer joy, it was Herta.

I rushed forward to embrace her and we clung to each other, weeping with relief – a gesture of life from two friends who had just escaped death.

Herta looked in horror at what had once been her home, now reduced to smouldering rubble. 'You know I stay at home when the bombers come, but today I'd gone to get cigarettes from the Italians in the camp near ours, and I just stayed with them when the bombs fell,' she said.

She looked shaken by what would have happened to her if she'd followed her usual habit of staying at home.

'It's fate,' she said. 'Just fate.'

***

February 1945 was surprisingly mild and we could sit outside gossiping with friends and workmates. The bombing had left us homeless. Herta returned to the camp while I found a room with a Ukranian family who had been brought to Germany to work in an arms factory. The daughter, Olya, and I became friends and soon enough I was working in the munitions factory as well. It was hard, dirty work drilling out parts for guns.

I only stayed in the hope of hearing from Julius, but that hope was beginning to fade. So much time had passed since I saw him in Komarom and we had heard so many terrible stories about the prisoners who were forced to march hundreds of miles through the harsh winter months to reach Germany that I wondered whether I had now lost him forever.

He may have died somewhere between Budapest and Germany, just another victim of a war that had already claimed so many.

I could hope or I could grieve. Sometimes it felt as if I was doing both.

And then, when Olya and I got back from work one day, we found Herta waiting on the doorstep, grinning happily. She was clearly excited about something.

'Surprise!' she cried out, running towards me waving an envelope.

My heart leapt. It was a letter and with trembling fingers I tore open the envelope. There inside was a single sheet of paper.

> Dearest Olga,
>   I am here in Germany and am doing well. The food is good. All I need is a toothbrush!
>   Your loving fiancé,
>   Julius

That was it. Just a couple of lines on a piece of paper, but the envelope told a far more poignant story. It bore a prisoner number and, on the reverse, an address.

I read all of it carefully, noting that it was dated early in January and had taken more than a month to reach me. I was elated that Julius was alive – he'd survived the journey to Germany – but, if I had been less naïve, I would also have been terrified.

There was one word in the address that now echoes through history: Dachau.

CHAPTER FIFTEEN

The towers of St Stephen's Cathedral had escaped the worst of the bombing of Vienna and although damaged the vast building on Stephansplatz offered a quiet haven from the war.

It was a long time since I had been in a church, but when in Vienna I found myself drawn to the peace and sanctuary of the cathedral. Sometimes I would pray; other times I would just sit and watch others coming to worship.

Herta often joined me on these visits. There were no synagogues for her and to declare her faith publicly was far too dangerous.

'I never pray,' she told me. 'I don't believe in anything. After I lost my parents and all we had I can only believe in myself and hope one day that when peace comes I can work hard and have a better life.'

It was easy to sympathise and difficult to cling to religious beliefs when surrounded by so much horror. I had now become so used to my life of constant danger that I lived day to day. I could not afford to dream of the future. One bomb could put paid to all of that.

My sole aim was to find Julius. He was in a concentration camp so I would have to go there. I didn't doubt it for a moment.

Herta and I had come to Vienna together for one last time. The camp near Modling was closing down, the factories were moving north to Germany and the workers dispersed.

I knew where I was going; meanwhile, Herta was going towards the border with Yugoslavia to make her way home. We paid our final visit to Prater where I bought some new spring clothes on the black market: a skirt, a white lace blouse and shoes.

We said our farewells in the city that had come to mean so much to both of us. Despite the war, the tragedies and the hardship, we had enjoyed some good times in Vienna. I gave Herta my antique bracelet: 'Here you've been a good friend to me. I'll always remember you.'

We embraced.

'Good luck. Just think how pleased Julius will be to see you, when you find him,' she said softly.

With that, we parted. I watched Herta walk away quickly through the crowds until she disappeared from view.

***

Just as I had escaped the Red Army in Hungary, now I had to do so again in Austria. By the end of March 1945, the city was gripped with panic.

The country had been part of the Third Reich since Hitler annexed it in 1938. Now the Red Army had crossed the border of the Reich itself and Vienna was a prime target.

Many of the people who had fled Hungary were now preparing to do the same from Vienna. When I went to an enormous refugee centre in an old administration building in the centre of the city, I heard as many Hungarian voices as Austrian.

Mattresses were crammed into every available space and I found one for myself in a room with 30 other women. The atmosphere – and the food – was surprisingly good; people talked and helped each other. Everyone was buoyed by the thought of getting away from the Red Army. Hardship can be a unifying factor, bringing out the best in people – but it can also bring out the worst.

We were told our journey would begin the following day when

we would move to another refugee camp on the outskirts of the city.

I slept soundly that night, comforted by the presence of the other women and finding my mattress was of surprisingly good quality.

When I woke, I was all alone.

I sat up quickly and looked around. There was no one there; every other mattress was empty and the building was eerily silent. I reached for my clothes – they had gone. I searched desperately but there was no sign of them.

'Come on!' the German woman in charge was standing at the door. 'Why are you still here? Everyone is waiting. Come on, get dressed.'

'I can't,' I replied. 'Someone's stolen my clothes.'

She ordered me to cover myself with a grey, dusty army blanket while she checked the rest of the building to ensure that everyone else was out.

After a few minutes, she was back, looking shocked. In her arms she carried what appeared to be a small bundle of clothes. I could tell straight away they weren't mine and was about to say so, when she interrupted: 'Look what I've found.'

Then I heard a baby's cry. A tiny boy, around five months old, lay wrapped in the clothes. His eyes looked up at me and the German woman, searching our faces, hoping to see his mother.

He had beautiful blue eyes, which reminded me of Julius, and I took him gently in my arms and held him close.

The woman unwrapped the bundle of baby clothes, finding some food and a note, written in bad German, which said the boy's father was a German soldier and his mother could no longer look after him. How desperate she must have been to abandon her child.

She must be among our group of refugees, I realised. If I cared for the baby I could find the mother and she would be reunited with her boy.

I recalled talking to a Hungarian woman with a baby the previous day. She had admired my clothes and was much the same size as me. Not even in times of war, surely, would someone steal clothes and leave a baby instead?

Slowly, we made our way out of the building. I carried the baby carefully, while still trying to keep the blanket wrapped around me to hide my nakedness.

A small lorry, full of women, was waiting outside. They helped us up into the back and soon we were on our way.

I looked around me at all the women. 'How could someone steal my clothes?' I said, beginning to cry. They were the best clothes I had had in a long time and their loss affected me deeply.

I held the baby closer and the German woman put her arms around me.

'Don't worry, in the new camp they will sort something out. We'll be there for at least two days. We can even make something out of this blanket. Can you sew?'

I remembered the evenings I'd spent with my mother, beneath the oil lamp in our house in Sisak, working carefully on our embroidery.

'Yes, I can sew,' I replied, but in truth I didn't want to make clothes from an old blanket.

As our lorry bounced along the potholed roads, my new baby slept peacefully in my arms. I looked down at his sweet face and wondered what would become of him – and, indeed, what would become of me.

We could hear the thump of artillery guns nearby and the rapid rattle of gunfire. The battle for Vienna was getting closer all the time and if we didn't make quick progress we ran the risk of being trapped in the city as the Red Army closed in.

It wasn't long before we stopped outside a large building and were told to get out. The driver helped me down, still clutching the baby and my blanket, and took me to a small office where I was told to wait. The baby stirred and I gave him some food, before rocking

158

him gently back to sleep.

The Germans brought me some food: bread, margarine and a hard-boiled egg. I stared in amazement. An egg? I hadn't seen one in such a long time, I'd almost forgotten what they looked like. Eggs, tomatoes and fresh fruit were virtually unknown.

I examined the food closely until one of the Germans said: 'Don't you like eggs?'

'Oh, yes,' I said, grabbing the egg in case someone took it away. This was food fit for royalty and I was determined to enjoy it. Throughout the war, and particularly for a refugee, food was an obsession; you just never knew where the next meal was coming from.

The German woman in charge appeared in the office as I was eating. She had questioned some of the girls and my guess about the young Hungarian girl was correct: she had taken my clothes and abandoned her baby before fleeing. No one knew where she was now.

I looked at the little boy and felt a rush of tenderness. How could a mother abandon her own baby? War has a terrible effect on people – and not just in the most obvious ways.

Two Hungarian girls who had heard of my plight appeared. One gave me a blouse, the other, a pair of shoes with rubber soles. They were hardly comparable with the clothes I had lost but I felt that help had arrived and I was grateful.

While I cradled the baby, they set about turning the blanket into a pair of trousers. The small scissors they had were hopeless but a passing soldier saw them struggling to cut the heavy material and offered his cut-throat open razor, which sliced through the blanket with no trouble. Of course, we didn't have any buttons or zips, so the girls just made the trousers big enough to slip over my hips and I used two safety pins to hold them up.

'Give us a twirl, Olga,' they laughed, proud of their handiwork. I did, but I felt despondent over the loss of my own clothes and was glad there was no mirror for me to see myself in the baggy trousers.

That night we once again each got a mattress on the floor. I wrapped the baby carefully in a blanket and held him next to me until he fell asleep.

Occasionally, he woke during the night and I would comfort him as his tiny blue eyes looked at me.

The next day we were told we were leaving Vienna and once again were loaded into the lorries, which began the slow crawl northwards through the city streets. We crossed the Danube by the Floridsdorf Bridge, which was destroyed a few days later by the Germans as they gave up the defence of Vienna and the Red Army took over.

As we travelled over the water, we all fell silent at the sound of heavy fighting in the city behind us.

***

By the afternoon of that day, the roads were packed with vehicles leaving Vienna. We were squeezed together on the floor of the lorry and I held the sleeping baby in my arms. I'd managed to get a small rucksack in which I kept the baby's food and clothes, but I had no spare clothes for myself.

Large numbers of Hungarian Hussars were travelling the same roads with horses and farm carts, their officers trying to clear a way through all the traffic. The soldiers with us wouldn't say where we were being taken and it was dangerous to ask too many questions.

When our lorry stopped and we all got down to stretch our legs, I picked up the baby and rucksack and slipped away into the crowds of refugees. It was risky travelling on my own, particularly as I now had the baby to care for, but it was important that I was free to get to Dachau and find Julius. Staying with the others meant I would have to go where I was taken. I wandered along the line of refugees with the baby who was still asleep but would soon need feeding.

I had some powdered milk and stopped at a house and asked for some hot water to mix it into a warm drink. The woman who answered my knock was kind and warmed some milk for the baby and gave me food.

Feeling refreshed by the warmth of our welcome and the food, I rejoined the tide of refugees and walked with a group of Hungarian Hussars for several miles, by which time tiredness began to set in. My constant travelling and caring for a child left me feeling mentally and physically exhausted.

In front of me, I could see an empty cart with one soldier walking in front beside the horse. There was an old blanket thrown in the back and I placed the baby carefully on it and then jumped up, ready to sit next to him on the blanket.

Suddenly, there was a loud shout from under the blanket, which began moving. A man's head appeared.

'What do you think you're doing?' he asked angrily, 'You nearly killed me with that heavy parcel of yours.'

'It's not a parcel,' I replied in Hungarian, 'it's a baby. He needs some sleep as we've been on the road for a long time.'

The man's expression softened when I added: 'I'm very tired myself. Can I please stay on the cart and have a rest?'

Realising my plight and the fact that I spoke his language, he apologised and helped me and the baby to settle on the cart before he jumped down and walked along beside us.

Of medium height, dark and with a small moustache, he introduced himself as Istvan and said he was from Budapest, where he had been a civil servant before the war. His wife, four-year-old daughter and son of 18 months had still been in the city as the Red Army approached.

'I hope somebody will help them if they're in need – you know how badly the Russians treat women,' he said.

He assumed the baby was mine and asked about my husband.

He was obviously concerned and treated me so kindly that I quickly warmed to him. As we continued our slow journey and darkness fell, I found myself pouring out my life story to this stranger.

When I'd finished, he said: 'Julius is a lucky man. Not many fiancées, not even wives, are travelling round the world looking for their loved ones.'

We smiled at each other, then he added: 'How will you find him in Dachau? It's a dangerous place.'

It wasn't the first time I'd been given that warning. I'd been told the same about Budapest and Vienna, but I didn't realise then that he knew far more than me about the nature of the camp. To me, it was just another prison; another place where I could find Julius. The full horror would only hit me later.

So in reply to Istvan, I just said: 'Oh, I don't know. I never make plans. I just let things happen.'

He laughed. 'It was good you made no plans for today, otherwise we'd never have met.'

The cart bumped along the rutted road and the Hussars carried on walking behind, with Istvan keeping pace with me.

'Do you speak German?' he asked me suddenly, and when I replied that I did, he said: 'We could be helpful to each other. Two other officers and I are in charge of about 30 soldiers and we're desperate for a good night's sleep, but none of us speak German so it's difficult for us to talk to the people at places where we could spend the night. You could help by translating for us…'

Istvan explained that they had plenty of food and in return for helping them they would make sure that the baby and I were well cared for and safe.

I agreed readily – and then immediately worried about the responsibility of having three officers and 30 soldiers relying on me to find them somewhere to rest for the night.

Istvan took me to meet the other officers, who seemed pleased with the arrangement. We chatted for a while, but they became evasive when I asked how far they were going.

'We don't know yet,' one replied, 'but I hope you won't have to cope with us for too long.'

It was unusual for an army unit not to know where it was going and I have since wondered if they were deserters. That might be unfair: they could have been the last remnants of the Hungarian army to make it across the border into Austria as the Red Army took over their country.

In any case, we had an agreement. When the officers spotted somewhere they thought would be suitable I approached the householders and asked them in German to help. We couldn't all stay in the same building, but with a combination of barns, stables and rooms in houses I managed to find somewhere for all the men on that first night.

Some of the householders, suffering hardships themselves, would ask if we had food to spare, in which case I would barter with them, suggesting a better room in return for food.

By the time the main column of refugees arrived in the small village on our first night, the soldiers were all settled in their billets. I felt very proud and Istvan took food around all the homes where it had been promised.

Istvan, the two officers and I were billeted with one family. Everyone made a fuss of the baby and helped me warm milk for him.

Sitting down to dine with the officers and the host family was a rare treat. After all the privations of the war, it was real banquet with plenty to eat and wine to drink. One of the officers noticed my caution about eating all the food – my instinct was to save some for the next day.

'Don't worry,' he said. 'You'll not be hungry with us.'

Even the baby was aware of the relaxed atmosphere, smiling up from his blankets at all the new faces and becoming even more excited when Istvan started playing a piano that was sitting in the corner of the room.

We all joined in the Hungarian songs – even though the family didn't know the words and when Istvan struck up a romantic ballad he seemed to be singing it to me. It was a relaxed, enjoyable evening despite the hard journey still ahead of us – a moment of relief from the brutality of war.

***

Over the following days our group settled into a daily routine. We would set off at dawn, I would sit with the baby in the back of the cart, Istvan would walk alongside and we would talk, while the remainder of the soldiers followed along behind.

As dusk fell and we approached a village or town I would jump down from the cart and begin knocking on doors, asking for rooms for the night, negotiating with offers of food. We were fortunate: the Austrians liked the Hungarian soldiers so I did not have any problem finding accommodation.

As we headed towards the border town of Passau, after which we would be on German soil, I began to worry more about the baby. He had long since drunk all the powdered milk his mother had left and while I was able to get milk along the way, the food the soldiers had brought was not suitable.

He was getting more restless and I was finding it harder to cope the more he cried. Much of his discomfort was probably nothing more than hunger, but what could I do?

A couple of days later a lorry pulled to a stop beside our cart. In the back, among many others, was a young Yugoslav woman from Smederevo who was nursing a baby much the same age as my little boy. We began talking and I asked if she had any baby food.

'I'm sorry – I'm breast feeding and have plenty of milk. Do you not have any?'

I explained that the boy wasn't mine and told her how I had

found him.

'Would you like me to look after him now?' she asked. 'I have enough milk and I will care for him. I know you must love him, but…'

Her voice trailed off. We both knew she was right. 'It would be better for the child and for you,' she added.

Sadly, I agreed. Of course, I'd grown to love the baby but I was worried about caring for him on such a perilous journey and the young woman looked kind and genuine in her offer to look after him.

With much fuss from the soldiers who had become fond of the baby, and tears from me, I gathered up all his blankets and clothes from the cart and passed them up to the woman. Finally, I hugged the baby for the last time, gave him a gentle kiss and held him up until eager hands took him into the back of the lorry.

Since leaving Zagreb I had lost almost everything. My rings, wallet, jewellery and clothes had been stolen; I had given my antique bracelet to Herta as a parting gift; all I had left was a St Anthony's medallion which my dear aunt Alice had given me for Christmas in 1940. Now I was giving up a little baby boy.

Shortly afterwards the lorry pulled away and I watched until it disappeared, then climbed back onto the cart, feeling strangely alone now without the baby in my arms.

***

The following days passed in our familiar routine as we followed the Danube west from Vienna towards our crossing point into Germany at Passau: a distance of about 200 miles.

We passed through beautiful scenery, with the blue river winding its way across countryside that in peacetime would have been tranquil and quiet, but now was swarming with refugees all fleeing in the same direction.

In the sky above, bombers still came and went, en route to Vienna and Linz, Hitler's home town, but the long columns of refugees were left alone. We were no threat to anyone.

Every day Istvan greeted me with a warm smile and a cheery 'good morning' and we would spend the days talking about our lives, what the future held, our hopes and fears. He gave me his address in Budapest and made me promise that if I went to his city after the war I would visit. He always behaved as a proper gentleman and I felt as if I had known him all my life.

Every night, I found accommodation for us all and Istvan organised a rota system ensuring that the better rooms were shared out fairly. All the men cared for me and I realised as we travelled that I had not felt so relaxed and protected for a long time.

It was easy to just take each day as it came, thinking little about the future. But I didn't have that option. I wasn't there for the same reason as the other refugees – simply to escape the Russians. I had a purpose.

Once we were through Passau and moving further into Germany, I began to wonder how I would find Dachau. The Hungarians still had not told me where they were heading and I began to suspect they had no set destination in mind, but I did and it was vital that I got there.

We continued to follow the river until Regensburg, where Istvan told me in a few days we would reach Nuremberg. There, we would have to part. He didn't explain why.

We reached the city two days later. Gazing out from high ground nearby, I was shocked by what I saw. Nuremberg was in ruins. It looked as if hardly a single building had been left standing by the bombers. The skeleton of the Frauenkirche was there in the main square but all around was rubble.

This was the city that had become so familiar in the 1930s as the site of the biggest Nazi rallies, but I looked at it and could see only Germany's defeat.

The Hussars were shocked into silence as well.

Istvan approached me, looking suddenly shy. 'We must part here,' he began, sounding very formal. 'We are all very grateful for what you have done and on behalf of us all I want to thank you.'

He paused and looked down, then he handed me a folded piece of paper: 'Here is a small poem I wrote for you last night when I knew that we would have to part today. Keep it to remind yourself of us.'

I unfolded the paper and read the neatly-written words:

We are going tonight to the front
I say to you
I hope we'll be all right
If some voice from the sky calls us
I will always remember you…

They were the lines from the ballad he had sung at the piano a few nights before. He watched me reading them and then said: 'Sorry, but I am in love with you…'

He looked uncomfortable; he was a married man, after all. 'Who wouldn't be?' he added. 'I hope you find Julius. He's a lucky man.'

I was shocked by his words but not that surprised. We had grown very close during our journey, enjoying each other's company and finding we had much in common, bringing each other comfort during terrible times. It is hard not to become close to someone in those circumstances.

I said my goodbyes to them all and headed down the slight hill to the town.

After a few steps I heard someone approaching. It was Istvan, who thanked me once again.

'If I wasn't happily married I would say more,' he added wistfully. We looked at each other for some moments while the Hussars stood around pretending not to know what was going on.

I took the St Anthony's medallion from around my neck and handed it to him. 'Here, Istvan, take this. May God help and keep you and let you return safely to your wife and children. I promise if I come to Budapest I will come to see you.'

My last piece of jewellery was gone and so was the man who had helped me and cared for me during the journey from Austria. I whispered farewell to him then turned and walked towards the ruins of Nuremberg.

CHAPTER SIXTEEN

By the time the train pulled into Munich, night had fallen. The city was in pitch darkness, tense with fear because the air raid sirens were wailing.

Everyone scrambled off the train and ran as fast as they could away from the railway lines and station.

The train had brought me from Nuremberg, via Passau, the very route I had travelled with the Hussars. A refugee centre in Nuremberg had given me a permit to travel as far as Miesbach, south of Munich, but I simply crossed out the name and wrote 'Munich' above it. The train conductor had not even given it a second glance. I suppose if your country is on the brink of overwhelming defeat, checking train tickets seems a rather futile occupation.

I was swept along in the crowd on the station platform, unable to stop to get my bearings until everyone had pushed and shoved their way through the exit and out into the street.

Then the crowd just seemed to evaporate, disappearing into the night. In a matter of minutes, I was left standing alone.

The only pinpricks of light came from the pocket torches the residents carried to find their way past the ruined buildings, around the craters and over the rubble.

Just then I heard voices shouting and the anti-aircraft guns began firing, their exploding shells lighting up the sky. The bombers had arrived.

I'd never been to Munich before and had no idea where the shelters were. I couldn't just stand there – I had to get away. I ran down a street full of destroyed houses, falling over the rubble, picking myself up and running on as I heard the bombers getting closer.

I had no time left so I hid beneath the ruins of an old house as a thunder of explosions hit the area.

I was still far too close to the railway station but didn't dare move to better shelter. Instead, I put my half-empty rucksack down, sat on the wet rubble, closed my eyes and put my hands over my ears – as if that would save me.

As the bombs crashed down, the ground shifted and the shattered building shuddered above me. A cloud of thick dust swept along the street engulfing everything. I could hear buildings near me collapsing.

'Please,' I thought. 'No more. Not again.'

I was terrified, alone and hungry. I had seen so much bombing and had so narrowly escaped death in Vienna. How long would it be before I became just another victim of war?

As if the bombs weren't bad enough, the rain was falling heavily and I was soaked to the skin.

It was past midnight and still there was no sign of the all-clear. Instead, from the sky came the drone of the bombers making another run over the ruined city.

The worst time was not when the aircraft passed overhead but the moments immediately after, when I knew the bombs were in the air, dropping silently towards earth. Towards me.

This time, however, the explosions were followed by the sound of the aircraft fading in the night as they turned and headed back to their bases in England. It was over – for a few hours, anyway.

I emerged from my makeshift shelter, soaking wet and covered in dust to see the devastation all around. I always felt a mixture of intense fear and anger at the bombers.

Everywhere I had travelled in Germany I had seen only destruction: buildings reduced to rubble and those who had survived living in the ruins. Many others were lying dead in the streets as the ambulances fought to keep up with the terrible number of dead and injured.

The danger was still not over once the bombers had gone. Many of the bombs dropped every night did not detonate on impact; they lay in the streets, or embedded in the rubble, primed and ready to explode.

I picked my way carefully past them as I saw the telltale torch lights of what was left of the population of Munich, emerging from their shelters. I had no papers, no passport and no money. I was 22 years old, alone in the Third Reich amid all this death and destruction.

I was desperately hungry and asked a passerby where I could get food. She directed me to a soup kitchen for refugees. I had little hope that it would be open in the early hours after a bombing raid. Amazingly it was not only open, but virtually deserted. I was given hot bean soup straight away.

The woman behind the counter watched me eat.

'Some more?' she asked as soon as the first bowl was finished, adding that the heavy bombing had kept people away that night. 'Oh, yes, please,' I replied gratefully.

The kitchen had been set up, the woman explained, to help those fleeing the Russian advance in the east. Not many had made it as far as Munich.

I said I too was fleeing – from Budapest, from Vienna, but most of all, from the Russians.

The woman was startled by my next question: 'Do you know how I can get to Dachau?'

She presumed she had misunderstood my German and asked me to repeat the question. I did, and she asked: 'Do you really want to go to Dachau?'

I nodded. The woman gave me directions but I could see the suspicion in her eyes so I finished my food and left.

I spent a miserable night back at the railway station, waiting for dawn to break. When the train to Dachau was announced, I lost myself in the crowd milling to get aboard. I hadn't got a ticket and felt tense, nervous and very tired. Many people were simply fleeing Munich for the relative safety of the countryside. It seemed as if every town I reached now had been smashed to the ground by a giant fist. I was moving through a devastated world, never spending a day without fear.

'Always the bombing, but I must get to Dachau. I don't know what to expect, but I have to find Julius,' I thought, sitting in the crowded train as it pulled slowly out of Munich.

Dachau is just ten miles from the city and if Julius was there, then my journey was over. I could stay in the town and wait. I had no idea what to expect but I couldn't give up after all I had been through.

Soon the train was moving through the outskirts of the town. I was sitting by the window and saw a group of men with shaved heads, dark caps and blue and white striped uniforms being marched along a road. It was my first glimpse of prisoners from the camp.

The enormity of what I was doing hit me and I could feel my legs trembling.

We passed another road and another group of prisoners. A man wearing the same uniform but bearing an armband with the word 'Kapo' on it was leading them. Who was he?

I began scanning the prisoners' faces, desperately hoping to see Julius.

A passenger in the train must have been watching me. 'Miss, you seem to take a great interest in all these prisoners – haven't you seen them before?' he asked.

I shook my head.

'You must come from far away. They are from the camp and

are going to work.' I had to be more careful; I couldn't risk drawing attention to myself. If I was caught, I dreaded to think what would happen.

I was relieved when the train pulled in at Dachau station and I could get off with the other passengers and escape from the inquisitive man.

Dachau was a small town, with a population of about 7,000. Cobbled streets led uphill to the old town where many of the houses were painted in pastel colours in the Bavarian tradition. Once up the hill, you could see Munich in the distance.

As I stepped out of the railway station I wondered if I'd made a mistake. This didn't look like the sort of town that would be home to a concentration camp. It seemed too quaint, too affluent, too respectable.

In fact, the journey I had just taken was the same as many prisoners in the early part of the war. Then the prisoners had been brought to Dachau town railway station and marched to the camp on the outskirts until a siding was built to take the prisoners directly to the camp.

Out in the street, my first aim was to find work. Without work I would still have no money and without money, nowhere to live. Once I had somewhere to live, I could decide how I would find out if Julius was in the camp.

Germany was being crushed rapidly between the twin onslaughts of the Americans and British in the west and the Russians in the east, and in Berlin Hitler had taken to his bunker never to be seen alive again. In Dachau, however, the local labour exchange was still open.

There was a woman sitting behind a desk who asked why I had come to Dachau, instead of remaining in Munich?

'It's the bombing. I was frightened of the bombing. Some people in the refugee café there saw how frightened I was and told me I should come to Dachau,' I claimed.

I could hardly tell the truth: that I was looking for my fiancé in the concentration camp.

In any case, my explanation was perfectly reasonable. Dachau was excluded from the Allied bombing raids because of the camp. There were still air raid alerts – the town was too close to Munich to escape entirely, but it was largely untouched.

The woman produced an index card with the details of a job. 'There is a chemist's shop five minutes from here; go in and ask for the pharmacist,' she said, writing the address on a piece of paper and handing it to me.

Back in the street, I soon found the shop. A small bell rang as I pushed open the door. The pharmacist was an Austrian from Vienna and was delighted when he heard that I had come from there. He was eager to hear the news about his old city - which areas had been bombed and what life was like there now.

I liked him and we chatted for some time. Then he took me to meet his wife. She prepared a room for me in their home, which was a large two-storey house overlooking the town. For the first time in months, I couldn't see any bomb damage.

She was taller than her husband and seemed less welcoming.

'I'm from Tyrol,' she said. 'Have you ever been there?'

'I spent a day in Innsbruck once,' I replied, eager to please.

'Did you like it?'

'Yes, but I couldn't see much in one day.' She gave me a thin smile.

I was thrilled with my neat, attic bedroom after so much time spent sleeping rough. Everything seemed so clean and comfortable. I longed to just lie down on the soft bed and sleep.

I gazed out over the rooftops of the town. Directly beneath was a garden where all the trees were in bloom, a beautiful display of bright whites and pinks. And flowers, so many flowers. 'The first I've seen for a long time,' I thought.

Back in the pharmacy, I was told to clean floors and shelves. I also had to wash out bottles. The toxic smell of the medicines gave me a blinding headache.

When we returned to the house in the evening, the pharmacist asked me more about Vienna. His wife was becoming visibly annoyed by our constant talking but I thought nothing of it.

I spent a wonderful night in my new bed, safe from the bombs and hoping that I was at last close to Julius. But the next morning at breakfast, when the pharmacist once more began talking about Vienna, his wife took him to one side.

He explained to me as we walked to the shop that morning that his wife was a very jealous woman and she didn't want me working with her husband.

'Don't worry, we will go to the labour exchange and I will find you another job,' he told me.

I said angrily: 'Don't bother, I'll find a job myself.'

I returned to the house, collected my belongings under the frosty gaze of the pharmacist's wife and went to a local café before once again heading towards the labour exchange.

I was upset – just when I'd found a refuge, I'd been thrown out, through no fault of mine. It was sickening.

As I walked, the air raid sirens sounded and I headed to a local park, away from the buildings that presented the biggest danger if they collapsed under the bombardment.

Sitting on a bench, I watched the bombers unleashing yet more destruction upon Munich.

A large plume of black smoke rose above the city but in the park in Dachau, spring was in the air.

A pretty girl in a pink dress with her blonde hair pinned back in the latest fashion appeared at the park gate and smiled at me. She sat on the bench and we watched the bombers together.

We began to talk. The girl was Dutch and introduced herself as Helga. I asked where she worked – and was stunned by the reply.

'I work in the concentration camp.'

'The concentration camp?'

'Yes,' she replied, matter of factly. 'Didn't you know there was one here?'

'No,' I lied. 'I only arrived yesterday.'

'What do you do?'

I told her I had come from Vienna and that I had spent the previous night in a good bed for the first time in months, but now I had lost my job – and the bed.

There was a pause, then Helga asked: 'Can you type? My boyfriend has a good position in the concentration camp; maybe he can give you a job. I'm not sure, but we'll try when the alarm is over.'

Frightened and confused, I wondered what to do. Could I really bring myself to work for the Germans in Dachau concentration camp?

I hoped the air raid would never end so I wouldn't have to make a decision. But by four o'clock the bombers had finished for the day and disappeared towards the horizon.

Helga and I began walking through the town in the direction of the concentration camp. She chattered, while I was lost in thought. When I saw the barbed wire, the prisoners and the armed guards, I remembered that I had no documents of any kind.

The one place where they were bound to ask for identification was at the gates of a concentration camp.

'I could turn and run,' I thought, as Helga headed towards the main gate, but it was too late. That would only attract attention, I would be easily caught and then would find myself in the concentration camp – as a prisoner. When they discovered I had no papers I would be arrested anyway.

I was trapped – there was no way out. Helga showed her pass to the soldier at the gate and told me to wait there while she asked permission for me to enter.

I was resigned to my fate. 'I've come this far, now I have to face the consequences,' I thought. The main entrance to the camp showed only too clearly the risk I was taking. The guards were arrogant and carried their guns as if they were used to firing them at prisoners.

I was scared. Dachau had been built in peacetime, the first of Hitler's concentration camps. Part of the site was a sprawling SS barracks and I could see some of the entrances built in massive concrete blocks bearing an eagle and swastika above the heavy wooden doors.

A much smaller area was devoted to the concentration camp. I waited nervously as the guards watched, wondering who I was and what I was doing there.

After 15 minutes, Helga returned smiling and waving a sheet of paper, which she showed to a guard. He called me forward and I stepped through the gates. We walked initially through part of the SS camp before coming to another area surrounded by barbed wire and with watchtowers standing stark against the grey sky. Poking out of each tower was a machine gun. There could be no doubting that we were now at the concentration camp.

The entrance gates were set into the middle of a nondescript two-storey block with a wooden tower on the roof. The gates themselves were unremarkable except for the chilling slogan Arbeit Macht Frei ('Work Makes Free') carefully spelt out in the wrought iron.

Once inside, the first building I saw was the main administration block off to the right and, directly in front of me, an enormous parade ground. To my left were the 34 huts for the prisoners, laid out in orderly straight lines. At the far end of the camp, there was a tall chimney from which smoke streamed. Those must be the kitchens, I thought.

Helga led me over to the administration block and into an office where a German officer was sitting behind a desk. The man, I assumed, was Helga's boyfriend. He was older than I expected with grey hair and a formal manner, but he looked at me and smiled.

This was the moment I has been dreading. He would ask for my papers and I would be found out.

He gazed at me shrewdly.

'Helga has told me all about you,' he said. 'You don't have to start work today. Tomorrow you will get a pass for all entrances and exits. You can share a room with Helga and two other ladies.'

With that he turned back to his work, pausing only to say: 'Helga will show you to your quarters.'

And that was it. No questions. No demands to see papers. I couldn't believe my luck.

Helga was excited and led me to a small block in the SS camp that housed the German civilian workers in the camp. The accommodation was surprisingly good and the girls who I was to share with asked lots of questions while helping me make up a bed.

They all seemed perfectly normal. Nothing in their manner or conversation suggested that they worked in one of the most infamous concentration camps in the Third Reich. To them, it was just a job.

That night, lying in bed in the darkness listening to the shouts of the guards while the other girls slept, I said to myself: 'I'm in a concentration camp and going to begin work tomorrow. So help me God.'

CHAPTER SEVENTEEN

The next morning, I woke early to the sounds of the concentration camp resuming its grim daily routine. Orders were being shouted; prisoners marched to their work while those awaiting punishment were taken to the underground cells in the Bunker – a concrete block behind the administration building – where executions took place.

The offices where I worked were just outside the main gate, in the SS camp, right next to the railway line where the prisoners would be unloaded and marched into the camp.

We also had to visit the administration block in the camp itself. As Helga and I walked towards it that first day, she explained the barracks were numbered 1–29 and from 2–30; others were identified by the letters B,C,D,E, and often used for the sick prisoners of whom there was no shortage.

Helga pointed out some windows in an administration block.

'That's the camp museum,' she said. 'It has photos and models of all the different types of prisoners.'

In fact, it was just a room with typical Nazi caricatures: criminals were always depicted with harsh scowling faces; Jews as crooked businessmen cheating their customers.

As we walked, I was amazed by how many prisoners there were. The camp was built for 6,000 inmates in 1933 and now, in April 1945, there were 32,000 crammed in. Many prisoners died through disease and starvation; epidemics would sweep through the overcrowded huts, decimating the camp population.

Executions happened almost every day, with shootings carried out by SS guards, often against a wall just outside the Bunker. Hangings were conducted by a fellow prisoner forced to act as executioner. Prisoners were often paraded past the body of their comrades, still hanging from the gallows.

The greatest cruelty was the medical experiments in which prisoners were literally frozen to death or where they were starved of oxygen to recreate conditions at high altitude.

Everyone in the camp lived in constant fear. If they were sent to another camp there was every chance they would die on the way. It was hardly surprising that suicide was common.

Helga kept talking as we walked, seemingly oblivious to the horror around her. It was as if she were introducing a new girl at work in any office anywhere in the world.

'All the prisoners have badges so that you know why they are here,' she told me. 'The yellow ones are for the Jews, the black for ordinary criminals.'

I wondered what, in such a place, constituted 'ordinary'.

The Nazis were obsessed with bureaucracy and there was a baffling range of more than a dozen different triangular coloured badges, including pink for homosexuals, red for political prisoners and violet for Jehovah's Witnesses.

I would never remember them all. Nor did I want to. I looked at the seething mass of pyjama-clad inmates and wondered which badge Julius wore.

The whole place was terrifying – far, far worse than the jail at Komarom and the cells on Andrassy Utca where I'd been held.

Here in Dachau the entire camp lay under a stifling atmosphere of terror, the air heavy with the stink of death. The prisoners – horribly malnourished and skeletal – shuffled rather than walked, as if every step might be their last. Their eyes flicked nervously away from eye contact with anyone – even us girls who worked in the offices.

In a bleak, cheerless location amid a clutch of buildings and empty horizons, this great mass of humanity struggled every day just to survive.

Helga led me to an office where long blue boxes were stacked on shelves. These were the index cards for all the prisoners: those still in the camp, those sent elsewhere, those who had died, those who had been executed.

A supervisor pulled two boxes from the shelves, one bearing the letter C the other D, and laid them on the table in front of me. I had to file the cards in alphabetical order and if the prisoners had been sent elsewhere, file those cards separately.

I looked up at the shelves and ran my eye along the rows of boxes looking for the one bearing the letter K. That was the one that would tell me what I needed to know; whether Julius was in the camp, transported or dead.

It was there, but I couldn't look – I had been given my work and would have to wait until an opportunity presented itself.

Helga reappeared at midday and announced it was time for lunch. She led me to the main dining room where we sat at a long table with SS officers and other staff. I didn't know what to say to anyone. It struck me as bizarre and frightening to be sitting down with SS men and listening to the buzz of everyday lunchtime conversation in the heart of one of Germany's worst concentration camps.

No one talked about the camp nor mentioned that the Americans were just days away. It was as if everyone had decided they would talk only of the most trivial matters, to keep the horrors at bay.

Prisoners who worked in the camp kitchens served our food. Two men, wearing the red badges used to identify political prisoners, brought out large tureens of soup. We all helped ourselves – the food was very good. The soup was followed by a main course of meat and vegetables. None of the others seemed surprised by the quality of the meal but I was amazed. After so long of never having enough to eat and needing ration coupons for the most meagre meal, the food in Dachau was a luxury. Clearly the Germans looked after their camp staff very well. For pudding, the prisoners brought round bowls of a green fruit.

'What's this?' I hissed to Helga.

She looked at me in surprise. 'Rhubarb. Have you never eaten rhubarb?'

I'd never even seen it before, let alone eaten it. It tasted slightly sour but I liked it nonetheless.

After lunch I was directed to an office where I could collect my camp pass, which turned out to be just a piece of paper – not a card. It bore my false Hungarian name, Kovach, and was stamped with a swastika. There was an illegible signature on it and the officer who handed it to me explained it gave me permission to use all four entrances to the concentration camp.

I said thank you and added 'Heil Hitler' just as Helga had told me to when meeting officers.

'It's safer,' she'd told me. 'They expect it.'

The words stuck in my throat.

A tall SS guard approached me as I left the office. 'Hello, I want to show you something,' he said. I didn't know what he meant, but you didn't say no to the SS.

I followed obediently as he led me to a large building, selected a key from a heavy bunch he carried at his waist, and unlocked the door. Inside, we climbed a steep flight of stairs to another locked door.

'Here we are,' he said, choosing a different key, 'there's plenty in here for a pretty girl like you.'

We stepped into a huge, high-ceilinged room where on our right was a flat table upon which was arranged a glittering display of jewellery: rings, bracelets, necklaces, watches – all gold or silver, all very expensive and of the highest quality.

The SS guard picked up a gold chain and held it up to the light.

'Look,' he said, 'isn't it beautiful? It would look good on you.'

I was speechless. The room reminded me of the grand department stores that my aunt Alice and I visited in Zagreb before the war. On one side were the men's clothes: racks of suits all neatly pressed, a shelf of bowler hats, another for trilbys and homburgs. Opposite were women's dresses, fur coats, skirts, blouses and lingerie. On a high shelf to one side lay stacks of human hair.

'Choose anything you like and take it,' the SS guard said.

Some new clothes would have been useful after losing so many during my travels but these clothes and jewellery could only have come from prisoners, some of whom would now be dead. I couldn't possibly take them.

'I can't...'

'Why not?' the guard asked, clearly puzzled. 'All the girls working in the camp offices come here for their clothes.'

'Oh, I had a lot of nice clothes and lost them in the bombings. It was so upsetting and I really don't want to go through all that again. I have enough.'

Even to my ears, it sounded a lame excuse and the SS guard looked disgruntled.

'If you don't want anything then I can't force you, but I am surprised a nice girl like you refuses good clothes like these.'

'It's really very kind of you. Maybe when I've been here a bit longer...'

He muttered something under his breath and led me out, locking the doors behind us. I said goodbye with a 'Heil Hitler' and escaped back to my office, glad to be away from the clothes and their missing owners.

I learnt later that when prisoners arrived they were taken first to the schubraum (shunt room) in the main block where they were stripped of all clothes and belongings and issued with the infamous blue-striped pyjama uniform. No wonder there were so many clothes in the store room...

For civilian staff the working day began at eight o'clock, lunch

183

was called at noon then there was a break until four o'clock. The work finished at seven in the evening.

There were bars and dining rooms in the SS camp and the office girls were in great demand as there were hardly any female guards in the camp. Relationships were frequent – Helga was by no means the only girl to find a boyfriend among the SS men. I was invited to join them in the evening but said I was too tired and went back to our room, grateful to escape.

I lay on my bunk as darkness settled over the camp. Outside the shouting seemed to become louder. Somewhere, among all those prisoners, were some who had spent their last day alive. Whenever a new day dawned at Dachau, there were those who had not survived the night. This night would be no different. Yet, not far from me was a group of young women – just like myself – singing and dancing with the SS. What had happened to us all?

When I heard the sound of footsteps and giggling heralding the return of my roommates, I quickly turned on my side and pretended to be fast asleep.

***

The following day the air raid sirens sounded. Instead of bombs falling from the sky, however, we were covered by a snowstorm of Allied leaflets, promising the Americans would soon arrive to liberate the camp.

The guards quickly gathered as many of the leaflets as they could and destroyed them, but no one was under any illusions: we would soon be in the hands of the Allies. It didn't seem to affect the running of the camp – the discipline and the work carried on. More and more prisoners arrived every day. As the German army was pushed back they took their prisoners with them. Some concentration camps further north had already been liberated, but not Dachau.

I resumed my work that day and, through the windows of my

office, I watched a train arrive. The guards threw open the doors of the cattle trucks and I expected to see people jumping down from them. Instead, there was a pause and then bodies fell out onto the dusty ground. Other desperately emaciated men and women were pulled out of the trucks more dead than alive. As soon as those able to stand were marched away to the schubraum, working parties of prisoners were sent into the cattle trucks to clean out the remainder of the bodies.

It was a gruesome, dreadful scene – and one that I've never forgotten. It was only when I saw that train arrive that I fully realised what went on in Dachau.

I was turning away from the window when a lorry delivering food pulled up near the administration block. The driver had failed to fasten the rear tailgate properly and some carrots slipped out onto the dirty ground. I watched, horribly fascinated, as a prisoner so starved he could no longer walk (known in the camps as a musselman) began crawling towards the dropped vegetables.

Just as his fingers reached out to grab the food, an SS guard brought the butt of his rifle crashing down on the prisoner's head. I heard the crack of his skull and he collapsed in the dirt, his arm stretched out.

Shortly afterwards, his body was dragged away.

I was sickened and terrified by such brutality. The guards and the staff in the camp seemed indifferent to the suffering of the prisoners, but I was not. The sight of such cruelty and of people so weak they could only crawl, so starved they looked like skeletons, was more than I could bear.

This epidemic of inhumanity had even spread to the prisoners themselves. The guards relied on the trusted, long-term inmates, known as Kapos, to carry out many of the day-to-day duties of the camp. The Kapos were put in charge of groups of prisoners and were just as quick to exercise their arbitrary power as the Germans. Some of the prisoners later told me they found the Kapos worse than the SS. When ladling out the daily soup, they would reach down to the bottom of the pot for those prisoners they liked or who had done them a favour, ensuring they got a good amount of vegetables in their tin container – the only possession the inmates were allowed. Those the Kapos disliked got a ladle from the top of the pot, giving them nothing more than hot water with a weak flavour.

I never saw a Kapo too weak to walk, but to be fair, they were victims of the system as well – any deviance from the strict rule the Nazis imposed and they would have been quickly demoted, to take their chances among the musselmen and work groups. For the prisoners, nothing mattered but survival.

The prisoners who were sent out of the camp to work were more fortunate and were given better rations, but those inside, particularly the political prisoners, got very little – just the thin soup and hard bread.

I remembered the letter I'd received from Julius in which he had said the food was good. Did that mean he had been sent out to work? If so, he must have still been in good health when he arrived in Dachau, or was he simply pleasing the censors or showing he hadn't lost his sense of humour?

On the way to my office or returning to the room I shared with the other girls, I noticed the kitchen chimney in the distance, always sending up a pall of black smoke into the sky.

I said to Helga how surprised I was that the prisoners' food was so bad, as the kitchen chimneys seemed always to be working. She looked at me in amazement.

'Those aren't the kitchens,' she said. 'That's the crematorium, where they take the bodies. Don't go there. It's best avoided.'

Death was so routine that it was no wonder the crematorium chimneys kept pumping out smoke, sending the smell of death across the camp.

I felt foolish and naïve for not realising but it made me more determined to find out what had become of Julius and then to get out of the camp as quickly as possible. I had to act fast.

***

As my first week in Dachau wore on, the mood in the camp changed from one day to the next. Demoralisation seemed suddenly to spread like wildfire among the guards as rumours of the American advance grew. Arriving prisoners – those that were still alive – claimed the Allies were just days away from the camp, but the inmates worried whether they would live to see the moment of liberation.

A dreadful new rumour swept the camp, suggesting that the SS was preparing a huge pit into which all the prisoners would be put and then concrete poured over them in a final act of vengeful mass murder.

As I was in the camp under a false name and with no papers I was frightened to do anything but my own job in the filing office. I avoided conversation with the other staff as much as possible, fearful of giving myself away.

There was one task I could not avoid: finding out what had become of Julius.

At the long table in the filing office, I was still faced just by the blue boxes bearing the letters C and D. The box for the letter K was on the table but in front of another girl who was chatting to her friend.

Even at that stage of the war, the German demands for bureaucratic efficiency were unstinting. Trains and lorries were arriving all the time with prisoners, some of whom only stayed for a few hours before being forced to move on, but all had to be recorded.

Eventually, the girl working on the K box went for a break with her friend, leaving me at the table. I waited for a moment when others in the office appeared distracted and then as casually as possible reached across to the K box and pulled it closer.

My nervous fingers flicked through the cards as quickly as possible, finding hundreds of Polish names and then finally, 'Koreny, Gyula'. My heart leapt – I'd come this far, but what would the card tell me? That he had been executed? That he'd died of disease? Or that he was still in Dachau, not far from me?

I took a deep breath, steadied my nerves and looked at the words on the card:

Koreny, Gyula 15/1/1913. Eger.
Nationality: Ungarn.
Prisoner number: 136232
21/12/1944 Transported from Hungary
20/1/1945 Transported to Ohrdruf

I was gripped by despair – I was in the wrong place and had been all along. Julius had been brought to Dachau after I saw him in Komarom but his letter had taken so long to reach me he had been sent on to another camp before I even began my journey.

I sat at the table in silent anguish. How could fate be so cruel? The trip to Dachau, the hardship and the suffering, all for what? Nothing at all. It had been a journey of the utmost futility.

Tears sprang to my eyes but I couldn't let my fellow workers see me cry. I looked at the card again. Ohrdruf was another camp – but I didn't even know where.

There was something worse. So many prisoners in the final days of the Third Reich had been sent on death marches from one camp to the next, just ahead of the advancing Allied troops. Anyone falling ill or being left behind was executed on the spot. Even those lucky enough to be sent by train often didn't survive – I'd seen that with my own eyes in Dachau.

I tried to think clearly: should I wait for Dachau to be liberated or move on quickly, while I still could? No one could know what would happen once the Allies arrived. We were effectively cut off from the rest of the world, with no official news, no newspapers and no radio bulletins. Instead, rumour, half-truths and fear were all we knew. Now that I had discovered what had become of Julius one thing was certain: I had no reason to stay any longer in this dreadful place. It was only a twist of fate that had brought me here, my only reason being to find the man I loved. I had no desire to help the Germans in any way.

As that day's work drew to a close, I gathered up what belongings I had with me in the office and, leaving everything else back in my bedroom, walked to the main camp gate. I showed my pass, stepped past the Arbeit Macht Frei sign and turned my back on the camp with its armed watchtowers, starving prisoners and smoking crematorium.

I walked to the town in the warm spring sunshine, determined to forget the horror that I had seen in Dachau.

I never have. It haunts me to this day.

CHAPTER EIGHTEEN

All was quiet in the Dachau labour exchange. The woman behind the desk was talking to an attractive well-dressed lady. Neither of them paid me any attention to me for some time, but eventually, the official turned to me: 'Yes?'

'I was wondering if there were any jobs available?'

The elegant woman smiled: 'Would you like to look after a four-year-old girl?' she asked.

I nodded and the woman introduced herself as Mrs Buchler. She explained that her parents had been looking after her daughter, Barbara, but they were now too old so she needed a nanny and had dropped into the labour exchange to advertise the job.

Tired of all the false names and dishonesty, I gave my real name of Czepf and we set off to Mrs Buchler's house. We talked easily and struck up an immediate friendship.

Mrs Buchler was a professor of English; her husband, who was much older than her, a retired lawyer. He met us at the door, a small, kind man who showed me round the house.

There was a large garden with a strange net hanging between two of the trees. I had no idea what it was.

'It's a hammock,' said Mr Buchler. 'You can lie in it when Barbara is playing in the garden, and rest while you keep an eye on her. Careful not to fall out, though.'

Just then a smiling, ginger-haired girl appeared.

'This is Barbara,' said Mr Buchler, obviously proud of his daughter, who bore a remarkable resemblance to him. She grinned up at me and I was delighted to be there. After the concentration camp, to meet such a lovely family was a blessed relief, a confirmation that not everything was bad in the world.

We all sat down to lunch, joined by the Buchler grandparents, and everyone asked me questions about the camp. I'd seen no reason to hide the truth from Mrs Buchler and I wanted them to understand why I had been working in the camp, so she knew all about Julius.

Even during the lunch and all the family chatter, there was no hiding from the war. We could hear the sound of gunfire and explosions in the distance. The Americans were coming.

***

The following day we had a birthday party for Barbara, whose fifth birthday we toasted with a carefully preserved bottle of sparkling wine that her grandparents had brought with them after being bombed out of their home in the Rhineland.

Mr Buchler, who cycled into Munich every other day to find food, had collected vegetables and even a small portion of meat for the meal.

Barbara was thrilled with the celebration and Mrs Buchler played the piano. It would have been an idyllic scene but for the sound of explosions as the retreating German army blew up bridges to slow the Allied advance.

The Third Reich had all but collapsed now and the townspeople of Dachau were obsessed with two thoughts: when would it all end? And what would become of them when it did?

The answer came sooner than any of us expected. Looking out of my bedroom window on Saturday April 28th, I was struck by an extraordinary sight: Dachau had turned white. All the houses in the town were draped in white. Sheets, tablecloths, pillow cases, even handkerchiefs were hanging from balconies, displayed in windows or fixed to roofs. The town looked as if it had been caught in a blizzard of white linen.

I ran to Mr Buchler: 'What's happening? Why is everyone hanging white sheets on their houses?'

He looked at me sadly: 'We lost the war. We don't want to fight in Dachau any longer. The white is a sign of surrender. Any minute now we will be occupied.'

He opened a cupboard and began looking for a sheet. 'I must hurry and put something white on our house.'

Outside, we could see the German troops pulling out of the town amid rumours spreading that the camp guards had gone already. Everyone was scared that the prisoners would take revenge on the local population.

Sunday morning brought the sound of more explosions and the streets were full of German soldiers hurrying through. Mrs Buchler stood Barbara on a window ledge to watch the troops and said, with tears in her eyes: 'Look, Barbara, what is left of our poor German army. Remember we fought hard, but we lost the war.'

Tears streamed down her face and she held her daughter close, but Barbara was too young to fully understand what was happening.

The last of the German soldiers disappeared and the sound of explosions faded to nothing. There was an eerie silence across the whole town. No one left their homes; there were no vehicles on the roads; everything was still.

Faces peered out from the windows all along the streets. Waiting.

At midday, I heard a deep rumble and a clanking of metal. Looking gingerly from behind a curtain, I saw the long barrel of a gun and then a huge tank, with a white star painted on its side, turning the corner into the main street. It rumbled slowly towards us as other tanks fell into line behind it. The air raid sirens wailed and we all scrambled down to the basement, afraid that the tanks were going to start shelling us. We sat huddled together for about half an hour before there was a loud knocking on the door and, as she spoke English, Mrs Buchler went up to answer it. On the doorstep was a group of eight, heavily-armed American soldiers who told her they needed somewhere to stay.

Mrs Buchler showed them up to the first floor and said they could stay there, although she didn't have beds for them all. They thanked her politely as we all emerged from the basement to stare at the first American soldiers we had seen.

One of them spotted Barbara and held out a hand: 'Here, have some chocolate,' he said, smiling at her.

The little girl reached out for it but her mother grabbed her hand.

'No,' she looked sharply at the soldier, 'no, thank you. We have our own chocolate.'

We didn't, of course. The soldier shrugged as he and his comrades took off their kit bags, guns, ammunition and helmets, dumping them all in one room.

'We're off to find something to eat,' one of them announced, before they all disappeared through the front door.

The army of occupation had arrived – and now they'd gone again. Our soldiers never reappeared and the next day Mrs Buchler ventured out to find an American officer to ask what had become of them. She was worried about the guns and ammunition left lying around in the house.

She found a Major Franck who came back to the house with her, but, on seeing it, decided he wanted to stay there so arranged for the soldiers' equipment to be collected. We never found out what became of the men.

Major Franck brought his batman, Private Bloom, with him and took up residence on the first floor. Although the major was frequently absent, Bloom seemed to be everywhere, constantly asking to borrow something, particularly the iron and ironing board and collecting water to wash his jeep. He tried as best he could to be friendly to us all – even suggesting that I should marry him, but I told him I was already married, putting an end to his ideas of romance.

In the house we felt safe and tried to make the best of our new circumstances. Outside in the streets it was very different.

Not only had we been invaded, but the town was scarred by the notoriety of the concentration camp. Dachau was not a name anyone would forget.

The Americans imposed a six o'clock curfew on the residents but were considerably more lenient with the occupants of the camp, who frequently rampaged through the town, stealing and looting from the Germans.

In the camp itself the Americans had shot some of the guards and discipline had broken down.

Prisoners called at the Buchler's home frequently and I would open the door to them, because as a foreigner they rarely demanded anything from me. Instead they often gave me items they had taken from other houses. They reserved their hatred for the Germans.

I must have heard all the languages of Europe on that doorstep, but coming from Yugoslavia helped. Tito's partisans were heroes to the Allies and the prisoners. Often I would come back into the house bearing bread, butter and even meat to find the Buchlers cowering in the kitchen.

However, I didn't go out – it was too frightening, even during the day. The American troops were flushed with victory and although they behaved well, they were an intimidating presence and often turned a blind eye to the behaviour of the prisoners.

On May 1st, late in the evening, we all gathered round the wireless to hear an announcement from Berlin. Sombre martial music was played before a sonorous voice told us that the Fuhrer was dead, killed in the battle for Berlin at the head of his troops. It was true that he was dead, but had died by his own hand in the

Chancellery bunker. Even at the end the Nazis were lying to their people.

The Buchlers showed no great emotion at the news: by then everyone knew the war was lost. Now it was a question of Germany's survival.

A Russian prisoner told me on the doorstep one day that the Americans were distributing food to foreigners at the camp, so Mr Buchler and I rigged up a large box on one of Barbara's old prams and wheeled it to the camp.

Mr Buchler waited outside – they weren't going to give food to Germans – while I trundled the pram past the iron gates through which I'd first walked when I worked in the camp. I saw the administration block where my office had been, but hurried on, shivering at the memory.

I joined a large crowd of mostly ex-prisoners and was eventually given tins of food, margarine, jam, powdered milk and powdered eggs. Mr Buchler's eyes lit up when he saw the laden pram and we hurried it all back to the house, unloaded it quickly in the kitchen and headed back to the camp to collect more.

By the end of the day, we had a good supply of food and were feeling very pleased with ourselves.

'You were sent to us by God,' Mrs Buchler said to me, gazing wide-eyed at all the food we'd collected.

Life settled into an easy routine for me. I enjoyed looking after Barbara and had mastered the hammock in the garden so I could swing gently back and forth while the little girl played.

The Buchlers were good company and I felt part of the family but I couldn't forget the reason I was in Dachau: Julius.

I was tortured by the thought of what had become of him. As the Allies advanced across Germany the full horrific truth about the camps was becoming clearer.

The Germans had treated those who had survived in the camps until the final days of the war with a vengeful barbarity, and deaths from disease and brutality had reached terrifying levels. Realistically, what chance did Julius have?

Mrs Buchler showed me Ohrdruf – Julius's last known destination – on the map. It was near a small town called Erfurt, about 250 miles north of Munich. There were no trains; all the tracks had long since been destroyed either by the Allies or the retreating German army.

Mrs Buchler did her best to persuade me to stay, at least until the situation became clearer, emphasising how difficult travelling would be for a single girl who could not speak English and had no papers.

On May 8th, Major Franck was in his room on the first floor and we could hear his heavy footsteps thumping on the ceiling above us.

There was the sound of a radio then silence, followed by the thunder of his heavy boots as he ran down the stairs. He came into the kitchen where we were all sitting and spoke to Mrs Buchler: 'Have you heard the news?'

'No, what's happened?'

'The war is over. Germany has surrendered.'

The Buchlers showed no emotion and Major Franck, himself a German Jew who had been taken to America as a child, said nothing more. He turned and left the room.

Like so many millions of others, I felt glad the fighting had stopped – it had never been my war – but full of anxiety over the future.

Leading Nazis were fleeing all across Germany. People with much to hide were on the roads and those who could not identify themselves were liable to arrest and imprisonment – at the very best.

The rule of law had broken down in many parts and was only slowly being restored; in the meantime gangs roamed, looting at will and attacking local people, particularly women.

What's more, the Soviets were insisting that Erfurt was one of the cities for occupation by them and that the Americans should withdraw. No woman wanted to meet the Red Army under any circumstances.

'I have to go,' I said. 'I've come this far, I have to find Julius – no matter what has become of him.'

Mrs Buchler was appalled. 'Your mother would turn in her grave if I let you go. You're heading into the unknown, with the army all around, all those refugees and all the concentration camp prisoners on the loose.'

She pleaded with me. 'What makes you think Julius is still in Ohrdruf? Don't let's think the worst, but he may have been dead for a long time.

'What happens to you if you don't find him there? You don't speak English and the Americans hardly know any German; the camp authorities have burnt most of their documents to destroy all the evidence so you'll be stuck even further away from home. How on earth can you get back to Yugoslavia with only a few Reichsmarks in your pocket? How long can you survive?'

Everything she said was correct and she spoke to me as if the words were from my own mother. We all listen to advice, but, particularly when we're young, we don't always heed it. I was young, in love, and had come so far and sacrificed so much that I could see nothing but continuing my search. One way or another I had to know what had become of Julius.

If it meant my journey ended at the side of a mass grave in a concentration camp, at least then I would know. I owed it to myself and to Julius to make that final journey.

Mrs Buchler was getting desperate and tears were running down her face.

'Don't go,' she begged me, 'stay here. I'll contact Ohrdruf when things are a bit more stable. The war has only just ended. We'll write to the authorities and find him that way – if he's not there, what's the point of you going?'

It was no use – my mind was made up. Mrs Buchler wiped away her tears. Seeing that no amount of arguing would dissuade me, she began gathering food and clothes for my journey. She dressed me in a green Bavarian suit and a pair of heavy walking boots, then she rushed upstairs to the Major Franck's room and begged a piece of official notepaper.

On it, she wrote in English: 'Please help Miss Czepf, she is trying to find her fiancé, who was a prisoner in Dachau concentration camp and was transported to Ohrdruf.'

She folded it carefully and handed it to me. 'Oh, socks,' she said. 'I'd forgotten, you'll need some good socks for all the walking you'll be doing or you'll get terrible blisters.'

I laughed. After everything I had been through, and who knew what was to come, only a mother could worry about socks. She reappeared with several pairs and insisted I put on a brand new pair of bright white ones.

'They won't stay white for long,' I thought, but once again I thanked her.

Then it was time. We held each other and cried. 'You can come back any time; if it's all too much, just come home to us,' Mrs Buchler said.

I was too upset to speak. I turned and, in my new white socks, set off once more, stepping out into the chaos, confusion and danger of Hitler's ruined Germany.

CHAPTER NINETEEN

The weather was growing warmer. My days of struggling through freezing snowstorms were gone – but the refugees were not. The whole of Germany appeared to be on the move. Those in the east were flooding west, preferring the prospect of a future under the Western powers to that of the Soviets; demobbed soldiers were slowly making their way home, not knowing what to expect when they got there; leading Nazis and Gestapo officers had thrown away their uniforms and were travelling incognito, hunted by the Allies; displaced people from the countries occupied by the Nazis were starting the long journey back to their home countries.

Feelings of despair, defeat and distrust spread like an epidemic along the roads and among all of us who had to travel them.

Only three hours after I had left Mrs Buchler's home in Dachau, I was tired and lost. The sun was beating down and the road ahead was frequently blocked, forcing me to take detours. There were no signposts on the roads and I soon lost all sense of direction.

Lorry loads of American soldiers passed me from time to time, waving and smiling, but I ignored them. The lorries carrying civilians, however, gave me hope.

When the exhaustion of walking became too much I tried to hail one of them, but they all sped past, the blank faces of the refugees in the back staring out at me.

By dusk, I could go no further and approached an isolated

farmhouse. The elderly woman who answered the door welcomed me in and would accept no payment for the food she gave me.

Her daughter-in-law arrived, dressed in a green and navy blue dress, which looked as if it had been made from odds and ends of material. We were all soon chatting. Both their husbands had been fighting on the eastern front and although they had had no news of them for some time, they hoped they would return home soon.

I felt for them. Who could know what had become of their men? Just as I did not know what had become of Julius. It seemed to me that in this war, the men did the fighting, the women the worrying – no one escaped the fear.

Part of the old farmhouse had been damaged by shells and the two women were living in the remaining rooms, but still they were friendly and welcoming. In my travels I had seen so many different people in so many different circumstances – from concentration camps to government minister's offices – but I was still constantly surprised by the variety of human nature.

Some people were greedy and mean, hoarding everything for themselves and prepared to steal your last crust of bread. Others were generous to a fault and would share whatever they had and help in any way they could. I'd met both sorts, but in that isolated farmhouse so soon after the war had ended, I saw once again the generosity and optimism of the human spirit.

My two hostesses put a record on an old gramophone player, produced a bottle of wine and began to sing and dance. Despite my exhaustion, I couldn't help but smile. When the record stopped, one of them would cut us each a slice of cheese, then the needle would be placed on the next record and off they'd go again, whirling round the room as I sat sipping wine and eating cheese, tired but happy – for a few moments at least.

The mother apologised that they didn't have a spare room for me to sleep in: 'But you can spend the night in the stable – that is, if you don't mind sharing with our two cows,' she said.

At that moment, I felt as if I could have slept in a field with a herd of cows so I thanked her gratefully and they led me out to a surprisingly small barn. The smell was dreadful and the straw looked anything but comfortable – I began to wonder if I would be able to sleep at all. My comfortable bed in the attic room at Mrs Buchler's seemed so tempting.

I lay down on the straw, my mind spinning with thoughts from the day and anxieties over what tomorrow would bring.

Then, suddenly, it was dawn and I was woken by a cow looming over me and mooing in surprise at finding a human companion in her barn. I'd slept dreamlessly right through the night undisturbed by my stable-mates or the over-powering smell. I felt refreshed for my journey.

The two women in the house greeted me with smiles and sat me down at the table for a breakfast of home-baked bread and fresh milk.

'Please,' I said to the older woman as I prepared to leave, 'let me give you some money for all your kindness. I have some Reichsmarks with me.'

'No, no,' she replied, 'I'm glad we've been able to help you. We couldn't take money from you.' Her daughter-in-law shook her head, too.

Wrapping me some cheese and bread, they wished me a safe journey and saw me out on to the road again, waving until I could no longer see them.

This time, I was lucky. I had not been walking long when a lorry carrying civilians pulled up next to me. An American soldier jumped down from the cab and through sign language asked to see my papers. I didn't have any but he seemed to understand when I said I was from Yugoslavia and showed him Mrs Buchler's note. He ordered his companion in the back to open the tailgate and help me up.

The first soldier gestured with his hands raised to his mouth, asking if I needed food. I shook my head and said that I had enough, but he didn't understand and returned moments later with a small parcel, wrapped in wax paper. He handed it over, saying 'Yugoslavia, good. Tito, partisans. Nice people.'

I didn't understand what he was saying, but caught the words 'Yugoslavia' and 'Tito' so accepted his gift gracefully.

Then, with a loud slamming of doors, the lorry moved off. Soon we were rattling along the road, passing lines of refugees trudging along, covering a lot of ground and, I hoped, going in the right direction.

We were travelling across a desolate landscape. The war was over but you couldn't help but know it had passed this way, leaving only ruins in its wake. The towns were destroyed, the bridges reduced to rubble in the rivers, the roads pockmarked by bomb craters and the railway lines twisted and bent. The tragedy of war is not just in the fighting of it, but what comes afterwards.

I was tempted to open my parcel but a lot of hungry eyes were staring at me. All the nationalities of Europe seemed to be represented in the back of that lorry, the babble of voices speaking in some languages I understood and others I'd never even heard before.

I kept hoping to see a signpost or anything to indicate the direction in which we were travelling. We were now a good distance from Dachau, but where?

The man sitting next to me just shook his head when I asked him. He spoke a little German and I gathered he was Estonian and had been freed from a labour camp, but he didn't know where he had been held, much less where he was going.

In any case, he was far more interested in my parcel, offering me a knife and indicating he would help me to open it and then we could share the contents.

The knife turned out to be blunt but after a long struggle, I managed to open the parcel and my fellow refugees watched with envy as I unpacked tins of meat, fish, coffee and chocolate.

When the lorry stopped to refuel,we all jumped down and I shared the food with those nearest to me, while others started to eat their own supplies. I kept one tin of pork with apple sauce, which sounded to me the strangest mixture. I wasn't sure I would like it.

The driver and his companion emerged from an army canteen next to the petrol station, smiling and looking happy. I was given another bar of chocolate; clearly I was becoming their favourite – not such a good thing to be among a group of refugees.

When the driver motioned for us all to get back on the lorry, I approached him with a small map Mrs Buchler had given me and asked him to show me where we were. After some difficulty, he understood what I was asking and marked our position on the map. We had travelled a long way from Dachau, and to my relief we were heading north-east, towards Erfurt.

The driver also seemed to indicate that they would not be taking us much further and sure enough after a few more miles the lorry stopped and we were all ordered out. The lorry drove off leaving us, in the middle of nowhere.

The Americans were not obliged to give us a lift at all; they'd picked up refugees out of kindness and I was very grateful for the lift and the gifts of food.

We stood there beside the road, about 30 of us, of different nationalities, speaking different languages and no one with any idea what to do next. We were at a country crossroads with no buildings in sight.

My companions looked subdued and depressed. I wondered where they were all going. God knows what they had been through and now that the war was over they faced an uncertain and equally difficult future. They must have looked at me askance, wondering why a girl from Yugoslavia was travelling in precisely the opposite direction from her own country. No one asked. Personal questions were not welcome in such circumstances. For all we knew some among us might have been escaping Nazis or prison guards who'd thrown away their uniforms.

We were all running from, or towards, something. Asking why would help no one.

Many of those people were destined for more refugee camps, more wandering across the country, more scavenging for food, more desperate struggles for survival.

All my love for Julius would not spare me those same hardships.

Gradually, members of our group began to drift away, carrying their belongings and heading along the road stretching out before us. Soon, there were four other women and just one man left. We waited beside the road in the hope of hitching another lift.

The man would occasionally try to speak to me, turning his whole body as he did so, revealing that he had only one eye. I shuddered every time he fixed his solitary eye on me.

I was relieved when another US army lorry appeared on the horizon and we all began waving. It pulled to a stop beside us and the driver indicated that we should jump into the back. We all scrambled up and set off once more.

The lorry was not going far and we were dropped off again just as darkness was falling. The driver told me I was going in the right direction for Erfurt so this time I began walking until I came to a small farmhouse where the family let me sleep in the outhouse.

For the next four days, I became an itinerant farm labourer as I walked and hitch-hiked through the Bohemian and Thuringian forests, digging carrots, helping in the fields, doing any work that would provide me with a meal and somewhere to stay at night.

On the fifth day, I was within a few miles of the town of Ohrdruf.

***

The first thing that struck me as I approached the concentration camp was how quiet it was. Everything was still; there were no voices, no shouts, no sounds of marching feet, no vehicles. Behind the wire were the remains of abandoned prisoners' huts, some of which had been burnt to the ground; others had collapsed as the wood rotted.

The camp was smaller than Dachau and I learnt later that it had been the first Nazi concentration camp liberated by the Americans. Prisoners had been slaughtered in a final outbreak of killing by the SS guards as the Americans approached. Those prisoners still fit enough had been sent on a death march to Buchenwald, 35 miles east.

The Americans had been so appalled by what they found – piles of bodies, some covered with lime, and others partially incinerated on pyres – that pictures of the camp had been sent round the world. For many, it was the first shocking insight into the truly horrific nature of the Third Reich.

Now all that was left was a wasteland. Areas of the camp were flooded and the watchtowers that had once stood threateningly over the prisoners had been demolished.

Whatever had become of all the prisoners? Surely they hadn't just been turned out onto the roads by the Americans and left to fend for themselves?

I sat down on the grass, with my rucksack, feeling close to tears. To come all this way to find only desolation was terrible.

There would be no records to check in this camp, no chance to search for the name 'Koreny' to discover what had become of Julius.

I heard the distant sound of a lorry, making its way along the narrow lanes and soon it came into view, bearing the now familiar white star of the US army. It pulled to a noisy halt in front of me; the driver looked down and gestured at me to climb up.

I passed him the note Mrs Buchler had written, which he took from me and read carefully, the piece of paper looking tiny in his huge hands. He smiled at me and through signs made it clear that the prisoners from Ohrdruf had all been sent to Buchenwald and that was where he was heading with a lorry load of vegetables.

I was grateful for the lift. It was my last chance to find Julius but, by then, my hopes were fading. For one man who had already spent a long time in prison and then been sent to Dachau, Ohrdruf and Buchenwald in the space of four months, the chances of survival were not just slim, but close to non-existent.

As I sat in the lorry heading for Buchenwald, I knew in my heart that it was over. I'd set out hoping to find the man I loved. Now I was looking for his grave.

CHAPTER TWENTY

The war had been over for a month and yet, there at the gates of Buchenwald, stood two men in German officers' uniforms.

The lorry driver let me down from the cab near the camp entrance, which we'd reached down a winding road lined by trees on either side. With a wave and smile, he drove off to deliver his vegetables.

I looked cautiously at the German guards who were staring at me. It reminded me of Dachau.

Why were the Germans still here? Just then the guards started talking to each other, looking at me the whole time, and one thing struck me immediately: they weren't speaking German. In fact, they were talking in Slovenian – they too were from Yugoslavia. Although I was a Croatian speaker, I understood Slovenian well and went over to say hello.

They were very surprised to meet another Yugoslav and furthermore a woman. By that stage there were no women in the camp. The moment I stepped through the gate I became the only woman in Buchenwald.

They greeted me with a flurry of questions: 'Who are you?'

'Why have you come here?'

'Are you on your way somewhere?'

Before I could answer, the older one introduced himself in a deep, commanding voice as Ivo, an actor from a theatre in Ljubljana.

His friend was Stanko, a doctor, from Maribor.

'Are there any prisoners from Croatia still in the camp?' I asked.

'Yes, there are some, towards the far end,' Ivo replied gesturing towards some huts in the distance.

'And Hungarians?'

'Oh, yes, lots of Hungarians,' he replied. 'But first, would you like something to eat? If you've been travelling you must be hungry.'

Except for a crust of bread for breakfast at seven o'clock that morning I had eaten nothing and now it was past midday.

'Why did you start so early?' Stanko asked.

They obviously hadn't been travelling across Germany in the way I had for so long.

'Most of the time I have to walk, so I wanted to cover as much ground as possible before it got too hot,' I said. 'You never know if you'll get a lift or not. I was lucky today.'

They were keen to hear more about what brought me to Buchenwald, but first they had promised me food and led me through the camp entrance towards their barrack hut. We passed through the iron gates above which was the slogan Jedem das Seine, which means literally 'to each his own' but was used colloquially to mean 'everyone gets what he deserves'.

Buchenwald was bigger than Dachau and appeared cleaner, brighter and with more trees – not surprising given that it was on the edge of the Thuringian Forest. Like Dachau, it was not an extermination camp but a work camp, which did not prevent deaths occurring with a horrifying regularity.

From its creation in 1937 to the final liberation in 1945 about 240,000 prisoners passed through its gates, including Allied prisoners of war – unusual in a concentration camp. More than 56,000 people died there including more than 1,000 Soviet prisoners who were sent to the camp between 1941 and 1942, and executed, one by one, with a single bullet to the back of the neck. The dreadful legacy was all around us. Many of the inmates still shuffled along in the blue and white striped pyjama uniform, some of them barely more than skeletons and with no more certain a future than they had under the Nazis.

Others had gone to great lengths to scrounge whatever clothes they could find, but with their strange attire, unwashed and unshaven they looked like tramps.

Even grimmer than the appearance of the inmates were some of the mementoes that the brutal regime had left behind. The SS were great collectors of human skin from their victims, using it for lampshades and book covers. In one room I later saw what appeared to be large, dark paperweights sitting on a desk, until I stepped closer and realised with a shudder of horror that they were the shrunken heads of murdered Soviet POWs.

The nearby town of Weimar was the home of Goethe, Schiller, Liszt and Bach, yet here, just six miles from the town centre, was a place of terrible barbarity and inhumanity.

Once we reached the barrack block of the Slovenians they introduced me to another of their fellow-prisoners, a Jewish doctor from Zagreb, Bela Cohn, a tall man, with dark curly hair.

We made a strange group: refugees, political prisoners, Jews, students, doctors, actors – a cross section of society uprooted and thrown across Europe to gather in this most dreadful of places.

The camp had its own structure, and when Ivo announced it was lunchtime I had no idea what to expect. I was pleasantly surprised.

'You've arrived at a good time,' Ivo said. 'We captured a pig in the forest last night and roasted him over a fire. There's plenty left.'

We began eating and the taste of roast pork was exquisite. A tall, good-looking young man joined us and was introduced as Stevan, the successful hunter who had captured the pig. He was lively and humorous, a typical Yugoslav, with an eye for a pretty girl.

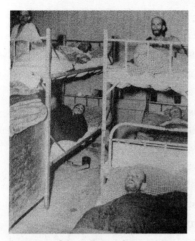

Inmates' infirmary barrack in Buchenwald at the time of liberation.

Stevan wore a jerkin, open at the top, and as they handed me a second plate with a large slice of bread and not quite such a large slice of pork, I noticed something moving inside his jacket.

A small furry head appeared and I screamed, thinking he was an eccentric who kept a pet rat. He laughed loudly at my reaction, showing his even, white teeth and roguish smile.

'Allow me to introduce my girlfriend, Vera, to you,' he said, carefully bringing out from beneath his jacket a small squirrel, whose wide eyes flicked around the group staring at each of us in turn.

I laughed. 'Well, they said I was the only lady in the camp,' I said, 'but now I see there are two of us.'

'Ah, but before you arrived, Vera was the only lady we knew,' Stevan replied.

Despite the light-hearted chatter, there was a note of sadness among the group. They knew each other well, having survived the most dreadful hardships, but they all looked older than their years (as I'm sure I did) and had lost so much it was no surprise that even with good food, there was a perceptible air of melancholy.

Occasionally, I would catch one of them staring at me, not in a hostile manner but in an inquiring way, as if to say: 'You know our stories, but what's yours?'

After all, what would bring a woman all the way from Yugoslavia through the collapse of the Third Reich to Buchenwald, one of the most notorious of all the concentration camps?

We each had a glass of apple juice after the meal (I had no idea where they had found such a delicacy) and everyone fell silent, looking at me with an air of expectation.

So I told them my story. I told them about my aunt Alice; my Jewish stepmother; the many lost to Jasenovac camp and the fear that haunted the streets of Zagreb. And I told them of the Hungarian diplomat who had gone with me on forged papers to visit a Jewish relative in Vrapce; who had taken money and letters to my stepmother's Jewish family in Budapest. All this and our love too.

Stevan looked at me gravely: 'But what made you come here?'

I explained how Julius had been detained in Budapest, presumably after someone betrayed him to the authorities, and how I had gone looking for him.

'I heard he was in Dachau and so I got a job working in the camp office there but then found out that he had been transported in January to Ohrdruf. I got there yesterday but was told that all the prisoners had been sent to Buchenwald just before the Americans arrived. So that's why I'm here…'

My voice trailed off. A circle of faces bearing expressions of amazement and disbelief stared at me; those that believed me clearly thought Julius would be dead by now; those who didn't must have been wondering what the truth was.

Bela Cohn broke the silence: 'What is his name? Most of the German records are intact and we should be able to trace him – if he's here.'

'Koreny. Julius Koreny,' I replied.

'Well, tomorrow morning we will look in the records and see what has become of him,' Bela said, with little hope in his voice.

That evening my claim to fame in the camp disappeared: three other women arrived. They were Serbs, one from Belgrade and two from Novi Sad. They had been in a work camp in Germany and were trying to make their way home.

Although the camp was nominally under the control of the

Americans, people came and went at will. After all, we were all refugees, all lost souls in one way or another.

The three newcomers were greeted warmly and a small storage room in the barracks was put aside for the four of us. I was exhausted and the others set to cleaning and tidying the room and making up four makeshift beds. They were far from comfortable but gave us a much-needed place to lie down. We slept in our clothes although I still had two nightdresses that Mrs Buchler had given me. This didn't feel like the time to wear them. No, I would save them for better days, far from Buchenwald.

I was desperate for sleep but I couldn't settle after such a hectic day. I'd surely reached my journey's end; either Julius was here in the camp, or he was dead.

If Bela was right and the records were more or less intact, then they would be similar to the ones I worked on in Dachau, recording the fate of all the prisoners. Julius's name would be there on one of the cards – and it would reveal all I needed to know.

I reflected that at last I had other people on my side, others with whom to share the burden of my search. With that comforting thought, I finally slipped into sleep.

***

I woke early, not to the noise of marching and German orders that I'd heard in Dachau, but to the sound of shuffling feet and murmuring among the inmates of Buchenwald.

The three other girls were still asleep, breathing softly in the dawn light. I lay there wondering how long I could depend on the generosity of the prisoners whom I'd befriended. I was not an ex-prisoner so the Americans had no obligation to me, no need to add me to the Yugoslav contingent's number for food rations.

I felt sure I would soon find myself alone again. The optimism of the previous evening evaporated. The quicker I found what had become of Julius the better. After that, I could make my own plans.

Taking care not to wake the other girls, I got up and made my way outside to find Bela. If he knew where the prisoner records were kept then he held the key to finding Julius.

Bela was standing outside the barrack block set aside for the Yugoslavs, who were proud to have their own accommodation – other nationalities were mixed together in other huts. My countrymen kept themselves separate from other prisoners and had little to do with the Americans either, mainly because of the lack of a common language.

Bela greeted me with a warm smile and suggested we go straight to the records office hoping, I suspect, that my futile search would soon be over.

The Germans had allowed Bela to work as a doctor among the prisoners and as we made our way towards the administration offices, he asked again for Julius's surname.

'Koreny? It sounds familiar. Maybe I've treated him – but I could be mistaken.'

We arrived at the offices where an American soldier sat at a desk guarding the entrance. Bela tried to explain what we were doing but neither he nor the guard could understand each other, so I handed over the letter from Mrs Buchler. The guard read it carefully, shrugged and allowed us through into the record office.

They were similar to the cards I'd worked with in Dachau and we selected the box marked 'K', divided the contents between the two of us and began searching.

Shortly after, Bela cried out: 'Olga, I think I've found him.'

He pulled the card from the box and there was Julius's name at the top, recording the date he'd arrived in the camp. At the bottom was the last recorded information about him:

'April 10th, 1945. Typhus.'

We stared at that one word: typhus. The Americans had arrived at the camp on April 11th; many prisoners had died following liberation from disease or malnutrition. I turned to Bela, my eyes filling with tears: 'If Julius was ill with typhus the day before the Americans arrived, he must be dead.'

'Don't be so pessimistic,' said Bela. 'We don't know what happened to him. This is the last entry the Germans made in the records; the Americans might have separate records and he might be in a separate barracks. Thousands of prisoners here caught typhus – I treated many of them. I might even have treated him – I just can't remember.'

Despite Bela's words, I was overwhelmed with a sense of hopelessness. There were tens of thousands of inmates still at the camp and Julius's card told me only that he'd been ill – nothing more. I was no closer to finding him.

We spent the rest of the day in a desultory search of other barracks, constantly repeating Julius's name in the hope it might trigger a memory in someone. But we found nothing.

That night I collapsed on my bed in the storeroom, exhausted and unhappier than I had been in a long time.

After a fitful night, I went to find Bela again, feeling low and depressed. We sat outside the Yugoslav barrack block and I poured out my heart to him. I retold every detail of my journey, including aspects I hadn't admitted before such as my voluntary work at the Horniphon factory and my time at Dachau.

'And after all this, what have I got? Just a memory,' I said.

Bela looked at me sympathetically, but I was speaking almost to myself now, as if all I had not dared think about before suddenly came flooding out.

'What do I really know about Julius? Only what he told me himself. Our meetings were mostly visiting Jewish friends and relatives and a few trips to the opera. We were never really a "normal" couple.

'He wasn't even my type,' I said, smiling at the memory. 'I only fell in love with him later. But was it really love? Or did I just feel guilty after all he'd done for my family?

'I came from a good home, had a good education and could have had a good job in Zagreb. My father and stepmother never loved me, I know that, but I could still have had a good life.

'What does the future hold for me now? I'm only 22 years old but I've wasted part of my life already.'

There was a long silence and then Bela said: 'I think that Julius was the only person apart from your mother and Aunt Alice who loved you. When he was arrested, you felt that he had done all these things he should not have done for your stepmother just to please you, because he loved you.

'Of course you felt guilty about what happened to him, but that doesn't mean you don't truly love each other.'

All around us the prisoners shuffled around, a living reminder of a world of hatred.

'No amount of guilt would make a young woman do all the things you've done and take all those risks to find him,' Bela continued.

'Only one thing could make you do that: love.'

CHAPTER TWENTY-ONE

The barrack blocks in Buchenwald were built from wood and laid out in lines, stretching away down the slope from the camp entrance towards the trees of the Thuringian forest.

I stood by the Yugoslav block and looked across the vast, chaotic wasteland of the camp. In one corner, just along from the entrance, was the camp's crematorium; in the far distance I could see the rolling countryside.

Between the forest and me lay more than 30 barrack blocks and tens of thousands of inmates. In the final weeks before liberation, the camp had been packed with 110,000 prisoners, but the numbers were falling all the time. Somewhere among them, surely, someone must know what had become of Julius.

It was a lovely June morning, with blue skies and sunshine to warm the dusty camp. All around, prisoners sat, soaking up the sun, building up their strength, chatting to their compatriots, waiting… always waiting.

I began my lonely trek round the camp, stopping at every barrack block, at each group of prisoners, asking them all the same question and getting the same answer: 'No, we haven't heard of Julius; no, we don't know where he might be.'

My days became a dispiriting round of unanswered questions and bemused expressions. There were so many nationalities in the camp that just making myself understood was a struggle and my search began to look increasingly desperate.

My new friends in the Yugoslav block did their best to keep my spirits up, sharing their meals and including me in their evening gatherings, where we swapped stories and sang songs.

As each day dawned, my spirits fell further knowing that all the hours of daylight would bring me was more depressing, fruitless searching among a prison population to whom the search for one person was a matter of utmost insignificance. Who could blame them?

I would scrutinise the prisoners who were still too weak to leave their bunks in the hope of seeing those piercing blue eyes and familiar blond hair.

It was not to be. After two weeks, I'd searched every inch of the camp and found not a trace of Julius.

I was coming to the final stage of my odyssey. Here in the dusty ruins of a notorious concentration camp my quest was to end in failure. Ahead of me lay only despair and the long, lonely journey back to Zagreb.

On a beautiful summer Sunday I finally admitted all this to myself. It was time to go home.

Reluctant to tear myself away, I walked along the long line of barrack blocks one last time. I had become a familiar figure, and some of the prisoners would nod a greeting to the strange lost girl from Croatia.

Eventually, I found myself wandering out of the camp down to a stream, where a group of Hungarians were sitting, dipping their feet in the cold water.

I listened to their lively chatter and one of them, still wearing the yellow Star of David on his shabby camp uniform, smiled at me.

'Where are you all from?' I asked.

'We're from Budapest,' he replied. 'Please, sit down, join us.'

While some of them carried on paddling in the water, the others gathered round, talking and asking questions.

I told them I was not Hungarian but was looking for one of their countrymen. I turned to the man wearing the Star of David: 'His name is Koreny; does it mean anything to you?'

He looked at me thoughtfully. 'Was his first name Gyula?' he asked. My heart missed a beat: it was the Hungarian spelling of Julius.

'Yes, that's his name.'

'I know him,' he said, full of excitement. 'We met when we were both in prison in Budapest and he told me that he had been working in the Hungarian Embassy in Zagreb and was engaged to a Croatian girl there.'

He looked at me quizzically and shook his head. 'I'm sorry,' he said.

'What?' I asked, my heart in my mouth. 'What do you mean?'

'He told me that when the war was over, he was going back to Zagreb to marry this Croatian girl called Olgi. If you're his wife, I'm terribly sorry but you've come here for nothing. Julius said he was divorced.'

I smiled at him. 'Oh, no, I'm not his wife,' I said. 'I'm Olgi.'

He looked at me in amazement. 'You've come all the way from Zagreb?'

So again, I told my story and how I'd arrived in Buchenwald.

'Now I need to find Julius,' I said. 'Did you see him here in the camp? Was he transported with you to Dachau and then here?'

Everyone had gathered round to hear my tale, but one by one they shook their heads. 'He's not very tall with blue eyes…' I said, desperately trying to jog their memories. 'Please think – did you see him here after the Americans came?'

The answer from all of them was sadly 'No'.

Tears ran down my face, I begged them to think, to talk to their friends, to see if anyone remembered him.

They all looked away. I could read their expressions. Julius had been a prisoner since the end of 1943, he'd been held at three separate Nazi concentration camps – what were the chances of his survival?

It was hard to live in the camps but very easy to die.

The meeting with the Hungarians was the final straw. I resolved to leave the camp the following day and head south. As I left them at the river bank, I asked them one last time: 'If you think of anything, anything at all, then I'll be at the Yugoslav barracks this evening. This time tomorrow, I'll be gone.'

***

It was a melancholy evening with my friends in the Yugoslav hut. They tried to persuade me to wait and travel back home with them. However, I wanted to visit Mrs Buchler and her family in Dachau, collect my belongings and thank them for their kindness. I knew how sad Mrs Buchler would be to hear that I had failed in my mission.

My friends made the best of it and tried to give me a memorable send off. We ate well and drank some wine before the singing began. In the dark night at Buchenwald our voices joined together to sing songs of home, of love and loss, our sad faces illuminated by flickering lamps.

Bela gave me his address in Zagreb: 'We must meet up when we are all back there,' he said.

Stanko, likewise, scrawled his address on a scrap of paper, and said, smiling: 'Here, I would like to get married when I find the right little woman…'

'You'd make a lovely couple,' said Bela, 'he would soon teach you Slovenian.'

We laughed but my mind was full of memories of Julius and how we thought we'd found the perfect love.

It was all I could do to stop myself from crying.

***

The day of my departure dawned bright and warm. The rising sun cast long shadows across the camp. I packed what few belongings I had and said my final farewells.

The gatehouse at Buchenwald was a grand affair: the iron gates were flanked on each side by low concrete buildings, while above was a two-storey timber structure with a row of windows, a wooden walkway round the outside and finally, on the very top, a clock tower.

It looked more like a hunting lodge than the gatehouse to a concentration camp and was far more impressive than the entrance to Dachau or Ohrduf.

I was becoming quite an expert on the sombre architecture of concentration camps, I reflected, as I headed towards the gate to begin the long journey home.

The day promised to be hot but it didn't lift my spirits. The best I could hope for was that the summer weather would make others feel happy and generous – willing to give a girl a lift.

The rest of the camp was going about its business. The former prisoners were eating breakfast while the Americans continued with the endless process of recording each one of them and preparing them for their onward journeys.

In one building at the camp the Americans had placed a ring of tables around a wooden post. Anyone in the camp could visit the room, take a small slip of paper and write down the country to which they would like to be sent. Many picked their home countries, of course, but I went in there often and chose a different destination each day. America, Mexico, England, Canada – all those exotic places that I doubted I would ever see.

I smiled wryly to myself – what had become of those choices? Instead I was heading to Dachau and then back to Zagreb. I hadn't written down either of those places as choices for my future.

Close to the gate, I glanced at a large, two-storey block, which the Americans used as offices. In a window next to the door a table lamp was clearly visible on the desk inside, the bulb illuminating the macabre lampshade decorated with a tattoo. It was made from human skin and sat there either as a reminder to the Germans of their barbarity, or as a grim souvenir collected by the soldier inside.

I stopped and stared at the lamp. The tall, blond American soldier sitting writing busily at the desk looked up and then turned back to his work.

Should I ask him about Julius? I had been in and out of all these barracks; I must have been here. 'What's the point?' I asked myself.

The soldier looked up again and I went in and presented the scruffy, dog-eared letter that Mrs Buchler had written for me all those weeks ago.

It was a futile gesture, I knew, but like a gambler who can't leave the roulette table because the last bet will be his winning one, I couldn't leave Buchenwald without one last attempt.

The soldier studied the letter and I pointed at Julius's name as if such a gesture would somehow aid his understanding. He stood, pulled a large ledger from a shelf behind him and flicked rapidly through the pages, each of which bore a long list of names.

Finally, he picked up his pencil, wrote on a piece of scrap paper: 'First floor, no. 23' and pointed towards the stairs.

I quickly climbed the unsteady wooden steps to the first floor but was faced by just one door. There was no room 23.

I pushed open the door, expecting to see another office. Instead it was a vast long, low room lined with beds on either side, in most of which were men lying motionless. The smell of disinfectant hit me. This was a hospital ward.

A few men were sitting up in bed, still wearing the striped uniforms of the camps. The room fell silent as all eyes turned to me.

An old man limped forward and asked me in Polish what I wanted. Hoping he could understand English, I passed him my tatty letter, which he studied closely, before indicating that I should follow him.

Slowly we walked along the line of beds, all eyes following our progress through the silent ward.

My Polish guide stopped at the foot of a bed, which bore a small sign with the number 23. He pointed to the man lying there and gabbled something to me in Polish.

The patient had one leg raised high in the air in a harness. He was tiny, very pale and thin, almost entirely bald and without teeth. The only colour in his face was the black of the shadows under his eyes.

But those eyes. Just as I was turning to look at the Polish man to ask why he'd brought me to the bedside of this elderly and presumably dying man, those eyes flashed blue. And then we both knew.

A smile of joy and amazement spread across the patient's face. I didn't know whether to laugh or cry but felt myself drawn by a great force towards him. We embraced, weeping, and held each other so tightly I was scared I would hurt him.

He clutched me as a child hugs a favourite toy and cried out: 'Olgi, Olgi! Oh, God, how did you find me?'

I choked back the tears, softly stroked his cheek and whispered: 'Julius, my love.'

CHAPTER TWENTY-TWO

The news of our reunion spread like wildfire through the hospital ward. Men who hadn't risen from their beds for weeks suddenly found the strength to make their way along the ward to the strange sight of this couple embracing and weeping.

'I love you Olga and I always have,' Julius whispered to me. 'As soon as I recover we are getting married.'

I was crying and laughing at the same time. All around us thin, shaven-headed men in striped uniforms stood watching, smiling and talking.

'How on earth did you find me?' Julius repeated. 'I was sure you were back in Zagreb. I was going to travel there to find you as soon as I was well enough.'

I laughed again, wiping tears from my eyes. 'I searched everywhere for you, every barrack block in the camp, and this was the last place I tried. We all thought this was just for American offices; the windows were always closed and there was no sign of life here… I never knew.'

'They brought the most seriously ill here,' Julius said. 'We're the ones they were expecting to die. None of us were fit enough to go out so I suppose the others in the camp didn't realise we were here.'

'I thought you were dead,' I said, holding him closer, painfully aware of how thin he was. I could have picked him up and carried him, he felt so light.

I didn't share my thoughts, but to myself I said: 'Oh God, he is a wreck of a man, he is in such a terrible condition.' At the back of my mind was the dreadful thought that he might still die.

The other patients began to drift away, granting us some privacy. Julius told me that he had collapsed with typhus in February while in a labour party working on the camp railway. The SS guards had beaten him so severely he suffered thrombosis in his leg and his hands were severely wounded when he tried to protect himself from the blows. He now had to keep his leg raised to avoid the thrombosis travelling to his heart. Meanwhile the Americans were treating the typhus, which had claimed the lives of thousands of concentration camp inmates during the final months of the war.

My struggle to find Julius would now be replaced by the fight to keep him alive.

Julius was exhausted by both the illness and the surprise of my arrival. We both had so much to talk about, so much to say, but we sat in silence holding hands. Eventually, I said: 'I've got to tell my friend Bela that I have found you. He's a doctor and he'll help us.'

Julius smiled weakly as I kissed him on the cheek and headed for the door. When I glanced back, he was already asleep.

***

Bela was surprised to see me rushing towards the Yugoslav barracks – and even more surprised to see me smiling.

'I thought you were leaving today?' he asked. 'Why are you looking so happy?'

'Bela, Bela,' I said breathlessly, 'I've found him!'

'What? Don't be ridiculous. We searched everywhere…'

'Come, come with me,' I said, grabbing his hand and hauling him towards the block where I'd found Julius.

The American soldier raised no objection to us visiting the ward after I told him that Bela was a doctor and we hurried up the stairs.

Julius remembered being treated by Bela when he was first diagnosed with typhus and they greeted each other warmly. Julius told us more about his illness – and how close he'd come to death. After he fell ill, the Germans had loaded him onto a lorry with other sick prisoners to be taken from the camp. Even in the delirium of his illness he knew that inmates taken away were never seen again, either dying during transportation to another camp or simply being abandoned somewhere and left to die.

Despite his high temperature and weakness, Julius jumped down from the lorry when it slowed during the journey away from the camp and was hauled up into another lorry carrying healthy prisoners back to Buchenwald. This brave move saved his life.

Although he was seriously ill by the time the lorry passed through the gates of the camp, the Americans were now advancing so rapidly the Germans could no longer send prisoners west.

After that, everything was a blur – long spells of unconsciousness followed by brief periods of coherence, and then nothing. He had woken in a hospital bed and been there for two months, his leg raised and his temperature fluctuating dangerously. His hair had fallen out and was only just beginning to re-grow and despite the treatment of the Americans he admitted he was still not feeling much better.

The ward he was in was a mixture of all nationalities and prisoner categories: Jews, gypsies, homosexuals, politicals and criminals. Treating them all were two Hungarian doctors.

'I'll talk to the doctors,' Bela said. 'Perhaps you can come to our barracks and I can look after you there.'

Unsurprisingly, the overworked doctors had no objection to one of their charges being cared for elsewhere.

Bela returned to give us the news and asked Julius if he had any clothes to wear other than the prison uniform.

'No,' he replied. 'I have nothing.'

Later that day two men from the Yugoslav barracks turned up to carry Julius back and once there, provided him with a German army summer uniform which had been left behind by the camp guards.

Bela administered some medication and soon Julius was asleep in his bunk, still wearing his new uniform.

***

After a few days of care from Bela and the other Yugoslav prisoners, Julius was beginning to show signs of improvement. His strength was returning and before long his leg could be freed from traction and lowered gently onto the bed.

As his appetite returned he began to gain weight and his hair grew more thickly on his head. He was no longer so exhausted and one morning when I arrived for my daily visit he smiled broadly and told me that he felt energetic and, what's more, he wanted to try to walk – something he hadn't done for at least two months. Bela found him some high, lace-up boots and we slipped them onto his feet.

Then, very gingerly, he put one foot down and then the next onto the floor beside his bed. With me holding one arm and Bela the other, we pulled him carefully upright. He swayed slightly but while we held him he took a few shaky steps along the wooden floor of the barrack block before making a tentative turn and returning to collapse on his bed.

We all laughed and applauded. Julius looked delighted – but exhausted.

Still, he had taken his first steps and now we all dared hope that he was on his way to a full recovery.

Over the next few days I helped Julius with his walking. He would lean on me and we would make our slow, stumbling progress to the end of the hut. Eventually, the day came when we went outside, into the early summer sunshine and Julius took his first walk in the camp since he'd collapsed in February.

Other inmates watched and smiled, some called out words of

encouragement. We had become the talk of the camp: the prisoner who was back from the dead and the mad young girl from Zagreb who'd come to rescue him.

Soon, we were walking slightly further each day, exploring the camp and eventually venturing outside into the forest and the countryside, sometimes taking a picnic with us.

Throughout these excursions we talked about our past and what our future held.

'Why were you arrested?' I asked him.

'I honestly have no idea,' he replied. 'I was told I was a political prisoner but no one told me what I was supposed to have done. In the beginning they questioned me but then they seemed to give up and I became just another prisoner.'

'Do you think it was helping my stepmother's Jewish family that got you into trouble?'

He thought for a long time. 'I don't know. I don't think we'll ever know, but I wouldn't change anything. I did it for you…'

I told him about my travels, the friends I'd made on the way and the risks I'd taken.

He looked close to tears. 'I would never have imagined anyone would do that.'

Julius told me about his terrible time in the camps and the long days and nights in cattle trains. Sometimes they were put in open freight wagons, exposed to the elements, and a frightening number died during the journeys.

'When I collapsed in February, I thought that was the end,' he said. 'So few people survived and by that stage I was almost ready to give up.

'It was only the thought of you that kept me going. I dreamed of going back to Zagreb to find you and what joy we would have when I did.

'Instead, I woke up one day here and there you were, standing at the end of my bed. I couldn't believe it. I still can't.'

227

We both laughed and talked of our early time together; the nights at the Hungarian club, the trips to the opera, the café in Vrapce and all that we had to look forward to.

The days were growing longer, the sun warmer but the memories of wartime were all around us. The death rate from illness in the camp was still high and refugees were arriving all the time. There was an air of expectation and anxiety among us. The world had changed, we had changed; what would become of us now?

Slowly the Americans were making arrangements for the different nationalities in the camps to be repatriated. Truckloads would leave each day, heading out on another interminable journey, but this time, hopefully, with a happier ending.

Julius would gaze at those convoys, lost in thought until one day he turned to me: 'Olga, we've been engaged since November 1943 when I rang your father in Zagreb and we've both been through so much…'

He paused and my heart was in my mouth; as I waited to hear what he had to say.

'I want to marry you here, now. We can't wait, otherwise I'll be sent back to Hungary and you will be sent back to Yugoslavia and who knows if we'll be able to marry then. I love you, Olga. Let's marry here.'

Here? I looked around me at a vast area, full of barrack blocks, surrounded by barbed wire and with thousands of skeletal people wandering aimlessly around. The guard towers still loomed over us and the chimney of the crematorium stood stark against the blue sky.

If there is a less romantic place for a marriage proposal then I have never heard of it.

I was delighted that Julius still felt the same about me, that we were still in love, but the thought of marriage in such a place filled me with dread. On the other hand, Julius was right – married, we could travel together to Budapest; unmarried we would be sent to separate destinations. I thought of the many requests I had submitted on the scraps of paper in the hut and the exotic countries I had chosen, all for nothing.

Still, I had not come all this way and taken all those risks to lose the man I loved, so I spoke to Bela and asked whether we could marry.

He went into Weimar to make inquiries, returning to tell us that the town had been badly bombed but there was a temporary register office.

Bela looked at Julius and me and said: 'Because everything is in chaos, I thought it best to just go ahead and make the arrangements…'

We looked at him and then at each other. Arrangements? We were about to be married.

We both laughed and hugged each other.

'When?' I asked.

'Three days' time, at 12 noon.'

So after 19 months, 2,000 miles, prisons, bombing raids, concentration camps, illness and betrayal, we were to marry in Weimar, the cultural heart of Germany and the home to so many Nazi rallies.

Our great love would finally be celebrated just as it had begun: under the shadow of the swastika.

CHAPTER TWENTY-THREE

As a child in Sisak, I loved to watch weddings.

At the Serbian Orthodox Church near our home there was usually one a week and it was a tradition after the service for the best man to throw small change into the crowd for the children. We would all shout 'kume izgore ti kesa', which, roughly translated, means 'to burn his pocket'; then there would be a mad scramble for the money, usually half-dinar coins, the size of the old British sixpence.

I would emerge from the melee, scratched, dirty, bruised and with my dress torn, sometimes clutching a hard earned half-dinar, other times with empty hands.

My mother was appalled that I would fight for money, but I was young and no child can resist a coin?

It wasn't just the money that drew me to the church. I also stood outside to see the bride, resplendent in her wedding dress, shyly beautiful and the centre of attention. One day, that would be me.

I knew exactly how my day would go: I would wear a long white dress with a flowing train while my four young bridesmaids would wear pink and blue. The organist would play Ave Maria and all eyes would be upon me.

The reception would be held in a ballroom awash with flowers; my family and friends would be there to send my husband and me off on an idyllic honeymoon in Nice or Monte Carlo.

Who knows how many of our dreams will ever come true? I had found Julius, we were getting married… perhaps I'd used up my luck with those dreams.

Our ceremony would be nothing like the one I had hoped for.

The three Yugoslav girls with whom I was sharing a storeroom in the camp were thrilled. A wedding? At Buchenwald? How exciting!

What would I wear? Between the four of us we had next to nothing and the only solution we could come up with was for me to wear one of the thin cotton nightdresses that Mrs Buchler had given me in Dachau. It seemed ridiculous but the weather was warm and the nightdress had plenty of lace – it would have to do.

The next problem was shoes. We all wore different sizes and none of us had smart shoes anyway. All I had was a pair of heavy boots and my now rather bedraggled white socks, which I had brought from Dachau. So I was to be married in a nightdress and walking boots.

Next the girls turned their attention to my hair, using shoelaces and pieces of paper as curlers and instructing me to sleep in them all night in order to look my best on my wedding day.

Julius fared better. The German uniform stripped of its insignia fitted him well and the black boots, which Bela had found for him, were relatively undamaged and matched the uniform. Watching Bela and Julius sorting out his clothes was like watching two men in a tailor's shop.

'Oh, I'm not sure about this jacket, Bela. Let me try that one,' Julius would say, pointing to one among the apparently limitless number of former German uniforms.

Bela would grab the next jacket and, entering into the spirit, say: 'Perhaps sir will find this one more to his taste?'

Julius was soon looking quite elegant. His hair had grown, but sadly he'd lost his teeth for ever.

'Don't worry,' Bela said. 'Don't laugh and just keep your mouth shut when you smile.'

What a sight we were. A toothless man in a German army uniform and his blushing bride in a nightdress and walking boots – hardly love's young dream.

Bela examined us. 'Look on the bright side,' he said. 'At least there won't be any photographers there.'

***

It was a dull, grey morning when we set out for the station in the village of Buchenwald for the short train ride into Weimar.

There were six of us: Julius and me, Bela and the three girls from the camp. My bridesmaids.

The sky was heavy with rain but it stayed dry and the 11 o'clock train into Weimar arrived on time. Bela led us from the station through the bomb-damaged streets, to a low, shabby building in a square. This was Weimar's temporary register office; the town hall in the Marktplatz, opposite the Hotel Elephant where Hitler always stayed, had been damaged by bombing, which had devastated the whole of the north side of the historic square.

The rubble outside the temporary register office formed a mountain higher than the building itself. Our path to the door was an obstacle course of fallen masonry and bomb craters. My wedding dreams receded even further.

Bela hurried us along. 'Come on. If you don't marry now, it will never happen.'

He knocked on the door. There was no answer. My heart fell. I could see the whole day ending in disaster.

Just as Bela was about to knock again, the door swung open and a woman wished us 'Guten tag'. We all filed into the tiny office where Julius and I were shown the paperwork. Bela had got my place of birth wrong, putting me down as coming from Gombos. I allowed myself a wry smile. After my travels under false names or with no papers, it hardly seemed to matter.

Unsurprisingly, there were no other weddings booked for that day and we waited quietly. Julius seemed nervous and I squeezed his hand.

Promptly at noon, the door to another office opened and the registrar called us in.

Julius and I stood in front of him as he began reading the marriage service in rapid German. He turned to Julius and asked whether he took me to be his wife.

'Ja,' he replied firmly.

He turned to me. Did I take Julius to be my husband?

'Ja,' I said.

He paused for us to exchange rings and then, realising we didn't have any, hurried on, announcing solemnly: 'Somit seid ihr Mann und Frau, bis dass der Tod euch scheidet'. ('You are now husband and wife until death divides you.')

Then it was over. The whole ceremony had lasted just three minutes.

I felt happy we were married at last and we would be together but sad that we were there alone with no family around us. Only our friends from the concentration camp were there for our great day. What would my father say?

How I wished my dear mother had been there. She would have been thrilled to see her little girl – 'too ugly to ever find a man' – married.

We stepped out of the register office building, smiling and laughing, and headed for a bar on the opposite side of the square to celebrate. As we did so, the heavens opened and we were caught in a torrential downpour.

By the time we flung ourselves gratefully through the door of the bar and gathered around an upturned beer barrel, which served as a table, we were all soaked.

I had suffered more than the others. My thin cotton nightdress was no match for the rain and was clinging to me, while my hair, so carefully curled by the girls, was hanging straight and limp. Bela had been right all along: thank goodness there were no photographers present.

We ordered drinks, only to be told the bar had nothing but apple juice, so we each raised a glass and Bela proposed a toast to 'the happy couple'. It seemed fitting somehow, that such a ramshackle wedding ceremony should be toasted in apple juice rather than champagne.

I turned to Julius and clinked glasses: 'To us, Mr Koreny', I said.

'To us, Mrs Koreny,' he replied.

The four o'clock train back from Weimar was delayed and it was evening when we finally returned to the camp to find that our Yugoslav friends had prepared a wedding reception for us. Another pig in the Thuringian forest had fallen victim to the hunters and was roasting on an open fire. Macaroni and spaghetti were simmering in large pans of boiling water.

We sat on makeshift benches and ate food that tasted better to me than if it had come from the most expensive kitchen. Someone had even found some wine, so everyone rose to toast us and we kissed, illuminated by the lamps and fires of the camp.

After the food, the singing began and Julius and I had the first dance, whirling across the hard-packed ground as the crowd chanted and clapped. In the distance, prisoners still in their striped pyjamas flitted through the dusk.

It was a strange, surreal celebration.

Everyone joked about where would we go for our honeymoon: was it to be the French Riveria or a world cruise? Julius laughed and told them it was a secret.

'No groom tells his bride where they are going on honeymoon,' he said, 'but I can guarantee that we won't bump into any other honeymoon couples in the place I have in mind.'

This was greeted with a roar of laughter and more applause but just then we were interrupted by shouts and cries of alarm from the cooks by the open fire. A strong wind was blowing across the camp and the flames were being blown onto our barrack block.

The flames swiftly took hold and one end of the wooden building was soon ablaze. A human chain formed to bring buckets of water to throw on the fire and we were joined by American soldiers, who helped bring it under control.

I'd had no flowers, no wedding dress and no ring, but I could hardly have had a more memorable wedding.

Buchenwald had everything: cells, barracks, hospital beds, electrified fences, dining rooms, watch towers, shower rooms, execution chambers, mass graves, offices, a crematorium, parade ground…

What it didn't have was a bridal suite. How, we joked, could the Nazis have been so remiss?

As the party went on into the early hours we were sent on our way amid great cheering towards an old storeroom, where all the clutter had been cleared to one side and a makeshift bed prepared on the floor.

We were to spend our first night of married life there. We embraced in the darkness with the raucous sounds of the camp all around us.

I looked at Julius and we kissed softly, illuminated only by the dying flames of a blazing prison block in a concentration camp.

CHAPTER TWENTY-FOUR

We woke to gentle sunshine seeping around the edges of the blankets that our friends had hung on the windows. We dressed and went, somewhat shyly, across to their barracks to thank them for the wonderful party.

Everyone was looking a bit the worse for wear, except, of course, Bela, who smiled at us both. 'Ah, the happy couple,' he said.

We joined them for breakfast and everyone gathered around to congratulate us again, before drifting away leaving just Bela and us.

He looked serious. 'There is something I need to show you both,' he said.

'You, Julius, have been too ill to really understand what has gone on here, and you, Olga, seemed so unhappy and lost when you were searching for Julius I didn't want to upset you further.

'Now, however, you are both safe and happy it's important that you know everything about this place. Then you will tell others and no one will forget what happened here.'

We sat in sombre silence until Bela raised a weak smile. 'It will be your honeymoon in hell.'

With that he stood stiffly and said: 'Come.' Julius and I glanced at each other, not sure what to make of this new, serious side to our friend. He led us through the maze of barrack huts to Block 46.

'This,' he said, 'is where they carried out medical experiments.

Prisoners were deliberately infected with typhus, smallpox, yellow fever, diphtheria and many others so they could track the progress of the disease. Even if they survived the prisoners were usually killed at the end of the experiments.

'They would inflict burns on prisoners here as well, just so they could try out different treatment methods.'

The block was empty of course, but its terrible legacy lingered. The air was still and sluggish, almost stifling.

I shuddered. Bela was right: the horrors of this place, and the others such as Dachau, defied human understanding.

That day in 1945 we had no idea of the true extent of all that had gone on in Buchenwald, never mind the extermination camps in Poland. All we knew was a very small part of it, and that was terrifying enough.

We walked back up the hill towards the impressive entrance gate, heading left across the roll call square towards a brick building with a tall chimney. I knew from Dachau, where I had mistaken a similar building for the kitchens, that this could only be the crematorium.

Here, Bela showed us the line of ovens and the long shovels used to lift the bodies into the flames. Next door was a grim room, with white tiles covering the walls. In the centre was a large concrete table also covered in the white tiles. At one end of the table was a sink. Everything was immaculately clean.

'What is this place?' I asked.

'Oh, this is the autopsy room,' Bela said. 'They would bring the bodies from the medical experiments here to extract the organs. Sometimes they took organs from other prisoners who had died to carry out further experiments on them.'

On the shelves some glass jars still stood with human organs preserved in alcohol. Cards covered with neatly written German lay next to them, explaining their origins.

I was glad to leave and get back outside. 'Thank God that's over,' I thought – but it wasn't.

Bela directed us towards a steep flight of stairs leading down the side of the building to a basement. Inside was a long, low, claustrophobic room with just one small window at the far end. To the left of where we stood was a wooden chute and in the far corner a strange, black metallic contraption. At the top of the walls, evenly spaced about two feet apart, were single black hooks.

'This is the corpse room,' Bela announced. 'The bodies were thrown down the chute here,' he continued, pointing to the wooden opening next to us. 'Then,' he said, walking towards the opposite end of the room, 'they were dragged along, put into this lift and hoisted up to the ovens above. Sometimes this room was so packed they had to dump the bodies outside behind the building until there was room to bring them in.'

We stared at the rudimentary machine, nothing more than a goods lift into which the bodies had been crammed with no ceremony, no care and no respect. For so many people the short ride to the floor above had been their final journey on this earth.

'The hooks, what are they for?' I asked, pointing at the walls.

Bela paused. 'They hanged people here as well,' he said. 'Some prisoners were executed on a portable gallows that they would put up in the camp so that we could all see their suffering. Others were just brought here and hanged on a hook, dying while the guards dragged the bodies around on the floor in front of them.

'Here at Buchenwald you didn't have to be dead to be brought to the crematorium…'

I could see scratch marks etched deep into the walls beneath the hooks, left by desperate hands trying to cling to life. The suffering in that room must have been unimaginable; the atmosphere, even after liberation, was suffocating.

Fresh air never tasted so sweet as it did when we climbed the steps out of the corpse room. Bela looked at us both: 'I'm sorry, but you needed to know.'

We walked further round the camp and into the adjacent

SS quarters where everything was different: carefully tended accommodation, extravagantly decorated dining rooms and comfortable beds. It was a world away from the horror on the other side of the barbed wire fence.

I realised with a terrible sadness that Dachau had been much the same. The girls and me in the SS camp, the good food, the dining rooms and the normal life – yet all the time this evil game of random death had been played out on the other side of the barbed wire.

Through all the difficulties and dangers of the previous 18-months, I had rarely prayed but that evening I did, fervently thanking God for saving Julius and me and praying for the souls of those who had died behind the camp wire.

CHAPTER TWENTY-FIVE

We all suffer alone. No one can fully understand the pain of another, just as they will never comprehend your pain. A couple can be so close, so in love, and yet there always remains a part of each that is separate and theirs alone.

This is what Julius and I had to learn after we married. There were times when he was full of cheer and good humour, and yet in an instant his mood would change and he would disappear into thoughts of his own, as if he were miles away.

He had been through so much in the camps – how could anyone know what that was like unless you were there?

Likewise, I had been cold and hungry, trembling with fear during bombing raids, living on my wits and constantly moving on, terrified that at any time I would be exposed and arrested.

These are experiences you don't forget. They become ingrained in your character, a mark on your personality that can never be erased.

In many ways, Julius and I were the same people who had met and fallen in love in Zagreb; in others, we had changed profoundly from those apparently carefree days.

Even now, like many of the wartime generation, I never waste food and I will share whatever I have got – lessons I learnt on the refugee trail through Europe, when I saw the very best of people and the very worst.

Inevitably, there was almost a sense of anti-climax. I had found Julius, the war was over, and the camp inmates were being repatriated.

New refugees were arriving all the time, many from the east with shaven heads and bearing numbers tattooed on their arms. Two sisters from Yugoslavia told me they had come from a camp near somewhere called Auschwitz in Poland and how delighted they were to be going home. They didn't speak about the camp, but they appeared haunted, troubled and desperate to get out of Germany. Tragically, we heard later that one of them died on the journey back to her homeland.

My Croatian friends in the camp were looking forward to returning home and would gather each evening to sing patriotic Croatian songs, tugging at my heart. I was torn between Croatia and Hungary, the land of my husband.

I loved Julius and we wanted to be together, but what would the future hold? And would I ever return to Zagreb?

The world was changing as well. The old certainties had gone to be replaced by fresh ones – and new divisions. In the post-war world, Hungary and the newly-reunified Yugoslavia were both to be under the control of Moscow. Having spent so long fleeing the advance of the Red Army I was now to return to them.

Bela laughed at me: 'You came to find Julius and escape the Russians – now you are going to meet them and give your Slav brothers a big hug!'

I found it hard to laugh.

Buchenwald was now one giant transit camp. Refugees from other camps were transferred there before being sent on to their own countries.

Eventually, our turn came. Those of us travelling to Budapest were told to be ready to leave in one week. It wasn't as if we had much to pack.

Bela found some German army woollen material, which he gave

to Julius, who was no longer so badly dressed because in addition to his German uniform he had some shirts, a good pair of boots and a long winter coat.

Women's clothing was in shorter supply but I hoped that when I reached Budapest I would finally be able to dress well again. I wondered what girls of my age were wearing and what the current fashions were. I rarely saw a newspaper and never read a magazine. If nightdresses worn during the day with walking boots were all the rage I would be at the forefront of fashion…

It was a warm July and as we waited to begin our journey, Julius and I would walk in the forest around the camp.

'It reminds me of Tuskanac in Zagreb,' he said, 'the woods and the peaceful walks.'

He was much stronger, walking well and putting on weight. The worst was over.

One day we hitched a lift in an American jeep to Leipzig, a once beautiful city but now reduced to ruins. On our return we stopped to see what was left of the Zeiss factory in Jenna, once the best in the world for lenses. Julius, who was always interested in photography, wondered what had become of the Leica camera I had so carefully brought him from Zagreb when he was first arrested. He picked his way carefully through the rubble of the factory, collecting optical prisms and lenses.

'They might be useful when we get back to Budapest,' he told me, but he didn't say how.

Although he had trained as an engineer he had no job to return to and no idea where we would live. It was going to be another journey into the unknown.

***

It began when ten lorries lined up at the camp entrance and all the Hungarian inmates were called forward. We were to be driven to a demarcation line with the Russians in Czechoslovakia and handed over.

I had a last look round the camp and as I did so, the tears began to fall. It was extraordinary that for so many people this had been a place of horror and cruelty, but for me it had been a scene of great happiness: the reunion with Julius, our wedding and our bizarre honeymoon.

This camp would be razed, I thought, new buildings would appear and all my memories would be gone.

Bela found me crying and joked: 'I never thought a young lady would cry for me…' I couldn't tell him the truth. Buchenwald was part of me; to leave it was to lose something that I would never get back.

We climbed onto the lorries, two old, battered suitcases between us – the sum total of all we had in the world. Julius had insisted that we pack the prisms he'd found in the ruins of Jenna as he had an idea that when we were home he could manufacture binoculars and we would soon be millionaires.

The Americans gave us two large food parcels wrapped tightly in strong wax paper, then, with some shouting from the soldiers and desultory singing from the passengers, the lorries set off in a long convoy.

We didn't have much chance to talk – the engine noise was too great – but we made good progress on the empty roads. The countryside flashed past in a way it never did when I was painfully making my way to Dachau and Buchenwald.

It was only about 100 miles from Buchenwald to the Czech frontier and soon our convoy was slowing down to cross the border before picking up speed on the road to our first stop 40 miles into Czechoslovakia at Karlovy Vary, a beautiful spa town.

We were allowed to get down from the lorries to stretch our legs. I looked around and thought how pleasant it would be to spend a couple of weeks there, in the late summer sunshine, strolling in the hills and taking the waters. It would be like a honeymoon.

Of course, we had no such opportunity. Soon the shouted orders told us all to get back into the lorries and we set off south towards Plzen, more commonly known around the world as Pilsner. We stopped again and this time we were given a tour of the local brewery, home to Pilsner lager. The tour included a free sample of beer.

We were getting back onto the lorries when I looked around but couldn't see Julius.

'My husband,' I said to one of the Americans. 'He's not here... We can't go without him.'

The Americans looked baffled and then did a headcount. It came up one short.

The guards headed back into the brewery shouting for Julius. After a few minutes, they reappeared with the familiar slight figure of my husband among them, looking very sheepish.

'I'm sorry,' he said to us all as he got back on the lorry. 'There was some machinery in there that I wanted to have another look at, and I got lost.'

Everyone laughed amid suggestions that it was the free beer that had detained Julius, rather than some obscure machines. For many of us, it was the first laughter since we'd left Buchenwald.

However the mood turned sombre again as we travelled further south and began to see soldiers from the Red Army gathered on either side of the road, guns still at the ready.

Somewhere in the Czech countryside we reached the handover point and we all got down from the lorries, pulling our belongings after us. Looking around there were no vehicles waiting to take us further; instead, standing in a siding, there was a long cattle train, identical to the ones I'd seen arriving at Dachau and in which Julius had been transported from one camp to another.

A deathly silence fell across our group. These were camp veterans; the cattle trucks meant only one thing to them. Soon the Russians were shouting and cajoling us all towards the carriages, sliding back the doors and ushering us in. When the doors closed behind us I listened for the sound of locks, but there were none. I breathed a sigh of relief.

Nonetheless the atmosphere among the 40 or so people in our carriage was tense – some openly wondered if our destination was another concentration camp, a Russian one this time.

The fear spread to us all. I wondered if I would ever see my friends or return to Zagreb.

As the train began its slow journey, the conversation inevitably turned to life in the camps. Each passenger, it seemed, had experienced a different camp, witnessed a different act of brutality, each more shocking than the last. The stories from the camps in the east were too horrific to believe. It was a painful, human record of all that had happened in the past six years across Europe.

Eventually, Julius told his story: how he'd been arrested in Budapest, and then sent to Dachau, Ohrdruf and finally Buchenwald.

'Oh,' he said, 'of course, I got married in Buchenwald.'

There was a stunned silence. Was this Hungarian man joking about the camps? He smiled broadly and explained.

Soon everyone was laughing and congratulating us on our wedding. After the litany of human misery we'd heard, our story relieved the tension and people began to smile again.

The journey, however, began to remind me of all those journeys I had made during the war: constantly stopping and starting, clanking along at walking pace.

It was painfully slow – but at least this time there were no air raids. As dusk fell on the first day the train ground to a halt, the engine was detached and we were left there to get what rest we could during the night.

The pattern of our days was set: slow progress in the daylight hours and a complete standstill at night.

Julius and I slept by the door, opening it slightly for the fresh air, and

A post-liberation identification card issued at Buchenwald, showing that Julius was interned there.

one night, unable to sleep, I was gazing at the full moon, which reminded me of my childhood in Sisak, when two Russian soldiers appeared and began shouting at us all.

The people behind me in the carriage started stirring; the Russians still shouting, demanding watches.

This was the Red Army we'd heard about during the war, stealing, looting and raping. The adrenaline shot through me; we were to be cast back to the worst days of the war.

A large, fat lady behind me (the first overweight person I had seen in many years) said loudly in Hungarian: 'Oh, no, not again!'

One Russian soldier demanded to know what she had said. He jumped up into the carriage and pushed past me to get to her. As he did so, I said 'Hello' in Russian.

He stopped and shifted his gaze from the fat woman to me.

'How do you know my language?' he asked, suspiciously.

'We are brothers, I am from Yugoslavia,' I replied.

He smiled at me and the tension was broken. He jumped down from the carriage but not before warning us they would be back.

They did return, but not in the way many of my fellow refugees feared. Instead they came with an accordion and began to play. The singing started and soon we were dancing in the carriage and on the ground around us, fuelled by the food and wine provided by the Russian soldiers.

The next day we headed further south and our Russian friends returned at one stop bearing a pencil and paper.

'What now?' Julius asked me. 'Are they going to write down the words of a Russian song?'

In fact, they invited us to visit them – one was from Vladivostock, the other from Moscow. I thanked them politely, promising we would do so, knowing full well that we would never get the chance.

The day dragged on, but before long we were approaching Kosice, in the east of Czechoslovakia, the gateway to the border.

A couple of hours later we passed some small border posts and we were once more on Hungarian soil. A ragged cheer went up, spreading from one carriage to the next as the train rattled on.

Eventually, we came to a halt beside another train – a proper passenger train – and we all gratefully jumped down from our cattle wagons and climbed aboard. It was packed with refugees and their belongings but our new Russian friends cleared some space for us and we settled in a compartment.

It was a lovely, warm day but I was feeling exhausted and nervous. The travelling had been hard and I was anxious about the future. Where would we live? Would we find work?

Julius was looking out of the window with growing interest as we entered the devastated outskirts of Budapest. As far as I could see, there were piles of rubble, collapsed roofs, shattered homes. Nothing but ruins. People were picking their way through the devastation.

I looked at my husband, his face shocked at the sight of his city.

'At least,' I thought, 'this time we're together.'

The train slowed and finally ground to a halt. Station porters were shouting 'Budapest, Budapest!' and we climbed down with our suitcases and walked along the platform.

We were home.

CHAPTER TWENTY-SIX

At the front of the station, groups of refugees stood looking around, dazed by the devastation and hoping to see a friend, a family member – anyone to give them shelter.

A loud voice was shouting: 'All who don't have places or relatives, follow me!'

I looked at Julius, who shrugged. We joined a small group and were taken in a van to a building where we were shown into a large room with mattresses scattered around. The place was clean and bright, but I thought: 'Oh, God, not sleeping on the floor again.'

Suddenly, having come all this way and after so much hardship, the idea of once again being reduced to this level seemed so depressing. I began to weep, and Julius put his arm around me and held me close.

'What happened to good beds,' I said through my tears. 'Did they bomb all the bed factories?'

We both laughed and then chose two mattresses side-by-side for the night. After a good meal, Julius wanted to go for a walk to have a look around but I was feeling unwell, so he went alone.

The next morning the lady in charge of the refugee centre began chatting with us. She said to Julius: 'You're obviously not Jewish, are you?'

'No,' he replied, in all innocence, 'and neither is my wife.'

'Oh, dear,' the woman said. 'I'm afraid in that case you will have to leave – this building is for Jewish people only.'

We were stunned. We looked around at all the other refugees and wondered why we should be treated differently, but that was the way it was. We packed our belongings and were sent along to a Red Cross centre – and further misery.

The accommodation was much worse. The room to which we were directed housed a long line of wooden bunks, without even mattresses or blankets.

The expression on Julius's face was a picture of horror.

'Dachau,' he said, quietly, 'this is just like Dachau. It reminds me of the times when we had to lie on our stomachs in the morning while the guards did the headcount. If someone had died next to you in the night, you kept the body there and didn't tell the guards they had died so we could keep getting their food ration.'

He looked again at the bunks. 'Not back to this again. Please, no.'

This time it was my turn to hold him in my arms. 'Darling, it's not the same, really. You're free now; we just have to get by for a couple of days and we'll find somewhere better,' I promised, with no idea how we would manage it.

Nonetheless, we began our search that afternoon. Prompted by the chilling sight of the bunks in the Red Cross centre we scoured the city, day after day. Julius tried everyone he knew, but people had moved on, their homes destroyed.

Finally, after almost two weeks of fruitless searching Julius ran into the ex-wife of an old friend who had been taken prisoner and transported to Russia. She directed us to an empty house near her home that had been damaged in the bombing, but, she said, might still be habitable.

We hardly dared hope but went to look and found a house that looked as if it were nothing but ruins. On the three walls still standing the authorities had pinned notices saying 'Danger Keep Away' and all the windows were boarded up except one at the front.

We climbed through and found a small room, still furnished, but with rotten floorboards. The air was stale and musty, but the room was dry, had a ceiling, four walls and a small window (broken, of course).

We knew it was dangerous and we were squatting in someone else's property but somehow it seemed preferable to the depressing Red Cross centre. We collected our belongings and moved into the wrecked house.

I'd been married in a nightdress and boots, spent my honeymoon in Buchenwald, and now our first married home was to be one room in a bombed out ruin.

So much for all those romantic dreams I had had as a little girl.

***

Everything gets worse before it gets better. Soon after moving into the house, I fell ill with an infection of my middle ear. The hospital turned me away because it was full of wounded Russian soldiers and there was no medication left.

I had to have an operation, without anaesthetic, at a private doctor's surgery. It took me two months to recover, every day spent in pain. Living in a ruin in a wrecked city and suffering with an illness that left me dizzy and nauseous made me more and more depressed. I cried day and night, while Julius did his best to lift my spirits.

Finally, there was a glimmer of hope. Julius returned one day and announced he had got a job in an electronics factory.

'We'll be able to find somewhere decent to live now,' he said, smiling.

Our first move took us to a room in the flat of a friend whom Julius had met at university; after that we found a tiny flat with cooking facilities in a poor area of Buda.

Once I had recovered from my illness, I found a job on the

production line of a factory making speakers for radios and also did some translating work when the Russians came asking for repairs.

My salary was paid half in cash, half in calories: oil, soya beans, butter, eggs and vegetables. It seems strange now, but when inflation was out of control, payment in food was a great help.

On my way to and from work, I began to appreciate being in Budapest – to this day it remains my favourite city – but I was shocked by the loss of so many beautiful buildings. The bridges, which had once been the pride of the city, were gone, military pontoon crossings stood in their place.

It wasn't only the city that was ruined; so many people's lives would never be the same.

Julius told me he had heard that one of his friends, Gabor, from the Hungarian Embassy in Zagreb, was now in a hospital in the city. 'We should go to visit him, Olga,' he said, his voice serious.

'Of course we'll go to see him, whenever you like. We can talk about life in Zagreb and remember the good times there.'

'Yes, but first there's something you need to know,' Julius said. 'Gabor was a pilot and was sent to the Russian front in 1941. When he was shot down in 1944 his plane caught fire and he suffered terrible burns. His injuries are very severe, apparently…'

His voice trailed off. Neither of us knew what to expect, but nothing could have prepared us for the man we saw a day later in a hospital bed.

Gabor's face was just livid scar tissue, his nose a lump of burned tissue. We were shocked beyond words – how could anyone survive such injuries? And what would he look like in the future?

If Gabor had lost his face he'd kept his personality and extraordinary courage. He joked about his looks: 'This must be the first time in our lives that you're better looking than me, Julius,' he said.

He was delighted to meet me: 'Why waste yourself on this one when you could have a handsome chap like me, Olga?'

251

We sat beside his bed and he demanded to hear our story. When we'd finished, he looked at me: 'You're mad!' he said. 'All that way for Julius? It must be love.'

We all laughed and chatted some more, but the image of his face stayed with me. During Gabor's lengthy spell in hospital a young Hungarian girl, Illy, fell in love with him and ultimately he underwent plastic surgery. Nothing would give him back his old looks, but at least Illy gave him happiness and love; they emigrated to Canada in 1956 after the Hungarian uprising. If anyone deserved a new start in life, then Gabor did.

***

Slowly, our new lives began to take shape. Julius was working hard but hoping to branch out on his own as a photographer and I took a new job in a firm making light meters for photographers. We were still living in one room, but we both dared to hope that it would not be long before we found somewhere better.

As Christmas approached I began to think about how we should celebrate the festive season. We had little with which to mark the occasion but at least this year we would be together for the first time. That, for us, was celebration enough.

Then Julius surprised me. 'My parents would like to meet you and they've invited us to spend Christmas with them in Eger,' he said.

I'd never met Julius's parents and he had always given the impression that he was somewhat estranged from them. His mother, in particular, did not approve of his divorce and I knew from my meeting with Shary all that time ago in Budapest that the family had been ashamed by Julius's imprisonment.

Nonetheless, I was thrilled. Not only had Julius told me that his parents had a lovely house, whereas we had just one cramped room, but it also seemed to mark my acceptance by the family.

'I'd love to spend Christmas with them,' I said. Julius looked delighted and rushed off to buy us rail tickets for the 85-mile journey.

I gathered together any smart clothes I could find to take with me. The next day we boarded the train at Keleti station in considerably happier circumstances than when we'd arrived a few months earlier.

We were like two excited children heading home for Christmas. Within three hours we were gazing out of the train windows at the historic town of Eger, famed for its spas and a towering minaret built by Turkish invaders.

Julius's family home was a revelation. Not only was it undamaged and bore no signs of the Russian occupation, it was huge, with 10 bedrooms and beautifully furnished throughout. Scattered on the parquet flooring were handmade carpets and the walls were hung with paintings by Julius's father, Joseph. He specialised in religious images and much of his work was on display in Eger's cathedral. He used his daughter, Shary, as the model for the angels in the pictures.

Joseph and I took an immediate liking to each other: he was kind, charming and obviously delighted to meet his new daughter-in-law. Julius's mother, Iren, however was cooler and more distant. Perhaps she thought I was too young for her son or was still hurt by his previous divorce. Nevertheless, she behaved perfectly correctly towards me.

'I do hope you like Eger,' she said when we arrived, and later added: 'Thank you for saving my son's life. He has told me all about what you did for him.'

Joseph was much less formal, laughing and joking and incessantly asking questions about my adventures in the search for Julius. 'He's a lucky man,' he said.

We would walk arm-in-arm around the streets of the town, Joseph introducing me to all his friends and telling them all that I was the girl who had saved his son from Buchenwald.

He took me along Kossuth Lajos Utca to show me the fine examples of baroque and rococo architecture and to the Minorite church in Dobo Istvan Square.

Back at their beautiful house, Julius had discovered that his parents had placed a small bottle of Hungarian brandy in each bedroom for their guests. We sat in bed chatting and sipping the brandy left in our room but all too soon we had finished it.

'Never mind,' said Julius, 'I'll go to the bedroom next door and get the bottle from there.' He carefully filled our dark bottle with water, put that in the next bedroom and returned with the brandy.

As soon as that was finished, Julius repeated the trick and reappeared with another bottle. And so the night wore on, with us giggling like children as we liberated bottle after bottle from the other bedrooms...

We slept late on Christmas morning.

The previous year I had eaten Christmas lunch with the SS; this time it was with a family – my family – sitting opposite my husband at the table and toasting the festive season. We wished each other great good fortune in the coming year.

I sat listening to the happy chatter and gazing at the man I had sacrificed so much to find. From time to time, Julius would catch my eye and smile softly.

It was the best of Christmases.

***

We decided to return to Budapest on New Year's Eve to be back in time for the turn of the year. In honour of our visit and to wish us well, Joseph bought a whole pig on the black market, had it butchered and smoked and gave most of it to us to take back.

It was packed in a large rucksack: two large hams; two smaller joints; chops and locally-made Hungarian sausages. It reminded me of our wedding celebrations in Buchenwald where roasting the pig had set the barrack block alight.

Of course, nothing in those years after the war was easy. Due to food shortages and in order to prevent black marketeering, permission from the authorities was necessary for transporting a sizeable quantity of food outside your home area.

Joseph said we would be all right. 'If you just smile sweetly at the Russians, Olga, they will let you through.'

I wasn't so sure. I rather thought that given the choice, the average Russian soldier would choose the ham over a smile from me, but after we'd discussed it Julius and I decided to go ahead with the journey.

Bearing in mind what his father had said, we decided it would be better if Julius carried our suitcases, while I carried the rucksack. I smelt like a butcher's shop on legs.

We said our farewells to Julius's parents, his mother still quiet and controlled, his father openly emotional, telling us to hurry back.

At the station, Julius led us to a ticket window where he knew the clerk and they exchanged the usual greetings. 'We'd like two tickets to Budapest,' Julius said, immediately beginning to look shifty. I wondered how he would ever have managed crossing borders during the war in the way I had done.

The clerk turned to me: 'What are you carrying in the rucksack?'

As he was Hungarian and a friend of Julius's family, I told him. 'You'll never get through to Budapest. The Russians are checking all luggage at every station.'

Julius looked crestfallen. 'I've got to try,' I said. 'The food is too good to waste.' The clerk looked at us both for a moment. 'Are you prepared to take a chance?'

We both nodded. 'Oh, yes,' I said. 'I'm used to taking chances.'

'Tonight,' the clerk said, 'there's a coffin on the train to

Budapest. The family aren't travelling with the dead man and we have permission to put the coffin in a sealed carriage at the front of the train. The Russians know all about it and have agreed. Someone will meet the coffin in Budapest, but if you were prepared to travel in the carriage with it, no one would bother you...'

Julius's face was a picture, I thought he was about to tell the clerk that we couldn't possibly do such a thing, so quickly I blurted out: 'Yes, we'll do it.'

My husband looked at me as if I'd gone mad, but said nothing. We waited by the ticket office and, shortly before the train was due to leave, a railway official escorted us to the carriage. If he asked what was in the rucksack, I was ready to tell him it contained the private effects of the dead man.

I could feel the eyes of the other passengers upon us as we walked the length of the platform to a carriage with the blinds drawn and a large notice stuck on the door: 'No entry, coffin inside.'

They looked on sympathetically as we boarded, doubtless thinking it was a sad way to spend New Year, travelling home with the body of a loved one in a coffin for company.

Inside, the carriage was dark and had no seating so we sat on the floor next to each other, quietly at first, but then I began to giggle.

It just seemed so preposterous, sitting there together with a rucksack of meat and a coffin. Julius began giggling as well and we were soon laughing as the train pulled out of the station and headed back towards the capital.

We sat in the darkness of the carriage leaning against each other, recalling our reunion in Buchenwald and all that we'd been through. The smell of the meat made me hungry so we opened a bottle of wine and shared some sausages.

It was not long before the train was back in Budapest. As soon as it pulled to a halt, we hurriedly climbed down from the carriage before anyone turned up to claim the body and wondered what this strange laughing couple was doing there.

'What a funny way to celebrate New Year's Eve,' Julius said, smiling at me, as we walked away.

'Don't forget we got married in a concentration camp,' I replied. 'This is nothing to us. We're not going to do anything in the normal way, are we?'

Prophetic words that one day would come back to haunt me.

CHAPTER TWENTY-SEVEN

On September 7th 1947, I married Julius again – this time in Budapest. The authorities had told us that I would not be granted Hungarian nationality unless we remarried in the country.

To do so, I had to return to Zagreb to get my birth certificate and various papers. Yugoslavia didn't have an embassy in Budapest at the time, just a mission, where I was told that I would not need documentation to cross the border.

The advice turned out to be wrong and with no proper documents I was detained at the border town of Subotica while Yugoslavia checked I wasn't an 'enemy of the state'. The process dragged on and a letter to my father went unanswered. Only when an uncle who lived in Subotica intervened and wrote to Ilona, my stepmother did anything happen. A few days later, Ilona arrived by train from Zagreb. Smartly-dressed as always and with much of her pre-war confidence regained, we greeted each other cautiously.

On the journey back to Zagreb she warned me that my father had still not forgiven me for my war-time exploits and marrying against his wishes. Nevertheless, as the train reached the outlying districts of Zagreb, I felt a rush of excitement at returning to the city that I had once feared I would never see again.

In comparison with many other European cities, Zagreb had escaped lightly from the Allied bombing and much of it was just as I remembered when I had left in 1944 onboard the workers' train for Vienna. Although I had come with the purpose of getting my birth certificate and other documents, I was looking forward to catching up with Marta and my other friends and talking about our experiences.

My father was hardly thrilled to see me, but grudgingly said I could stay with him and Ilona until everything was sorted out. He expected it to take no time at all, and I had expected the same. Instead, everything dragged for an infuriating length of time. Although I got my documents, my records had become confused with those of someone else of the same name so the Government refused me a passport or a permit to travel back to Hungary.

Julius was despairing – I had been away from Budapest for months rather than weeks and neither of us could see a way out of the problem. I met Marta regularly and she tried to help but there's a limit to what friends can do. My father, however, had no interest in helping.

'Why should I?' he asked. 'You're married now, you're not my responsibility anymore.'

Eventually, exhausted and frustrated by the bureaucracy that had kept me away from Budapest and Julius for so long, I wrote to Marshal Tito himself, asking for help.

When my new passport was finally granted it came with the authority of Tito. My journey back was suddenly easy. Sitting on the train from Zagreb to Budapest, I looked at my ticket and my passport and realised that, for the first time, I was travelling legally – I needn't have any fears about the border.

Once again, Julius and I married in a register office, but at least for our second wedding I had a beautiful navy blue dress, grey and white high-heeled shoes and a new hairstyle. The clothes had come courtesy of aunt Alice in Havana, to whom I had written. She had responded with great affection, sending me money and suggesting that Julius and I should go to live in Havana. Shortly after, Alice was stricken with cancer and died by the end of the year. I was sad

(Left and above) Myself and Julius pictured on September 7th 1947, the day we married for the second time – this time in Budapest. (Below) Our marriage certificate.

Házassági anyakönyvi kivonat.

that I had not seen her since the moment she left the flat in Zagreb with the Ustasha official all those years before.

For our second marriage, Julius was dressed in a smart suit and had bought me a silver wedding ring. So in front of a few friends we repeated our wedding vows, Julius slipped the ring on my finger and we celebrated properly this time in a restaurant with roast lamb and bottles of Tokay wine.

It felt strange – a ritual we had to go through, but lacking the emotion and feeling of our first, bizarre ceremony in Germany. Today, if anyone asks me where Julius and I married, I always reply 'Buchenwald'. It rarely occurs to me that we married in Budapest as well.

Our luck slowly began to change for the better. Julius began working as a freelance photographer with his friend, Laci, and they would spend days away from home seeking clients. We had a flat in a shared house in Buda near the Kelenford railway station. One room was converted into a photographic studio and I became used to seeing Julius working with prints hanging from lines suspended across the room.

I was proud of the furnishings in the flat, which had come thanks to a win on the lottery after I bought a ticket with the number 2023 – my birth date March 20th, 1923.

I had also found work thanks to my 'friend' Marshal Tito. I had written thanking him for helping with my passport and thought no more about it until I received a letter from the Yugoslav Ambassador Karlo Mrazovic summoning me to the embassy in Andrassy Utca.

Only as I approached the embassy did I realise that it was the same street in which I had been imprisoned when I first came to Budapest to find Julius. The memory brought back old anxieties. Why had I been called to the embassy?

In fact, it was good news. The embassy needed Yugoslavs who could speak Hungarian and my correspondence with Tito's office had led to them suggesting my name to the embassy. I was delighted. Julius and I now had work, a decent home and at last we could begin to look forward to the future – maybe even plan a family.

I think we could both be forgiven for thinking that the worst was over, that the hardships which both of us had suffered were enough. It was our turn for the good life.

Although we couldn't know it, hundreds of miles away in Moscow wheels were beginning to turn which would not only prevent us enjoying our hard-won life together – but crush us completely.

***

The telegram arrived in May 1948. It was from my stepmother, telling me that my father, who had suffered from angina for many years, was very ill and she feared the worst. If I wanted to see him again, I had better go to Zagreb – there might not be another chance.

I was torn. My father had not shown me love or support when I needed it. My letters home had gone unanswered and when I'd returned home from Osijek during the war I had been turned away. However, a sense of duty prevented me from simply ignoring the message. Who can turn their back on a dying parent?

I packed a small suitcase and went to have my passport stamped for the journey. The date was May 18th; Julius was away working so I scribbled a quick note saying I would be back within a couple of weeks and left it with Margitka, our friend in an adjoining flat.

The journey to Zagreb passed without problem and I arrived at my father's home to find him critically ill in bed. He acknowledged me with a smile but was too weak to talk. The big, strong man I remembered seemed shrunken and frail beneath the bedcovers.

My stepmother had not exaggerated the crisis and was clearly struggling to cope. She had looked genuinely pleased to see me when I arrived and the warmth of her welcome was a surprise.

I began helping to care for my father, expecting to be there for perhaps two weeks. Julius and I exchanged letters. His always began 'My Darling Olga' and gave me excited details of the photography business and all the news of our friends in Budapest.

As I began to make plans to return, my stepmother approached me: 'Please, Olga, can't you stay a bit longer? I need help to look after your father and you've been so kind…'

It was a heartfelt plea, yet I wanted to go back to Budapest and Julius – my life was there, not in Zagreb.

'Please, Olga…' she said again.

I agreed to stay longer and wrote to Julius to tell him I had postponed my return. He replied that he understood but to hurry back as soon as I could.

It was a fateful decision. If I had returned when I'd intended then the subsequent heartbreak would never have happened.

The moment I agreed to Ilona's plea to stay I threw away all that I had risked so much to achieve.

CHAPTER TWENTY-EIGHT

Our lives are often dictated by events beyond our control. In 1948, I was 25 years old and in many respects, wise beyond my years. I was tough, a survivor – but not a politician.

If some people in Yugoslavia knew what was about to happen, then I didn't.

Our leader Marshal Tito and Soviet Leader Josef Stalin in the Kremlin were rapidly running out of patience with each other. Both considered themselves heroes of the Second World War and Tito, who unlike Stalin had actually fought, was certainly not going to bend the knee to the dictator in Moscow. Yugoslavia was his country, independent and strong. We had defied the Nazis and if necessary we'd defy Moscow too.

Stalin was furious with such insubordination from a country he considered to be nothing more than one of his satellite states. Relations deteriorated rapidly and on June 28th 1948, while I was still in Zagreb, what bond there was snapped.

Moscow expelled Yugoslavia from Cominform, the international organisation of Communist parties, sparking immediate fears that we were to be invaded again. The borders were sealed swiftly, the armed forces put on full alert.

Suddenly, we were completely isolated from the rest of the world. There was no way into the country – and no way out.

I immediately applied for a visa to return to Hungary but was met with blank refusal. It didn't matter that I was married to a Hungarian and my home was in Budapest. What did the fate of one young woman matter to the men in Belgrade or Moscow?

Julius and I tried desperately to make contact, but letters were censored – or simply didn't arrive. Getting mail from an 'enemy' country was frowned upon so no one took the trouble to ensure a good postal service. The phone lines between Yugoslavia and the rest of the Eastern bloc were cut. We were condemned to silence.

I sat in my room in the house behind the walls of the Res factory where I had grown up. My father lay fighting for life in his room. I could hear my stepmother bustling around, fetching and carrying for him.

This was the very place from which I had started my journey of love. It was here that Julius had charmed me and my family and it was here that I had been told of his proposal of marriage.

Zagreb was the city which had formed me. It was the place I had tested my courage and resolve by helping aunt Alice escape from the Gestapo and travelled on a false diplomatic pass with Julius to visit the old Jewish lady in the lunatic asylum.

We'd fallen in love in this city, enjoyed our first kiss on a trip to Vrapce and spent nights at the opera.

Everything had begun here: my journey to Osijek; my betrayal in Budapest; our meeting in jail in Komarom; the horrors of Dachau; our marriage and honeymoon in Buchenwald. So much done, so much achieved… and all for what? To have it all swept away by one final cruel twist of fate.

As I sat in the small, dark room of my childhood, the radio news was reporting daily on the latest developments between our Government and the Soviets. It was going from bad to worse. The Iron Curtain had been tightly drawn around our country. I was trapped.

I gathered all the letters I'd received from Julius over the years and read them one by one: words of love, words of devotion, words heavy with all our hopes for the future.

Julius and me in Zagreb in 1943.

By the time I'd finished, the sheets of paper were wet with tears.

***

The news grew grimmer by the day. Stalin was determined to strangle Tito's independent Yugoslavia at birth. At the borders, mines were laid and armed guards posted in watchtowers. Yugoslavia and its Eastern European neighbours faced each other across a no man's land that bristled with anti-tank defences, trenches and guns.

It was a scene that would one day become familiar in Berlin when the city was cut in two by the wall and those trying to cross illegally were shot.

I gazed at the maps once more, the ones I had looked at before I began my journey. How much had changed in the world since those days yet here I was, in the same cruel trap.

The news made matters clear: crossing the borders without papers during the war had been hard; under the Soviets it was impossible. My constant pleas to the authorities to allow me to return to Hungary fell on deaf ears. Julius and I were condemned to a separation that was even more stringent than the one when he had first been arrested and jailed.

Our letters were subject to the whims of two inefficient postal services and two belligerent governments. Although there was a telephone in my father's house we didn't have one in the flat in Budapest, so phone calls were virtually impossible.

Slowly, inexorably, our means of communication faded away. There was only an unbreachable silence.

After a while the Yugoslav authorities became increasingly annoyed by my marriage to a Hungarian national, an enemy state which had invaded us once before and could well do again. No one would employ me – they couldn't take the risk.

While my father's health improved, his temperament at home did not, so I moved out. Needing work to survive, I went to see a lawyer and asked his advice.

He was blunt: 'You will have to divorce – '

'But,' I interrupted him, 'I love Julius and after all that we both went through during the war, surely there is something we can do to be together again. Could he come and live in Zagreb?'

The solicitor smiled at me. 'No, no. That will not happen at the moment, but who can tell what will happen in the future? I'm sure you will be able to get back together, but in the meantime, if you want to work, then divorce is your only option.'

I left the solicitor's office full of despair. The sheer unbelievable injustice of our situation hit me with shattering impact. I wanted to scream my anger at all the forces ranged against us, from the Nazis, to Stalin, to the smiling bureaucrats. I hated them all.

Standing in that street in Zagreb I knew that my great voyage of love was over. It had survived the jails of Hungary, the concentration camps of Nazi Germany, the lethal Allied bombing raids and the collapse of the Third Reich but now we were separated by an Iron Curtain, every bit as impenetrable as the name suggests.

Whoever said love conquers all was wrong. It can conquer much more than any one of us would believe possible. It can give us extraordinary strength, remarkable resilience and unexpected courage. It can give us great hope and ecstatic joy – but there are still forces that cannot be overcome. Sometimes the enemy is just too strong.

I was divorced 'by proxy' from Julius in the Divorce Court in Zagreb in 1950. My final, futile gesture of love was to insist on retaining my married name. My solicitor advised me to drop the 'y' as too obviously Hungarian, so I left the court as Olga Koren.

I stepped from the court into a light drizzle and grey skies, which reflected my mood. I had lost my great love, my husband. I had no work and as far as I could tell, no future.

Zagreb was my past. It was where the great adventure of my life had begun and ended.

I would have to leave, to find my way in the world. I was alone again.

CHAPTER TWENTY-NINE

Vienna, September 1985

We travelled by train from London and booked into a small, comfortable hotel in the centre of Vienna, not far from St Stephen's Cathedral.

As soon as we'd checked in and dumped our bags, we headed into the city to see some of the sights I remembered from my past. First, the cathedral, restored to its former glory after the damage it suffered in the war; then the shops of Kärntner Strasse and later, Prater park for a spin on the ferris wheel.

On an evening stroll along Mariahilferstrasse, I looked at all the shops and said to my husband: 'I remember when all these buildings had been destroyed by bombs; those left standing stood out like broken teeth from the rubble.'

Now, the trams clanged along the street and the shop windows were full.

We stopped at one of the many little food kiosks and ate a frankfurter before continuing our walk.

The following day we resumed our tour of the city's sights before strolling back towards the hotel in time for lunch. As we turned the corner, a slight, elderly, grey-haired gentleman was waiting outside the hotel entrance.

My husband touched my arm. 'Look, Olga, there he is. I'm sure of it. I recognise him from the photographs.'

I looked more closely and just then the man turned, looked at me and showed no sign of recognition. Our eyes locked and then he realised.

At that moment on an anonymous street in Vienna, Julius and I were reunited for the first time in 37 years.

***

It had been a long journey from that day in Zagreb where everything had come to an end.

I worked, first for an export/import business and then for the Central Bank of Croatia, and there was even a marriage proposal from a successful pharmacist. But I was unsettled, feeling estranged from my home city and no longer so comfortable there.

Marta was married and although I still had my old friends around me, those post-war years were ones of uncertainty in Yugoslavia. After the breach with Moscow the country was isolated: rejected by Eastern Europe and viewed with suspicion by the West.

When I left my father's house, I moved into a room with a doctor's family in a beautiful flat in the heart of the city across the road from the music academy.

In 1954 I was 31-year-old divorcée, living in a rented room with only my shattered dreams for company. Was this it? Was I going to spend the rest of my life wondering what had become of Julius and dwelling on what might have been?

I'd never been afraid to take a chance, to make a move and see what fate had in store for me, so when some friends showed me an advertisement for a young woman to work as a nanny for a family in England, I thought: 'Why not?' I could spend a year away, learn to speak English and then come home.

So one day in September 1954 I arrived in London: a huge city, full of rushing people speaking an incomprehensible language. I worked as a nanny for a while, then turned to the couture business to make a living – those lessons from my mother in Sisak stayed with me.

It was tough. I found it hard to make ends meet and sought a domestic job that would give me live-in accommodation. I had little contact from home. Marta and I kept in touch as old friends do, but the only letter I got from my father was to tell me that my stepmother Ilona had died following surgery. He had remarried almost straight away.

The news saddened me. Although we had never been close, without Ilona I would never have met aunt Alice and never have made those trips to Vrapce with Julius. Another connection with that era had gone. My past life was drifting away from me.

In 1958 I began working as a cook and housekeeper for Field Marshall Sir Gerald Templar, the Chief of the Imperial General Staff, and his wife. They were a kind and civilised couple, who treated me well. I began to feel more comfortable in London at last.

By 1963 however, my thoughts were turning to home. It was almost nine years since I'd left Zagreb for what was only supposed to be a 12-month stay. It was time to go home.

I booked a ticket and began my preparations. I visited friends, went out dancing and set about enjoying my last few weeks in London.

And then, one evening, I went with my friends to the Empire ballroom in Leicester Square where a softly-spoken Irishman asked me to dance. In less than a year, we were married.

Gerry Watkins, a civil servant, was the man who finally made my childhood dreams come true. He arranged everything for the wedding at the Church of the Sacred Heart in Quex Road, Kilburn, and the reception was at an elegant hotel. Just as I had always wanted, the church was awash with flowers and I walked up the aisle to the sound of Schubert's Ave Maria.

Standing in front of the altar in a London church on January 9th

271

1964 it seemed a world away from the day I married Julius at the temporary register office in the ruins of Weimar in 1945.

For once everything had been conventional. And maybe convention works: Gerry and I are still happily married today.

***

We built a new life for ourselves in London, now my adopted city. As the years went by, my past life during the war receded even further. I never forgot Julius but we had lost contact for good after the Hungarian uprising in 1956 when communications in and out of the country became even more difficult.

I told many people about my experiences and we would all wonder what had happened to Julius and how my life could have turned out so very differently.

But I was not unhappy, far from it. Gerry made me happy – he still does. We had a wide circle of friends, many of his in London's large Irish community and mine among the Yugoslav exiles.

My knowledge of languages meant that I was often used as an unofficial translator among friends from East Europe.

So, as the years went by, my past became just an exciting piece of my long gone history. It was only when we befriended a young couple, who moved in near us, that my link to Hungary was resurrected. In a twist of fate, the husband was Hungarian, and his mother, who regularly visited from her home country, did not speak English. I would, therefore, chat to her in her native tongue when her son was at work.

We talked, of course, about Budapest and I told her the story of Julius. 'What became of him?' she asked.

'We lost touch long ago, during the years when it was so difficult to communicate with Eastern Europe…'

'What's his family name?'

'Koreny,' I replied.

'Oh, there's a family by that name in my street,' she said. 'I'll ask them when I'm back if they know of him.'

I thanked her and thought no more about it.

Months passed and the conversation slipped from my memory, so I was puzzled when a letter arrived at our home in north London postmarked Budapest.

'Who's writing to me from Hungary?' I thought, tearing open the envelope.

It was from Julius.

'Dear Olgi,' it began. After 30 years, I was once again reading the spidery handwriting that had once been capable of lifting me to the heights of joy or casting me down into the depths of despair.

It all came flooding back - the letter that stuck in my mind the most was the short one he had written from Dachau that had set me on my journey across war-torn Germany.

Now, Julius's letter told me how a woman had knocked on his door asking if he was the Julius Koreny who had once been married to Olga Czepf. Shocked, he invited her in and she had given him my address.

His letter gave me news about Gabor and his parents; how he'd despaired when we were separated but how he had remarried in 1955. Was I married now? he asked.

I felt a mixture of shock, elation and doubt. After so much time, I was delighted to hear from him, but so much had happened to us both since then – did I really want to go back to that time of my life?

I talked to Gerry who encouraged me to write back. And so began an exchange of letters with the man for whom I had once risked so much. We wrote about all that had happened since our sudden separation, how our lives had taken very separate paths.

Inevitably, we discussed the subject of meeting again.

And so, eventually, we found ourselves in Vienna in

September 1985 and on that street outside our hotel we came face to face for the first time in almost 40 years.

***

Julius was very thin and the boyish looks of his early years had faded. But those lively blue eyes, which had always been his most striking feature, still sparkled. For a moment we were both lost for words. The pedestrians rushing past paid no attention to us. The traffic roared and Gerry stood to one side.

I greeted him in Hungarian and he replied 'Hello' before kissing me on the cheek.

We felt as awkward as two strangers meeting for the first time.

'Oh, Julius, this is my husband, Gerry,' I said.

The two men shook hands, Gerry polite and amiable, Julius cool and reserved.

I didn't know what I had expected, but not this. Perhaps I thought Julius would greet me with a bunch of red roses. But no, instead, I found myself translating the conversation between my two husbands, while my mind was full of memories.

We moved to a small café for a coffee where Julius asked me all about our journey and our life in London. Neither of us mentioned our shared past; it seemed too soon. The date was September 7th 1985 – exactly 38 years since our second marriage in Budapest.

When we took a walk before dinner that evening, Julius wanted to hold my hand – but somehow I could not. It seemed disloyal to Gerry, who was with us as we walked.

'I'm so pleased to see you again, Olgi,' Julius said. 'You were always my best friend and always will be. You're so special to me.'

His words took me back to those years when we had been together, preparing for our future before it had all been taken away from us.

Still there was the question: why had Julius been arrested during the war?

Even after such a passage of time, 40 years later, he was still no nearer knowing the truth.

'There was a woman who worked as a translator in the embassy in Zagreb who I have my suspicions about,' he told me. 'We had been friends and she knew about you, Olgi, and perhaps she was jealous. I don't know. Maybe she found out about our visits to your Jewish relatives…'

Julius mentioned her name, a woman who I had bumped into in Zagreb after the war – and who had fled the moment she saw me. Was she the one who had betrayed us?

Once he had reached the concentration camps, Julius had been given a red star to wear, indicating he was a political prisoner. His camp records show his category as 'Schutzhaftling', meaning he'd been arrested on the instigation of the Gestapo.

After the war, the new communist rulers of Hungary had offered Julius a position at one of the embassies, but on a lower grade than his wartime work. He turned them down.

It all suggested that somewhere along the line Julius had been identified as less than enthusiastic about the Nazi regime, possibly even a subversive.

We would never know; it was all such a long time ago.

As we sat down to dinner that night in the Austrian capital, Julius told me about Illy, the woman he had married in 1955, who had died in 1980. I felt relieved that he had remarried as I had.

'She was a good woman and we were happy together,' he said. 'But she would never have done the things for me that you did. If you and I were still together, Olgi, we would be living in Vienna or another Western city. You're too adventurous to have settled for Budapest. Illy didn't want to take any risks, even in 1956 when many Hungarians left the country and fled to the west after the uprising.'

He was right, of course. I would never have settled under the dour rules of East Europe - my adventures during the war had set my course for life. I look back now and realise that very little of my life falls into the category of 'ordinary'.

And my feelings for Julius? I could remember the love for him that had taken me on that perilous journey and I could still see much of the man with whom I had fallen in love in 1943. But the passage of time had changed me and him. My life and my future was with Gerry in London, Julius belonged only to my past.

The war years and our marriage had happened almost 40 years previously, and all the danger and struggle we had faced together had united us. Time, though, separated us now.

I had never been someone to make careful plans, to live a life governed by caution. I had been impetuous, always believing that fate would decide my path and that somehow everything would work out for the best. I thought more about the past during those days with Julius and Gerry in Vienna and realised there was nothing that I would have done differently in my life.

You do what you do for the best of reasons at the time. You make choices, choose your route, follow the road you're on. But at the end, it's fate that decides your destination.

With Gerry and my home in London I had arrived at mine.

***

Our final meeting came a few days later, when we had dinner with Julius and his son Gabor at a Yugoslav restaurant in Vienna. We chatted easily, like a group of old friends, retelling old stories and discussing our plans for the future.

At the end of the meal Julius suggested coming to the station the following day to see Gerry and me off. I said no. For some reason I didn't want another painful parting at a gloomy railway station.

Instead, the four of us said our farewells in the flickering candlelight of the restaurant. We each raised a glass of brandy, and Julius said to me: 'Olgi, I wouldn't be alive if it were not for you. You saved my life and it's a great pity everything turned out so differently from what we had hoped.'

Then we each raised our glasses in a sad toast to lost love and broken dreams.

Together again... Julius (left), pictured with me and my husband Gerry, in Vienna in 1985 – the first time Julius and I had met in 37 years.

EPILOGUE

Olga, now 88, still lives in north London with Gerry, now 80. They have been happily married for 47 years. They have no children.

Julius Koreny died on June 6th 1994 in Budapest from cancer. His son, Gabor, remains in touch with Olga.

Her father, Josip, died in 1960, several years after the death of her stepmother, Ilona.

Istvan, the Hungarian Hussar who did so much to help Olga on the roads to Germany, was taken prisoner by the Russians at the end of the war and released in 1946. He returned to Budapest and was reunited with his family.

Herta survived the war and emigrated to Israel.

Bela Cohn finally made it home to Zagreb from Buchenwald and set up his own medical practice.

Olga bumped into Lenka in Budapest after the war. She was married and expecting her first child.

And the little abandoned baby boy? He was taken back to Yugoslavia by his adoptive mother and raised as one of the family. The last Olga heard, he was doing well and was unaffected by his difficult early days.

When Olga and Gerry married they went on honeymoon to Paris, Italy and Croatia. Buchenwald was not on the list.

(above) Myself, aged 20.
(below) Myself, today.

Splendid
BOOKS

www.splendidbooks.co.uk
www.facebook.com/splendidbooks

If you enjoyed this book please "Like" it on
Facebook
www.facebook.com/agreaterlove

More from
Splendid Books

Compiled by Steve Clark, bestselling author of *The Only Fools and Horses Story*, and television expert Shoba Vazirani, *The British Television Location Guide* reveals the settings for dozens of top television shows.

From *Only Fools and Horses* to *Doc Martin* and from *Emmerdale* to *Doctor Who*, the book gives details of how you can visit the places you have seen so many times on the box.
Just **£9.99**

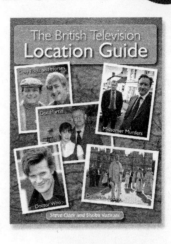

Read the real story of life behind the scenes at *The Bill* by the show's Graham Cole, who played PC Tony Stamp, in this frank autobiography.
£17.99 (hardback) or
£7.99 (paperback)

Read actor Derek Martin's fascinating real East End life story from growing up during the Blitz to starring as Charlie Slater in *EastEnders*.
£17.99 (hardback)

To order:
By phone: **0845 625 3045** or online: **www.splendidbooks.co.uk**

By post: Send a cheque (payable to Splendid Books Limited) to:
Splendid Books Limited, The Old Hambledon Racecourse Centre,
Sheardley Lane, Droxford, Hampshire SO32 3QY

1923

2011
1923
―――
"88

1913
201.

1923

1913 + 1994

Гашиб 99
―――

2011
1913
――
99

1994
1913
――
8 1